W9-BVD-797

SAUDI ARABIA EXPOSED

SAUDI ARABIA EXPOSED

Inside a Kingdom in Crisis

John R. Bradley

palgrave
macmillan

First published 2005 by
PALGRAVE MACMILLAN™
175 Fifth Avenue, New York, N.Y. 10010 and
Houndmills, Basingstoke, Hampshire, England RG21 6XS.
Companies and representatives throughout the world.

PALGRAVE MACMILLAN is the global academic imprint of the Palgrave Macmillan
division of St. Martin's Press, LLC and of Palgrave Macmillan Ltd. Macmillan® is a
registered trademark in the United States, United Kingdom and other countries.
Palgrave is a registered trademark in the European Union and other countries.

ISBN 1-4039-6433-5

Library of Congress Cataloging-in-Publication Data
Bradley, John R., 1970–
    Saudi Arabia exposed : inside a kingdom in crisis / by John R. Bradley.
        p.   cm.
    Includes index.
    ISBN 1-4039-6433-5
    1. Saudi Arabia—History—21st century.   2. Saudi Arabia—History—1932–
I. Title.
DS244.63.B73   2005
953.05'3—dc22

                                                                                    2004065487

A catalogue record for this book is available from the British Library.

Design by Letra Libre.

First edition: June 2005
10   9   8   7   6   5   4
Printed in the United States of America.

For

Nicolas Buchele

CONTENTS

ACKNOWLEDGEMENTS

David Pervin at Palgrave Macmillan was everything any author could wish for, and much more besides, in an editor, and I owe him an immense personal debt of gratitude for his willingness to go far beyond the call of professional duty while guiding this project from the proposal stage through to completion.

Nicolas Buchele was a constant pillar of support, and this book could not have been written without his help.

Sheldon M. Novick, a fellow Henry James scholar, offered invaluable suggestions in the early stages about how to make the material in chapter 1 more accessible to the general reader.

Anthony Paul's input on the Saudi youth chapter was timely, and much appreciated, and I am grateful to him too for helping me to work through some of my ideas about the kingdom during our coffee breaks.

My trips to Asir and Al-Jouf were undertaken in the company of Roger Harrison, whose enthusiasm and sense of adventure were truly inspiring. The material on Al-Jouf and Asir in chapters 2 and 3, some of which we worked on together for a special supplement in *Arab News,* has benefited still more from his subsequent input and advice. I am especially grateful for his permission to draw on the *Arab News* material.

All the opinions expressed in this book, and any errors that may have crept into it, are of course entirely my own responsibility.

INTRODUCTION

The Kingdom of Saudi Arabia, so extraordinarily introverted and completely closed to outsiders, is perhaps the world's last great, forbidden country. For most Westerners, it exists only in the realm of the imagination, with images feeding off tales of both the exotic and the violent: Oriental clichés of the sensuous, secretive, and tempting East that have, somewhat incongruously, combined with the continuous clamor and bang of the "war-on-terror" rhetoric in the wake of the September 11, 2001 attacks.

That said, there are thousands of Western expatriates inside the Islamic kingdom, some of whom claim that they always knew they were somehow destined to live there. Unlike the vast majority of expatriates who had hoped against hope that they never would have to live in Saudi Arabia, but were finally tempted by the high salaries, this other small band of romantic fatalists is rarely driven to distraction by the restrictions imposed by local customs and traditions: the mind-bogglingly inefficient bureaucracy; the shops and restaurants pulling down their shutters five times a day during prayer time; the prowling religious police; the kind of reckless driving that can only be described as suicidal. They feel, perhaps despite themselves, an almost tangible sense of privilege to have gotten in. And they experience a correspondingly immense sadness when, at last, it is time once again to move on—emotions complicated and deepened by the knowledge that, because Saudi Arabian tourist visas for the independent traveler do not exist, there is no way of returning, once passport control has finally been cleared.

When I moved to Saudi Arabia to join the editorial team of the kingdom's main English-language newspaper, *Arab News,* I was not one of those who always believed that fate, or *kismet,* would lead me to the kingdom. My interest in the Middle East, however, had already led me to learn Arabic and to travel in many other countries in the region and then to settle for a year and a half in Cairo. One day in late 2000 I overheard an Egyptian colleague at *Al-Ahram Weekly*, a respected Cairo-based newspaper I worked for while studying Arabic more intensively at a local language school, mention that he had been an editor in Jeddah for many years on *Arab News*. After September 11, the newspaper would for a time be one of the—if not *the*—most quoted in the world, as its website would provide the only window onto the kingdom and regularly get in excess of 2.5 million hits a day. It would be championed by liberals in the West as a voice of Saudi sanity, but damned by neoconservatives as a mouthpiece for the Saudi regime, which appoints a prince as chairman of the company that publishes the newspaper. I asked my colleague to write a letter of introduction on my behalf to the newspaper. He agreed. But he held out little hope of success. In late 2000, a year before the September 11 attacks, Western journalists were almost never given visas to visit Saudi Arabia. If they were, it was on condition that they were "accompanied" everywhere during their three-day visit by a minder from the Ministry of Information. The minder made sure that nothing unpleasant was seen by the journalist, and that he heard nothing other than the official line from carefully vetted individuals: Saudi Arabia is a land of peace and harmony.

Six months later, I was sitting in the *Arab News* office in Jeddah. For the next two and a half years I worked for the newspaper, as news editor and then managing editor. During that period I spent only five weeks outside the kingdom, choosing to spend most of my annual vacation time traveling to the remoter regions inside it. Other Westerners had previously gotten jobs as copy editors on local newspapers in Saudi Arabia, including *Arab News*. But they were typically part-timers who worked officially as English teachers; and, even if they were not, they usually had "researcher" or "lecturer" written on their residence permits, generally did not write articles, and were limited (as were all foreigners, until recently) to traveling only in approved areas. In contrast, my own residence permit, which I received a few months after my arrival, had "journalist" written in it. Stranger still was that I had not been asked even to go through the formality of signing a piece of paper in order to receive it, let alone been required to undergo the notoriously thorough medical examinations that are, by law, a prerequisite for the submission of any work visa application.

And so, a few months before September 11, when everything inside the kingdom was pretty much just bumbling along as normal, I found myself the only permanent, accredited Western journalist in a country that everyone in the world, and especially Americans, would suddenly want to know so much more about after the attacks took place. The two and a half years I spent in Saudi Arabia turned out to be not only the most tumultuous of

my life, but also a period of unprecedented political and social turmoil for
the kingdom itself, with a crisis in U.S.-Saudi relations and the stirrings of
a home-grown Islamic uprising. Fate would have it, too, that the law banning expatriates from internal travel, without first seeking permission from
their sponsor, was abolished almost on the day of my arrival. I was therefore able to travel throughout Saudi Arabia, from its remotest village mountains to its least accessible city slums, without any restrictions, and (just as
importantly) without a minder. And I could talk to anyone who would
agree to talk to me.

While I was not one of those expatriates who believed they were always
destined to live in Saudi Arabia, what I did share with such folk was a romanticism about the kingdom as a land that was intriguing. In the first
hours and days after my arrival, though, reality succeeded in undermining
all my preconceptions. It succeeded, too, in the months and years that followed, in extinguishing the last remaining flames of my misconceptions.

Jeddah, in June 2001, was no longer "the bride of the Red Sea," as it had
historically been referred to, but rather, at first glance, nothing more inspiring than a bland Chicago suburb: so Westernized and modern with its flashing neon lights, its massive shopping malls. What had I expected to find?
Something, I suppose, between what I had read in the seductive pages of
Seven Pillars of Wisdom and the nightmarish reports on human rights abuses
regularly issued, to great international fanfare, by Amnesty International.
There were, it later became obvious, elements of both at play inside Saudi
Arabia, and often—especially when it came to the Amnesty International
reports—not in ways that were manifested subtly. What became clearer in
time, though, was that, hidden beneath its superficial veneer of modernity,
the kingdom was not merely like nowhere in the West, but nowhere on
earth. Even other Arabs consider it an enigma—as, for that matter, do many
Saudis themselves.

Arab News provided a housing allowance, as apposed to accommodation
in a residential compound of the kind usually given to foreigners hired by
Western companies. That left no choice, after two weeks in a hotel, but to
look for somewhere to live in the local community. Such an option suited
me fine: I have never been able to understand why someone would travel to
a new country and then choose to live and socialize there only, or for that
matter at all, with his fellow expatriates. Moreover, having spent years traveling throughout the Middle East, I had every reason to expect that Saudis,
like Arabs I had encountered on my previous journeys, would by and large
prove welcoming, an assumption that turned out to be correct.

Someone suggested I should move into a studio in the working-class Al-Ruwais district, because I still had only a "visit visa" and the owner uniquely did not require a resident permit (something landlords of apartments and villas required their tenants to have by law). A desirable quarter at the height of the oil-boom years of the 1970s, Al-Ruwais has become one of the last places any Saudi would choose to live (and since Westerners have become the targets of Islamists they, too, would now be well advised to avoid it). At that time, though, it merely proved unpleasant, with its crumbling villas and dingy, pot-holed lanes that lead from the main roads to pockets of slum housing, where trash remained uncollected for weeks and sewage trickled down the crushed, rat-infested gutters. Its inhabitants were still mostly Saudis, but almost all of them were not only poor but also black: an early hint of how the endemic racism in Saudi society is not directed exclusively at Third World immigrants.

There were other hints, too, that such poor Saudis were facing the kind of social problems outsiders rarely get to see, and about which the Al-Saud regime at the time did not allow discussion. During my walks to a local shop in the late evenings after work, for instance, I would see young men lying on cars, presumably to escape the stifling heat of indoors, and obviously stoned out of their heads. More unsettling was the occasional sighting of a Westerner pulling up in his car, into which one of those young men would then disappear after exchanging a few words with the driver.

Drug abuse, male prostitution, slums, racism: hardly what one expected to discover on one's doorstep having just arrived in "the land of the two holy mosques."

As soon as I got my residence visa I moved into an apartment in the historic center of the city, and then into a small villa in another nondescript neighborhood in the north. The viewing of the latter villa in the company of the landlord gave another insight into the presence of the forbidden inside the kingdom, but this time into that which exists in the social world inhabited by many of the super-rich. The villa was in the grounds of a mansion owned by a member of one of Jeddah's leading merchant families, who worked for the Saudi royal family. He had built it for his own use, he said, but then found himself spending most of his time living outside the kingdom, so decided to rent it out. He advertised for a Westerner because, he explained, it was not suitable for a Saudi family, since it contained no room into which the female members of the household could be herded in the once-in-a-lifetime event that—horror of horrors!—a male who was not a relative should unexpectedly pay a visit.

The landlord was married, and when in Saudi Arabia lived most of the time in the mansion. The small villa he had built was nothing more and nothing less, it was perfectly obvious, than what would have been called in nineteenth-century London a "fucking pad," complete with a secret door that led out onto a side street and through which, it could safely be assumed, many a young lady of the night had been able quietly to slip in unnoticed, and then just as quietly slip out again a few hours later.

Showing me around the villa, he opened the wardrobes in the bedroom. At the bottom of one of them were more than a dozen bottles of hard liquor. When he switched on the TV, to demonstrate that the satellite dish worked, the channel that came on was dedicated to hardcore porn. Not that he was embarrassed by any of this. "Where does it say in the Qu'ran that I cannot enjoy looking at beautiful women's breasts on satellite TV?" he asked me, without a hint of irony. "That," I replied, "is the kind of interpretation of Wahhabism that should be promoted in the West." I added that I would indeed like to rent the villa.

Female prostitution, 24-hour access to hardcore pornography, a stash of hard liquor that would keep an alcoholic satisfied for at least a year: again, hardly the kind of things one expected in a rented villa in "the land of the two holy mosques."

Then again, Saudi Arabia is marked by a breathtakingly contradictory embrace of the universal and the unique, the ultra-traditional and the defiantly modern, the tediously mundane and the truly bizarre. It is commonplace to note the vast changes—certainly material, in terms of buildings, roads, infrastructure—that oil wealth has brought. But while the Arabia that has always captivated outsiders is for the most part no longer, the hodgepodge, mishmash of contemporary life in Saudi Arabia continues to intrigue. This is not least because of the juxtaposition of the modern environment with the anachronistic—or, to a Westerner at least, decidedly odd—attitudes held by so many of its people: even, perhaps most disorientingly, by many of the Saudis who seem at first glance to be the most "Western."

That is, of course, a generalization. But contrary to the temptation of ideologues of all kinds to see or portray the country as monochromatic and uniform in thought and belief—something, ironically, the Saudi regime also peddles, because it perfectly serves its political ends—there is no single culture that defines what Saudi Arabia is and who its people are, just as there is no single culture that alone could be said to define what the United States is and what Americans are. Talk to five randomly selected Saudis about their personal lives and their aspirations, and you will likely be told five very different life stories. Visit the different regions of the kingdom, meanwhile, and you will for sure encounter many distinct and still, in many respects, despite seven decades of Wahhabi-Al-Saud hegemony, fiercely independent entities.

While there is more than one Saudi Arabia, the only one that has caught the attention of the West in recent years is the "Wahhabi kingdom." It is home to 15 of the 19 hijackers who partook in the terror attacks on September 11, governed by perhaps the most corrupt family the world has ever known, a place teeming with extremists, where children are taught that "the Jews" are the eternal enemy, and where Westerners are periodically blown up in their residential compounds or gunned down in the street by attackers filled with hatred for them and seeking martyrdom. It is a place that treats Third World immigrants like slaves, where Saudi men never get to see a woman who is not a direct (and usually very close) relative, and where Saudi women themselves cannot leave the house without a male chaperone, let alone drive, and live for the most part in absolute purdah.

However, there is another Saudi Arabia, where Westerners with an open mind and sense of adventure can—and often do—encounter the finest traditions of Islamic hospitality, generosity, and kindness. In this Saudi Arabia, they may spend an evening sitting with liberal-minded, and even secular, Saudi friends, drinking coffee in Starbucks while talking about the latest Western movies. Princes and princesses, selfless and incorruptible, can talk passionately of the need to introduce sweeping reforms that would limit their own power. Teenagers surf the web in Internet cafes while watching the World Cup or Superbowl on widescreen TVs, or play soccer in the street. Women, shed of their long black cloaks in the home, can quickly prove themselves to be as independent and single-minded as any in the West (having become, moreover, the owners of most of the money deposited in the local banks). You may be invited to listen to an anti-Wahhabi lecture given by a local Sufi activist. And, increasingly, this other Saudi Arabia is a place where the main concern for perhaps the majority of the population, the one thing in addition to their faith that binds them, despite their many differences, is the question of whether they and their children will be able to find a job, and if they are likely to recover their status in the world that was so profoundly undermined on September 11 by one of their own: Osama bin Laden.

The following pages open a window onto both of these Saudi Arabias.

PART ONE

Chapter One

LIBERAL VOICES OF THE HIJAZ

One humid evening in the fasting month of Ramadan two dozen Saudi men and women gathered in the garden of a villa belonging to one of Jeddah's oldest merchant families, having been carefully selected because of their liberal inclinations. The men and women, sipping orange juice and fanning themselves, chatted in English and Arabic as they settled down to listen to a lecture attacking Wahhabism, the kingdom's official and uniquely austere brand of Islam.

A young British man had spent the afternoon under the blazing sun, setting up a makeshift lecture theater in the middle of the modern villa's carefully landscaped garden. He surveyed the rows of chairs just beyond the trickling fountains, drinking a glass of Coke filled with ice while, with a pinched finger and thumb, pulling a short-sleeved, sweat-soaked shirt away from his skin.

Now, he said, everything was finally ready, including a projector hooked up to a laptop computer.

The villa, a sprawling concrete and marble building in a style that blended local Arabian motifs with a superficially Western design, was built—as are most on the west coast of Saudi Arabia—to maximize the movement of the air through the rooms. It belonged to the Alireza merchant family, and was shut off to the outside world by a high surrounding wall. It was located in north Jeddah—a series of anonymous residential, shopping, and commercial districts that are a world away from the charming, rundown atmosphere of the historic downtown area of the city.

In the north, both lavish and jerry-built villas are hidden from prying eyes by massive walls, often topped by extra corrugated iron sheets: a manifestation of the Saudis' obsessive regard for their privacy. The streets between them are empty of people day and night, except for an occasional street cleaner from Bangladesh.

A stone's throw from the Alireza villa is Jeddah's sea road, or *corniche,* famous for being the longest such road in the world. Hundreds of outdoor sculptures are dotted along its 16-mile stretch. Over the years, they have slowly transformed it—and much of the rest of the laid-back Red Sea port city—into an accidental outdoor art museum. However, in keeping with a strict Wahhabi aversion to recreating or displaying the human form, there are no images of people to be found there; such images are forbidden given the loathing of graven images or anything that interferes, or is seen as having the potential to interfere, with a person's devotion to Allah. Even human forms in the advertisements plastered between the neon lights throughout Jeddah and the kingdom's other major cities have an eye missing or part of a foot painted over, although you would have to look closely to notice the deliberately introduced mark of imperfection. Only with such alteration can it be argued that the human form is not being reproduced, let alone adulated. Thus an uneasy compromise is reached to reconcile conflicting pressures between form and substance, between Wahhabi austereness and the reality of modernity.

Back on the patio, in the garden of the villa, immaculately liveried waiters were offering cold drinks to the men and women who were still arriving. Most had rushed to the villa from exclusive parties where, an hour or so earlier, they had broken the daylong traditional Ramadan fast at an *iftar*—literally, a break-fast meal.

Iftars can be simple occasions, with poor families eating dates and sipping tea before settling down together to watch TV soap operas specially produced for the Ramadan season. But they can also be ostentatious displays of wealth and indulgence, events at which great crowds of relatives meet up in spacious gardens to indulge in a lavish array of food that has taken the villa's servants most of the day to prepare.

The lecturer, Sami Angawi, was busy in the garden fiddling with his laptop. A large man who had studied architecture in Britain and America, Angawi leaned heavily on a beautifully carved walking stick. He is from another respected Jeddah merchant family, and in 1975 he founded the Haj Research Center. It documents the more than 1,350 years of history of the annual pilgrimage to Mecca, a 45-minute car ride from downtown Jeddah.

Angawi is described by those who know him as the undeclared leader of the vast swath of Saudi Arabia known as the Hijaz, which runs along the Red Sea from Jordan in the north to the Asir region bordering Yemen in the south. He is also a reputed follower of Sufism, the mystical Islamic belief system based on the idea that love is a projection of the essence of God to the universe. Perhaps that was why he was not wearing a long, white flowing *thobe*—the bland Wahhabi national dress—but rather a darker robe decorated with beads and toggles and a woven, colored pattern just below the neck.

Being a follower of anything other than strict Wahhabi Islam, secretively or otherwise, is a risky undertaking in Saudi Arabia—as, for that matter, is wearing a traditional Hijazi robe and giving a lecture. Such acts, public and private, are subtle but powerful political statements, suggesting as they do the cultivation of independent belief and action, luxuries in a quasitotalitarian state—Islamic or otherwise. In Saudi Arabia, any direct, untempered criticism of the Al-Saud family or the Wahhabi establishment it rules alongside might easily be overheard and reported by a person sitting nearby, who might even himself be a member of the feared secret police.

Constantly interrupting himself, as the pious in the Muslim world are in the habit of doing, with religious mutterings, and vaguely distracted by working through worry beads dangling from his right hand, Angawi talked in his lecture about how Hijazi culture had historically thrived on balance and moderation, tolerance and diversity. It was all, he said, being wiped out by the influence of hardcore Wahhabi ideology, imported by the Al-Saud family when it conquered the region in the 1920s. Architecture, Angawi digressed, is a reflection of society, of its principles and priorities and deepseated trends and beliefs. He advised his audience to think about how Mecca, Islam's holiest city in the heart of the Hijaz, is fast becoming one of the most crudely unplanned and overly commercialized cities in the world. Then they should ask themselves, he said, what that indicated about the psychological state of their sons and daughters and the sociopolitical environment in which they were being brought up.

Since the 1920s, he continued, the Wahhabis had even demolished places where the Prophet Muhammad himself had prayed. Their motive was a fear that such places would give rise to a cult that was tantamount to polytheism, the worship of multiple and equal gods or divinities, or idolatry. The Wahhabis have always despised polytheism and idolatry above and beyond every other Islamic "aberration" they condemn. It remains, in theory at least, punishable by public beheading. The Wahhabis' central belief is the concept of "tawhid," meaning the unity of Allah and reverence only for Allah. Even today, a theology text that 14-year-old Saudis study states "it is the duty of a Muslim to be loyal to the believers and be the enemy of the infidels. One of the duties of proclaiming the oneness of God is to have nothing to do with his idolatrous and polytheist enemies."

Angawi—an infidel perhaps, by such criteria—had personally excavated what may have been the Prophet's own home and discovered underneath public lavatories in the early 1990s, but the authorities had hushed up the find to avoid a rush of pilgrims to the site.

At the climax of Angawi's slideshow, a photograph was projected onto the far right of the screen that showed a beautiful Turkish building in Medina, four hours' drive to the north of Jeddah. The roof was being crushed by the yellow arm of a crane. Then, on the left of the screen, an image appeared of the giant Buddha statues in Afghanistan destroyed in 2001 by the Taliban, whose numbers had been swelled by thousands of Saudi mujihadeen, or freedom fighters, as they fought Soviet occupation. Finally, slowly, an image of the Twin Towers, in flames after being hit by planes taken over by mostly Saudi hijackers, came into focus between the first two photographs.

Angawi's message was clear: The roots of global Islamic terror can be traced in a very direct way back to the fanaticism of the Wahhabis, who to this day rule Saudi Arabia in partnership with the Al-Saud ruling family. Just as the United States is reassessing its own oil-for-security alliance with the Al-Saud as a consequence of those attacks, he also seemed to be hinting, ever so subtly, that it could be time for his Hijazi audience to think about reassessing their relationship with the Saudi royal family.

He had been careful throughout the lecture not to mention the Al-Saud by name.

The great sweep of the Arabian Peninsula known as Saudi Arabia is home to several ancient cultures: from the Hijaz on the Red Sea coast, which includes the city of Jeddah where Angawi gave his lecture, to the Shiite-majority Eastern Province on the Gulf; from the central Wahhabi bastion of Al-Najd to the largely tribal Asir region on the Yemeni border.

As the Ottoman Empire expanded from the thirteenth century, the Hijaz and Asir fell gradually under Turkish rule. But these, and all the other regions, managed to retain their cultural and national character, both during the reign of the Ottomans and within the Saudi state after its emergence in the 1930s in the wake of the Ottoman Empire's collapse. Today, this stubborn regionalism, though glossed over in official Saudi propaganda, is reflected even in the most popular Saudi TV comedy series, *Tash Ma Tash* (No big deal), which broadcasts during Ramadan after *iftar* and in which regional accents and customs especially are mocked to hilarious effect. Other topics dealt with by the satirical comedy series deal with the restrictions and contradictions of the kingdom's daily life, from women who find themselves unable to leave the house because they do not have a male guardian to accompany them to young men who cannot find a job. The religious police hate the show, but—perhaps because comedy is viewed as an acceptable safety valve for social, regional, and other frustrations by the powers that be—it runs and runs and continues to get spectacular audience ratings, while the actors continue to get death threats.

Under the Ottoman Empire, the Hijaz, home of the sacred shrines of Mecca and Medina, was run by the House of Hashem, or Hashemites, descendants of the Prophet, and they had considerable autonomy. Turkey sided with the Germans in World War I, however, and their defeat meant the end of centuries'-old reigns, in this part of the former Ottoman Empire as elsewhere. In 1916, at the height of World War I, when France and Great Britain were conducting secret talks known as the Sykes-Picot agreement to carve up the Middle East into zones of influence, Sherif Hussein bin Ali, the Hashemite ruler of the Hijaz, initiated the Arab revolt against the Ottoman Turks. At the Cairo Conference of 1921, the British rewarded Sherif Hussein, naming one of his sons, Faisal, king of Iraq, and another, Abdullah, ruler of modern-day Jordan—both countries imperial creations carved out of the sand. However, Sherif Hussein himself was double-crossed by the British, who were privately also backing his rivals, Ibn Saud and his Wahhabi followers. Ibn Saud was viewed as the leader most likely to pacify rival tribes in the Arabian Peninsula and had already proved himself very willing to cooperate closely with Britain in order to achieve his goal of carving out a state for his family to rule over. Hussein, then, was forced to abdicate in favor of his eldest son, Ali, and he went into exile—first to Cyprus and then, after falling ill, to Amman, where he died in 1931. Ali's rule itself lasted only one year, and in 1925 he followed his father into exile. Ibn Saud and his forces meanwhile were sweeping across the region, and he prepared to declare himself the new ruler of the Hijaz. Many of the lower-ranking members of the Hashemite family, however, stayed put, after promises of protection from the Al-Saud (which were subsequently kept).

This was the third time the Al-Saud dynasty had tried to establish an empire across the Arabian Peninsula, and the third time proved lucky.

Back in 1744, Mohammed bin Saud, a local ruler from the central region of Al-Najd (and from whom Ibn Saud was descended), had signed a pact with a religious reformer, Mohammed bin Abdul Wahhab. Their aim was to bring about, through force if necessary, the reign of the word of God. Abdul Wahhab had begun his preaching some years earlier. Wahhabism, his legacy, advocated a literalist and legalistic stance in matters of faith and religious practice. It damned Shiites as not being true Muslims and was particularly hostile to Sufism, because Wahhabis adhere to the most cautious opinions and shun any form of worship that is not literally attributed to the Prophet. For example, Wahhabis judge it sinful for Sufis to sit in circles and mention the name of Allah as a group or recite the Qu'ran melodiously; and they damn Shiites because they recall the martyrdom of the Prophet's grandson, Hussein. Wahhabism claims to "purify" Islam from such innovations, superstitions, deviances, heresies, and idolatries. Unsurprisingly, Abdul Wahhab condemned as well modern and ancient "innovations," such as listening to music and smoking.

During the time of Abdul Wahhab, the people of Al-Najd were in fact practicing Islam in these and many other ways contrary to hardline Wahhabi beliefs—such as invoking prophets, saints, or angels and not simply Allah in prayer; worshipping at graves; celebrating annual feasts for dead saints; and wearing charms. These practices he regarded not as mere sins but as acts of apostasy that merited the maximum penalty, and he justified the slaughter of all who stood in the way of Wahhabism's domination of the entire Muslim world.

Abdul Wahhab's religious fervor and his partner Saud's military skill proved to be a potent combination. After conquering and converting most of the tribes of Al-Najd to Wahhabi doctrine, the Wahhabi–Al-Saud forces swept out across the Arabian Peninsula. By 1806, the first Wahhabi state stretched as far as Iraq in the north, and into parts of the Hijaz. It was, however, soon dismantled by Mohammed Ali, the sultan of Egypt, who had been delegated the task of doing so by his Ottoman masters. Since the Hijaz was already part of the Ottoman Empire, and much of that empire's legitimacy came from ruling over Islam's two holiest shrines, the Turks instructed Mohammed Ali to spare no effort in forcing the Saudis back into Al-Najd. He succeeded in doing so, and finally that central region also fell to Mohammed Ali's forces. By 1818, the Saudis were crushed, and the lands they had ruled over were pillaged. Thus the first Saudi empire was brought to an end.

An attempt by the Wahhabi–Al-Saud alliance to retake lost territory resulted in the less ambitious, but more stable, second Saudi empire. It suffered various political and territorial fortunes between 1824 and 1891. Its establishment was not so much important for the territory it encompassed as for the loyalty it garnered from those it ruled over. Slowly, many of them embraced Wahhabism, as the Wahhabi–Al-Saud pact itself—in terms of intermarriage between the Al-Saud and Abdul Wahhab's descendants—was consolidated over numerous generations. But this second empire, too, was finally crushed—this time by a rival clan, the Al-Rashid. They were based in the city of Hail, to the north of Al-Najd, a relatively easy-going place that, like the Hijaz and Asir, had always fiercely resisted Wahhabi-Al-Saud domination, and in many ways continues to do so.

The Al-Saud family's third revival began in 1902, when Ibn Saud captured Riyadh back from the Al-Rashid. That victory ushered in a string of conquests to the east, north, and west, which laid the foundations of the modern Kingdom of Saudi Arabia. When, after World War I, the extraordinarily skilled diplomat Ibn Saud finally deposed Sherif Hussein in the Hijaz, his army was also moving south to colonize the mountainous Asir region that had historic links to Yemen. By 1932, Ibn Saud was able to declare himself king of Saudi Arabia, a country the size of Western Europe to which fortune would soon grant untold wealth in the form of more than a quarter of the known oil reserves on the planet.

Wahhabi atrocities against non-Wahhabi Muslims had punctuated the Al-Saud's rise to power in every region of the country. One historian, Said K. Aburish, claims in his book *The Rise, Corruption and Coming Fall of the House of Saud* (1996) that no fewer than 400,000 people were slaughtered during the formative years of the Saudi state. That is probably an exaggeration. But the Hijazis in the west, the Asiris in the south, and the Shiites in the east did all suffer massacres, witness their Islamic monuments destroyed, and have their various Islamic beliefs damned as apostasy by the new official ideology: Wahhabism. Although all were eventually cowed into submission, many of these diverse people Ibn Saud finally ruled over were not historically Wahhabis, and their loyalty had been bought, or promised, or indeed compelled under threat of beheading.

Jeddah's own residents had given up without a fight, for instance, only because stories had filtered through to them of how, in September 1924, the hill town of Taif about a hundred miles from the Red Sea coast had been the scene of a yet another massacre. Hundreds—men, women, and children— were slaughtered by the Wahhabi zealots, a repeat of a massacre in the same city during the first years of the nineteenth century. The earlier massacre, too, had been carried out by Wahhabis, also employed as warriors and bandits by the Al-Saud.

To this day, the Al-Saud rule in partnership with the direct descendants of Abdul Wahhab, known as the Al-Asheikh family. The Al-Saud princes hold almost all the key government posts. Members of the Al-Asheikh family hold almost all the key positions in the religious establishment and are responsible for enforcing Islamic orthodoxy on the streets. This they do through intimidation by the Committee for the Promotion of Virtue and Prevention of Vice, or "religious police," which is feared and reviled both because of its wide reach and because its members are drawn from the lower classes. Their resentment of the rich, combined with their freedom of action, results in a dangerous combination and adds to the hardline religious social atmosphere sanctioned by Wahhabi doctrine, which is spread by clerics in the mosques and teachers in the schools, and which guides the verdicts handed down by Wahhabi "justice" in the courts.

The September 11 attacks, in which 15 of the 19 hijackers were Saudis, has increased the pressures on these fragile religious, tribal, and regional alliances established during Saudi Arabia's bloody formation, as was testified to by the content of Sami Angawi's lecture. These tensions, however, are rarely manifested in the body politic. Rather, they reveal themselves in changed mindsets, odd comments, and behind-the-scenes social and political developments. Because they usually manifest themselves in places off the beaten track, they generally do not get reported. They are, though, now as great a threat to the survival of the Al-Saud regime and unity of Saudi Arabia as they were an obstacle to the establishment of the state. In fact, along with a huge generational gap between the rulers and the ruled, a crime wave, and an ongoing economic crisis, these religious, regional, and tribal tensions represent perhaps a greater challenge to the continuing rule of the royal family than the crisis in post–September 11 Saudi-U.S. relations, which grabbed the outside world's attention. As with other culturally and religiously diverse regions conquered by hostile foreign forces in the first half of the twentieth century, such as those under German and Soviet occupation, the people of Saudi Arabia seem only to be waiting for their own chance to throw off the superficial layers of the imported ideology—in their case, Wahhabism.

By the time it was conquered by Ibn Saud and his Wahhabi army, Jeddah had developed into the most cosmopolitan city in the Muslim world. Its residents hailed from Java, the Middle East, India, and Central Asia. Jeddah's cosmopolitanism was largely the result of it being both a major commercial port and the gateway to Arabia for pilgrims on their way to Mecca and Medina. The city had benefited, too, from the fact that many pilgrims had stayed behind after the Haj to become teachers, preachers, and traders. The latter set up trading companies, which established links with their home countries—entwining Jeddah ever more intimately into the rapid globalization of the late nineteenth century and leading to the heyday of its historic role as an international port city.

Only the relative shortage of drinking water had kept the city confined to the square mile of the old town, now known as the historic Al-Balad district. These foreign cultural and commercial influences created a tolerant Muslim social environment. Despite their privileged closeness to Mecca and Medina, the easy-going locals were not, historians agree, particularly strict in their religious observances. Indeed, they even had a taste for democracy. Although they were cut back after the Al-Saud imposed their rule on the area, various kinds of local elections continued to be held for the town councils in the Hijaz until the late 1960s.

The Alireza merchant family—best-known for acting as the local agent for the American car giant Ford, and in the garden of whose villa Sami Angawi had been invited to give his lecture that evening in the fall of 2002—have been in Jeddah for more than 160 years. They trace their local history back to an individual named Zainal bin Alireza, who arrived in Jeddah in the 1840s as a 12-year-old in search of work.

As historian Michael Field has shown, Zainal traveled all the way from Iran on his own and in Jeddah was fortunate enough to be taken into a local household to work for their family business. He was joined by his younger brother, and together they set up the Alireza trading establishment. Legends abound about the charitable acts, deep but not extremist piety, and intellectual distinction of various Alireza family members in the century and a half since then. During that period, the family has been at the center of every economic, political, and social development in Jeddah.

One of the best-known tales, and the most frequently recited, involves a young man named Mohammed Ali Alireza.

In the early years of the twentieth century, like many of the family's offspring at the time, Mohammed was sent to help out in a branch of the family firm in Bombay, India. But, even before setting off, he had gained a reputation for bringing Jeddah's poor children into his family home and encouraging them to learn to read and write from teachers he had managed to persuade to give free lessons. Long before the Saudi state was established, education was still a little-considered ideal for the vast majority of Jeddah's impoverished children, as it was for children throughout the Arab world— and, for that matter, for most of those in the West.

After returning to Jeddah from India, where he had grown bored and homesick, Mohammed was given some capital by his father as encouragement to set up a school. Eventually, that school grew into a chain, which spread throughout the Gulf and India. In his element, Mohammed would, it is said, walk through the streets of Jeddah in the morning with a bag of silver piasters to give to children, as a way of encouraging them to make their way to his classrooms. Mohammed's later career as a pearl merchant—which he went into with the understanding that, at that time in the Gulf, it was the only sure way to get rich quickly—did make him fabulously wealthy, and he plowed almost all of the profits back into his educational institutions.

Mohammed was the rule, the Alirezas say, rather than the exception. His story does typify what the Alireza family is most respected for in Jeddah and beyond—quite aside from its business acumen: a love of education and culture, coupled with an Islamic belief in the importance of *zakat* (the support of charitable causes through personal donations that is one of the five pillars of Islam). As late as the 1940s and 1950s, Field writes, Western guests at dinner parties at the Alireza villa were struck by the family's habit of cooking ten times more than they needed, in order to distribute what was left over to Jeddah's poor. Even in those decades, after the oil boom had kicked in, there were still enough of the poor to form queues outside the villa, where they waited patiently for hours with begging bowls in hand.

In 1925, Haji Abdullah, then head of the Alireza household, was chosen to lead the delegation of locals that entered into negotiations with Jeddah's new ruler, Ibn Saud. Immediately, he gained a concession that would guarantee the continued livelihood of much of Jeddah's middle class: As well as leaving the remaining Hashemites and their property alone, all the civil servants who had served under the previous government would, Ibn Saud promised, be allowed to keep their jobs. Field has written that in a photograph of Ibn Saud and Haji Abdullah, which hangs in the Alireza's main office in Jeddah, the fact that the two were drinking the sweet, Turkish coffee of the region out of cups rather than the thick bitter coffee out of bowls (as would have been customary in Al-Najd) also implied a promise of regional autonomy.

Just two days after Jeddah's surrender, Ibn Saud agreed to still another proposal put forward by Haji Abdullah: that the Hijazis should not be incorporated into Al-Najd, but instead form part of a new state called The Kingdom of Al-Najd and the Hijaz, with clear implications of semi-autonomy for the latter region.

The Alirezas emerged from all of this wheeling, dealing, and horse-trading with their prestige greatly enhanced. They had helped guide the citizens of the city through a difficult period, and they were initially to take care of the government finances under the new Al-Saud regime.

As a city, Jeddah also initially managed to avoid the worst cultural excesses of the Wahhabis, for the zealots who made up Al-Saud's army did indeed withdraw back to the central Al-Najd region from whence they came. Since the local merchant families did not seek political power for its own sake, they mostly just continued to go about their business as usual—albeit under the Al-Saud's watchful eye. When times were bad, they hunkered down, waiting for a light at the end of the tunnel. Then it came, more dramatically than they could ever have dreamed, in the form of the discovery of oil. Nevertheless, Jeddah's local culture was slowly transformed by its alien rulers. Their radical Wahhabi partners were brought back to the city in the form of preachers installed in local mosques, teachers in schools, and religious police in the streets. The Wahhabis regarded the Hijazis as lesser Muslims, and even lacking true manly Arabian characteristics. Such prejudices stemmed in part from the conquerors' fanatical religious beliefs, pared down during centuries of a simple desert lifestyle; and these were complicated by town-desert rivalry. As one historian, quoted by scholar Joshua Teitelbaum, put it: The townspeople like those in Jeddah felt the Bedouin "to be dangerous robbers who were irreligious, uncouth and barbaric," while the Bedouin conquerors in turn viewed the townspeople as "defiled by their intermarriage with foreigners, unhealthy, effete, and cowardly."

Only one thing was certain: Jeddah's independent inheritance had come under threat from the colonizing ruling family, the Al-Saud. Decades of Wahhabi-Al-Saud hegemony, and private but consistent Hijazi resistance to it, was inevitably set in motion. Local resentment persisted, even as the economy grew and the lawlessness that had marked life under Sherif Hussein—which resulted, for example, in pilgrims regularly being mugged on their way from Jeddah to Mecca—was brought to an end. Families like the Alirezas, although firmly aligned with the Al-Saud, did not shy away from expressing dissenting opinions whenever they felt that things were getting too extreme. Indeed, that they invited Angawi to give an anti-Wahhabi lecture in their villa in 2002 was proof that their habit of asserting their independence had in no way diminished over time.

The destruction of historic monuments that Angawi had drawn attention to was the most obvious, physical proof that Wahhabism, with its hatred of polytheism, had eventually succeeded in undermining the Hijaz's historically tolerant culture. However, a few details from that evening in the Alireza villa's garden were also proof that, in Jeddah at least, some of that cultural inheritance had been kept alive. Men and women, for instance, had sat next to someone who might not have been a direct relative. And only a few of the women were veiled. In Riyadh, the capital of Saudi Arabia in what is still the ultra-conservative Wahhabi heartland of Al-Najd, such casual intermingling of the sexes would have been unimaginable. Moreover, despite the controversial content of the lecture itself—all "political" gatherings inside the kingdom are strictly illegal—no one in the audience revealed the slightest trace of fear. Indeed, quite the reverse: They had the air of a people who took pride in the fact that this was their city, and that a liberal Islamic tradition that respected religious and cultural diversity was their rightful inheritance.

Of course, even in the confines of the garden no one was bold enough to actually criticize the ruling family. But it remained their right to say whatever they wanted to say about the Wahhabi religious establishment—although, again, within the protective confines of the villa's high walls. In a sense, Angawi, by giving his slideshow, was taking his audience back to 1925, when Haji Abdullah—from the same Alireza family—had quietly insisted that the Wahhabi zealots be withdrawn from the Hijaz.

Nasif House, Jeddah's best-preserved old building, is now a museum documenting how Ibn Saud set up a court in it for one and a half years after his forces conquered Jeddah. The Nasif family—connected to the Alireza by two important marriages in the early twentieth century—was of modest Egyptian origin, and its famous patriarch in the nineteenth century was Omar Nasif. The family prospered in Jeddah as merchants, and Omar built the largest and most prestigiously appointed house in the city, famous for having outside its front door the only tree (which is still there today) inside the city walls.

Back in the 1920s, the house was a kind of social salon. Jeddah's merchants gathered there, and foreign consuls visited. That made it ideal for Ibn Saud as a base for his new government. But there may also have been another reasons for its selection. The most prominent Nasif in Jeddah before the city fell to Ibn Saud was Omar's grandson, Mohammed Hussein. British documents, unearthed by Teitelbaum, note that Mohammed was a Wahhabi by conviction even before the Saudi invasion, having been influenced by a "reformer" while visiting Egypt. On his return to Jeddah, he fell into the habit of attacking local Sufis, usually by throwing stones at them. This influential man clearly held strong beliefs that made him sympathetic to Ibn Saud and his Wahhabi backers.

A labyrinth of alleys and the occasional squares and numerous marketplaces, cloaked in differing kinds of shade as the day progressed, formed the heart of Jeddah when Ibn Saud entered the city, and—like the famous tree—they remain. Al-Balad was founded in the seventh century and owes its uniqueness to its traditional buildings, which now date back mostly to the eighteenth and nineteenth centuries. These crumbling houses lining the narrow, winding streets are made of white coral, cut from the Red Sea reef, and decorated with bow windows carved from Indian or Javan teak. The green and brown shutters contrast dramatically with the walls to which they are attached, and their intricate designs allow the women of the households to sit and observe the street without themselves being seen.

Although Al-Balad's defensive walls were torn down in the late 1940s, the area remained largely unchanged until the 1970s. Then the oil boom did change Al-Balad, as it did virtually everything else in the kingdom. Jeddah's population, a stable 25,000 for 45 years, reached 1.5 million by the end of the 1980s. It has grown 60-fold during the last two generations, the result of a local baby boom, an influx of immigrant workers, and mass urbanization. However, when Jeddah expanded in the 1980s, it did so almost exclusively northward.

In the 1970s and early 1980s, when Saudi Arabia was at the height of its drive for modernization, Al-Balad was largely erased from local consciousness. Many Saudis, especially the wealthy merchant families, moved to the north into newly built villas. At the same time, Third World immigrants moved into the traditional dwellings, which for generations had housed the local merchant families. These buildings' gradual, partial demolition was not the result of the kind of religiously inspired process that so angers Sami Angawi. It was pure economics. Al-Balad's narrow streets afforded too little parking space for a Saudi family, which by then typically owned three or more cars, often massive tank-like monstrosities. Its traditional markets did not stock the designer clothes young Saudis had become used to wearing. The houses could not compete with all the modern, air-conditioned luxury the oil money had bought. Amenities were lacking, since everyone of importance was relocating, or establishing, their new headquarters in the north of the city. Al-Balad was a reminder of leaner times, and most locals thanked God they were seeing the back of hardship.

For a while, it seemed that Al-Balad's very existence might be threatened. Steel and glass structures, not infrequently built on the site of demolished white coral houses, appeared almost overnight. The reflections of the older, traditional dwellings in the new shiny facades symbolized the kingdom's dramatic transformation. When the boom had passed its peak, however, the relentless expansion neared its end, and a sudden eagerness emerged among some locals to demonstrate that traditional Jeddah culture had not been undermined by the modernization process. The restoration of Al-Balad, so long out of the public eye, became a serious concern, and today it is the most wide-ranging and ambitious cultural project initiated inside the kingdom.

In 2002, $4 million was promised for the Jeddah Historical Preservation Society, established by the Jeddah Municipality in 1991 to protect and preserve Al-Balad's buildings and traditional way of life. The municipality had been making tentative moves on the preservation front since the 1970s, and the creation of the preservation society was the result of proposals put forward by a British architect hired to devise a workable preservation strategy. In the same year, the municipality chose to extend the boundaries of Al-Balad in a way that reflected the seriousness of the undertaking. A number of areas not previously part of the district were, by government decree, incorporated into it. This meant that they, too, would become part of the new preservation drive.

I sat one evening at the top of Nasif House in the main street of Al-Alawi Souq, which winds its way through the heart of the district, as a guest of Sami Nawar, the head of the Jeddah Historical Preservation Society. Born and brought up in Al-Balad and an engineer by profession, he is a small man with a humble demeanor but an obsessive, infectious personality. He had learned English by acting as a guide and interpreter for the first Westerners who lived in Jeddah. As we sipped the first of many glasses of tea, he recalled charming stories from his boyhood, which he illustrated by pointing from the window to the locations where the events he was narrating had taken place.

Nawar was on a high that evening following the recent news of the huge cash injection. "We originally planned to restore 200 houses in the next ten years," he said. "Now, we may do it in five. We will also rebuild most of the old south wall, which excavations have recently uncovered. And we have discovered 50 percent of a water system that an old man told us about and now we plan to buy the shops sitting on it and turn it into a major tourist attraction."

The department quickly realized that it had to help young craftsmen acquire the skills needed to restore the buildings. "When we started, the youngest workman was 60 years old and there were only 11 of them," Nawar recalled. "Now there are 25 young Saudis, and the fact that they are Saudi is very important. We have 600 buildings on our preservation list and they are all architecturally unique. If younger Saudis don't learn the old crafts from their elders, everything will disappear."

He recruited from among the boys who live in Al-Balad. The idea, he said, was that in time they would form a team of specialists who could be contracted out for other work. "We're doing this for Al-Balad's preservation, but also to cultivate a specialist skill that can give these young men a decent, independent future," he added.

He could have mentioned that the training also helped, however little, ameliorate the unemployment problem, and demonstrated that at least some Saudi youths are willing to work in what are perceived as menial positions.

If measured in terms of crude numbers, the preservation project could by 2003 be judged a success. The owners of some 250 houses had agreed to restore their properties at their own expense, in return for permission to open up commercial premises on the ground floors. Only three businessmen, who together own 14 properties, had at that point refused. Saudi Arabia is "a normal country," Nawar continued. There are people who emphasize business over culture, and others who are happy to lose money if it is for the cultural good. But the majority of owners, he said, had eagerly decided to restore and maintain their houses, in partnership with the society.

The fact remains, however, that the battle for preservation has not yet been won. Fires, in particular, have been a regular occurrence. A huge fire in August 2001 destroyed five old buildings, causing millions of riyals in damage. Their owner, former Jeddah mayor Muhammad Saeed Farsi, had spent $2 million on their renovation, which was completed only a few weeks before the fire reduced them to ashes.

A fire also gutted the first building to have been selected for preservation by Nawar's society after it had originally been earmarked for demolition. Harat Al-Sham, where the building was located, is a densely populated area of Al-Balad almost exclusively inhabited by Somalis, many of whom live on the poverty line. It is better known among the locals as "Al-Mudloom" (the framed). Public beheadings used to be carried out in the area. Legend has it that when a Saudi man, who was sentenced to death for murder but had maintained his innocence to the end, was finally beheaded, his blood spurted out from his neck and spelt out on a wall in front of him the word "framed" in Arabic. The executioner is said to have wept at the sight, and refused to carry out any more beheadings thereafter.

Nowadays, the preoccupations of Al-Balad's residents are less gruesome, even as the beheadings continue a stone's throw from their doorstep in the new "chop-chop" square. They include the contradiction between the drive to preserve the historic nature of the Al-Balad district and the fact that most of its inhabitants are now Third World immigrants—many rumored to be illegal overstayers—whose top priority is hardly treating historic buildings with the respect they warrant. The last big fire was caused by a kerosene cooker, for instance, knocked over in a house occupied by a Somali immigrant family. It follows that few officials have any incentive to care for the infrastructure supporting what they see as parasites. The smell that greets visitors to the area on hot evenings is of the raw sewage that runs freely down the middle of its streets.

For Nawar, though, the solution to this and other problems is to remain positive and push on with the development drive as vigorously as possible. His words are backed by speedy actions. It took just seven weeks from the time the fire destroyed the 200-year-old building to when its residents moved back into it. During that time, it had been completely restored.

His general philosophy is that once the area has been upgraded, more responsible citizens will be drawn back to it.

"We won't initiate any forced demographic change," Nawar insisted. "We want things to happen naturally. We will not have any massive evictions. People rent these buildings legally. If it is true that some of the residents are illegal overstayers, there are other departments in the municipality to deal with that. Our concern is for the safety of the buildings, and their restoration. I believe it would be criminal and against our religion—indeed, against humanity—to throw these people onto the street."

The logic behind the project is crystal clear: If you have a beautifully restored house in a restored street, it will fetch a much higher rent. This, in turn, will attract a more wealthy kind of tenant, who will be more likely to take care of the building. When the owners themselves see that the buildings will bring in as much rent as the modern buildings, but at relatively small expense, Nawar is convinced that most of them will go for it. After all, to restore a building costs only five percent of the cost of demolishing the building and starting again.

There thus exists, in the middle of what has become typically depressing Third World conurbations, an inner city revival program to rival any similar efforts in the West. This honoring of the past stands in stark contrast to the Wahhabi disregard of the physical history of the country now called Saudi Arabia, even while they claim adherence to a historically pure and unadulterated Islam of a long ago past. That this revitalization is also influenced by Western conceptions of a beautiful city, and in part overseen by Western planners, adds a touch of irony. But the central symbolic effect should be kept in sight: By restoring Al-Balad, the people of Jeddah are reminded of the cosmopolitanism that was once theirs, and can again be. Out of the ruins of a once-tolerant and pluralistic civilization can come some kind of brighter future for people who live in the dreary modern environment that surrounds them.

From 1964, Saudi Arabia was ruled by King Faisal, a son of Ibn Saud, but he was assassinated by a nephew in 1975. Back in 1926, Faisal had been appointed the first governor of the Hijaz, immediately after the region was conquered by his father in battles Faisal himself had played a crucial role in leading. As king, Faisal continued to be based a great deal in Jeddah, as did much of the working government—although the capital was officially moved to Riyadh in 1961.

Faisal's assassination was to prove a devastating blow to the merchant families of the Hijaz, and the Alirezas in particular, from which in many respects they have yet to recover.

After being appointed viceroy of the Hijaz, Faisal had quickly recognized the importance of fostering national unity. He was always particularly mindful of doing whatever was possible to prevent his Hijazi subjects from becoming overtly resentful of what he recognized was considered by most of them to be Wahhabi-Al-Saud colonization. Faisal's reign as monarch was a period of unmatched harmony between the Hijazi subjects and the royals who ruled over them.

Inevitably, he eagerly sought to cultivate friendships with the Alirezas, the Hashemites, and other leading merchant families in the region. Most of these became lifelong friendships, spanning the generations, which made the families trusted personal allies in Faisal's eyes. They were also rich, and Faisal periodically requested "loans" from them. While it was implicitly understood they were never to be paid back, handing over the cash meant that the merchant families could later call in personal favors from the royals.

In the 1930s and 1940s, when Faisal was appointed foreign minister—while retaining his post of viceroy of the Hijaz—the young Alirezas' chief value for him lay in their fluent English and their frequent trips abroad. Sometimes, when they traveled, Faisal would ask them to deliver messages, and occasionally even carry out diplomatic assignments on behalf of the crown. A number of Alirezas were made ambassadors—one of them to Cairo, for instance.

The foundation of this harmony was Faisal's political agenda, which was of a kind the liberal Hijazis could not only relate to but eagerly embrace. He prioritized education reforms, as the Alirezas themselves had done. He abolished slavery, while shaking up the bureaucracy of the government and limiting the amount paid in stipends to the ever-expanding legions of princes and princesses. At the same time, he ruled with absolute power, after abolishing as well the position of prime minister. And he consolidated the role of the Wahhabi religious establishment in the state bureaucracy by formalizing its partnership with the Al-Saud ruling family in the form of creating specific government posts for them. Faisal himself was a descendant of both the Al-Saud and the Al-Asheikh families.

In 1973, Faisal became a major force behind the oil embargo against the United States in protest at that country's support of Israel. Although in practical terms the boycott had a limited impact, it led to oil prices (and Faisal's personal popularity) skyrocketing. As a result, everyone in Jeddah—and throughout the kingdom—suddenly found that they were getting rich beyond their wildest dreams. All differences were put aside.

From the time of Ibn Saud, the Saudi state had been characterized by a system of patronage and subsidies: first to tribal and religious leaders, then in the form of a generous welfare state. After the 1973 oil embargo, the kingdom's health, social, and infrastructure indicators began to improve faster than in any other developing country. Saudis started to enjoy, and take for granted, ever-improving levels of free social welfare.

By 1975, the year of his assassination, Faisal was on the cover of *Time*, having been chosen as the magazine's Man of the Year. He had been respected even among the world's Muslims as clean living, incorruptible, and a true defender of the faith. At the height of his popularity, the domestic Saudi media, too, venerated him—not with the kind of silly sycophantic front-page coverage afforded by editors (under threat of dismissal) to senior princes these days, but in a way that genuinely elevated him to the status of true Muslim king. A deep nostalgia among many Saudis continues to exist for the period under his rule, as is evidenced by the comparatively large number of boys still named Faisal by their parents—especially in the Hijaz.

After his assassination, Faisal was succeeded by his brother, Khalid, a member of the powerful Al-Sudairy branch of the ruling family, which includes the present King Fahd and his six full brothers. Known as the Sudairy Seven, they include Defense Minister Prince Sultan, Interior Minister Prince Naif, and Riyadh Governor Prince Salman. The seven make all the important economic and political decisions in Saudi Arabia, with King Fahd's favorite son, Abdul Aziz, increasingly standing in for his father. Khalid, and then Fahd, the brother who succeeded him to the throne, consolidated the shift of the government bureaucracy from Jeddah to Riyadh. Foreign embassies had no choice but to follow suit. In the process, the Al-Sudairys consolidated their own private power base, awarding each other all the top positions in government. When it came to granting key, second-level positions to those who were not members of the royal family, they were usually given to fellow Najdis.

The Al-Sudairys are said to be highly distrustful of the Hijazis, as well as the Al-Faisals, and one consequence of this closing of the ranks among the Al-Sudairys was the deliberate marginalization of the Al-Faisals. Their reputation for being liberals who favored the "sophisticated" lifestyle and bureaucracy of the Hijaz did them no favors. Nor did championing Jeddah's way of doing business, and caring about the well being of their subjects. Today, the only member of the Al-Faisal branch of the ruling family to still hold a top position in the government is Prince Saud Al-Faisal, the foreign minister who is a son of King Faisal, and he has ironically described himself to a foreign journalist as a "tea boy."

In a villa in a different district of Jeddah, but in the same year that Sami Angawi gave his lecture at the Alirezas, an informal discussion group on the fall-out inside Saudi Arabia from the September 11 attacks was convened by Princess Reem Mohammed Al-Faisal, a granddaughter of King Faisal. The villa where this gathering took place belonged to her father—Faisal's son, Prince Mohammed Al-Faisal—who is chairman of the Jeddah-based National Commercial Bank.

Mohammed had been named in a $100 trillion lawsuit brought by lawyers acting on behalf of victims of the attacks on New York, who claimed that he and other Saudi individuals and organizations had for years secretly helped finance Saudi dissident Osama bin Laden's Al-Qaeda terror network. Although Mohammed had won a series of libel suits in Europe against a French-language book that had first named him as a potential funder of terrorism, the book was still everywhere on sale (outside of Saudi Arabia, of course), and—as is the case with all such smears—the damage to his reputation had been done. But although it was a pyrrhic legal victory, in the sense that it had not stopped readers from getting hold of the book, it was one that seemed to matter a great deal to the family. In 2004, the U.S. lawsuit brought on behalf of the families of the September 11 victims was dismissed.

The Al-Faisals, then, had found themselves at the center of the claims and counter-claims that were putting at risk one of the twentieth century's most enduring security alliances, between the Al-Saud and the United States. That afternoon, Reem was articulating the liberal Saudi perspective on life, religion, and the impact of the September 11 terrorist acts on Saudi-U.S. relations. She had been joined by half a dozen or so other upper-class Hijazi intellectuals, who included local media personalities, other members of the royal family, and members of Jeddah's merchant families. "I don't want things to reach a point where there's no dialogue at all between us," she said afterward, in reference to the people of the United States and Saudi Arabia.

The guests trickled out, and we settled down to a long conversation interrupted only by a succession of green teas and a break—for her—for evening prayers.

Reem is perhaps best described as a free spirit—a princess who wears the airs and graces associated with that title lightly. She mixes easily with all classes of Saudi society and considers the Hijaz her home. She is also a woman who has earned a niche for herself, both in Saudi Arabia and abroad, in the traditionally male-dominated art of photojournalism. Like her grandfather, Faisal, she is a conservative Muslim; but she feels equally at home in the artistic milieu of Paris (she spends half of each year in France) as she does in Mecca (where she has photographed the Haj).

The fact that even photographing women is strictly taboo in Saudi Arabia is an indication of how groundbreaking was her own decision to take to the streets with her camera. "It's a double indemnity," she laughed, when the practicalities of her undertaking photographic projects was brought up. "What do they hate more: the woman because she's a photographer, or the photographer because she's taking photographs of women? It's true that one encounters a lot of volunteer defenders of the social mores. And, by the way, it's usually the women who raise objections and cause problems, not the men—they simply hate having their photograph being taken!"

When she exhibited her photographs of Jeddah's port in Paris, another cultural stereotype had to be overcome, when the news broke that she was a Saudi princess.

"They suddenly expected me to arrive dressed in fine silk robes with an army of slaves in tow, carrying things on their head," she recalled. "And then it turned out that the press weren't as interested in my photos as they were in my presumed lavish lifestyle. They wanted to come and photograph me sitting at home in my luxurious surroundings!"

She raised her arms and looked around herself in vague bemusement, and I got her point: It was a nice place, to be sure, but hardly justified the label "decadent." In fact, it was characterized more than anything else by an obvious love of the arts, Islamic and Western, and by its shelves of books.

Reem's major subject in her photographs is "divine light," historically at the heart of all Islamic art, and this is especially evident in her collection "Diwan Al-Noor." The black-and-white photographs in that monograph feature solid objects that are always presented as reflections of the light that gives them form and content. An orb is circular in the photographs because of the light which curls round it. An archway is so tall because of the light streaming through it.

"I go through the world trying to find places and people where there is a sense of a touch of the divine," she said. "And I want that to be reflected in my images. I don't believe in giving them captions afterward, because I want people to have the sense that those who figure in them are citizens of the world."

Reem does not necessarily have to travel far in her quest to document the common threads of humanity that bind people of different cultures into the divine whole. In her on-going project documenting the Haj, for instance, she is trying to capture it as a human, rather than a strictly ritualistic, event. What has so inspired her photographic imagination is the manner in which so many races, speaking so many different languages, manage to cope with the experience of being forced to co-exist in such a small place while undertaking the intense, physically draining, and life-defining Islamic obligation.

She was most surprised, she said, by the extraordinary level of mutual tolerance she observed as she moved through streets swarming with men and women.

"It's like a little lab of humanity," she continued. "It's an amazingly successful coexistence. I was surprised. When you do the Haj yourself, you're concentrating so much on praying and the rituals that you really can't see the whole picture. But when you're an observer you can see the great sense of discovery. At some point, it seems logistically impossible: when you see three million people thrown together for four days in one place, you realize that nothing can work if they don't adapt to each other, and give one another space and respect."

So what, I wanted to know as a non-Muslim forbidden from entering Mecca, is the real story of the great coexistence of the Haj, which remains at the cultural, commercial and religious heart of the Hijaz?

"The first story is that these people can coexist. The second is that they can do so without being saintly. Everybody assumes that those who do the pilgrimage are perfect little beings who drop from the sky and don't have their history and baggage and misconceptions and culture and desires. You have pick-pockets in the Haj. You have uneducated people. You have rude people. You have saints. And yet all these people, with their little quirks and mistakes and problems and saintliness, still manage not to be at one another's throats. The reason is that for the one time in their lives they all sublimate themselves, suspending their own beings to a higher goal which has nothing to do with material gain. It's a Haj culture, and it's been going on for centuries."

What is perhaps most striking about Reem is the way she balances, again like her grandfather, sometimes radical criticism of the United States (especially its—to her mind—unconditional support of Israel) with equally forthright remarks about the obstacles that Saudi Arabia itself must acknowledge, and strive to overcome, if it is to succeed in its push for modernization and reform.

"There are major problems here in Saudi Arabia," she interjected at one point, straightening her veil and pushing a lock of hair that had come loose back underneath it, an act of instinctive modesty. "There is corruption. There is an unequal distribution of wealth. There are many people who do not have the necessary skills to perform their jobs properly, and many who have the skills needed but can't actually get a job. And the work ethic among Saudis—both men and women—is frankly zero."

Like so many other Hijazi intellectuals who feel equally at home in American and Arab cultures, Reem seemed to have been personally shaken by the events of September 11. She herself did not put it that way, but it was obvious both from my general conversation with her and from what I heard of the exchanges between her and a *New York Times* journalist who had left shortly after I arrived. Hijazi intellectuals feel that there were two victims on that day: the Americans who died in the attacks and the liberal tradition of Saudi Arabia, which has subsequently been marginalized as a result of the American media onslaught against the kingdom when it became known that 15 of the 19 hijackers were Saudis. Reem and like-minded Saudis shifted their focus away from promoting debate and reform at home to defending Saudi Arabia's reputation abroad, as it became labeled the "kernal of evil." There was a dramatic closing of ranks, coupled with a great deal of self-denial.

This latter charge Reem partly accepted, but she saw a parallel in the American media's refusal to look squarely in the face at what she insists at the same time was the root cause of the attacks themselves: America's foreign policy.

"It's true, all of us Saudis have been thrown into the front line because of the collective blame," she said. "Everyone thinks that because 15 Saudis were on those planes, all Saudis are criminals."

So if the American media had treated differently the fact that 15 of the hijackers were Saudis, would Saudi Arabia itself have been more introspective and willing to engage in constructive dialogue?

"Of course. Something obviously was very wrong that these 15 terrorists came out of Saudi Arabia. But instead of addressing it as a social ill, in the same way that the American schoolchildren who went on shooting sprees did so because of a social ill in their society, it was suddenly portrayed that they somehow represented Saudi Arabia, that they are the majority. We have social ills, sure; but we are human beings who form part of the global society. We are not abnormal people who have ills that don't exist elsewhere in the world."

A few hours earlier, I had seen Reem and her companions refuse to admit to the visiting *New York Times* journalist that 15 of the hijackers were definitely Saudis. Now here she was, openly admitting to me that they were. Presumably, the trust was there because she had read a number of my previous articles and felt confident that I was unlikely to write yet another hatchet job. Whatever the reason, I suppose I should have been pleased; but in fact I was deeply saddened. It was a glimpse into a constructive cultural exchange we can only reflect on as a "what might have been"—in which Saudis and Westerners actually listened to what one another were saying, while not hiding behind the facade of superficial denial.

Not that, according to Reem, there had ever been much of a chance. She had been photographing in the United States for two years before September 11, traveling on her own from state to state.

"I saw the hatred of Saudi Arabia before September 11," she claimed. "The reason is that it was so easy to tag the Saudi. We replaced the Semite of the nineteenth century. Because of our dress and because we are physically so Arab, they could label us medieval and dark and shifty. Of course, the perception was that all Saudi women were slaves, that we're corrupt, spending money blindly without even knowing it."

But was all that cultural misunderstanding, if that is the correct description, not the fault of Saudi Arabia? The kingdom closed itself off to the world with the discovery of oil, told itself it did not need to change and open up.

"We are at least 50 percent to blame," she admitted. "I remember talking to Saudis about how we have to address the issues, and they told me 'No, no, no, the rest of the world can see things in Saudi Arabia for itself.' But it couldn't. Ninety percent of humanity doesn't even know where Saudi Arabia is on the map, let alone what's going on inside it. The Saudis have a problem explaining themselves."

Of course, not admitting to a foreign journalist that the majority of the September 11 hijackers were Saudis hardly helped matters, combining as it did denial with a refusal to address underlying causes.

Reem's independence has been a trait among the female members of her close family since they came to the Hijaz in the early twentieth century. Her grandmother, Queen Effat, the only wife of King Faisal, was brought up and educated in Turkey, and was a forceful and dynamic matriarch within the royal Al-Faisal household. She endured much suffering and pain in a land that was then an undeveloped backwater, watching helplessly as many of the 12 children she bore sickened and died for want of proper medical attention. She lived through the wars of Saudi unification and numerous wars in the Middle East. She experienced the widest extremes of poverty and wealth. And, after all that, she had to come to terms with the assassination of her husband in 1975, by which time Reem herself was being brought up by her and the larger extended family.

"I've never seen an oppressed woman in my family," Reem remarked casually in the course of recalling tales of her grandmother and mother's powerful, guiding presence during her childhood.

"Growing up, I was always surrounded by my grandmother and my aunts and great aunts, and they were all women of tremendous character and independence."

But that was a closed and very privileged world, I told her, and as such was hardly representative of what the vast majority of Saudi women experience.

"If you are born with a silver spoon in your mouth, many doors in life open automatically for you," she readily acknowledged. "This is true wherever you are in the world. But no, as far as Saudi Arabia specifically is concerned, I've mixed with women from all classes in society. I've lived, eaten, and spoken with them as a matter of course, and I would say that the hardships poorer women here face mainly have to do with their lack of opportunities, not with their sex. Men and women in that sense are encountering the same problems: their lack of good education and their limited wealth. There has to be a good education system, and a fair distribution of wealth, in any country if its people—both men and women—are to achieve their full potential."

Reem's brother, Prince Amr Mohammed Al-Faisal, a businessman and a columnist for the Hijazi newspaper *Al-Medina,* settled down next to Reem on the sofa.

A clean-shaven man who is proud of the fact that he was educated exclusively in Jeddah, he speaks perfect English and considers himself proof that the Saudi education system cannot be exclusively to blame for the extremism in Saudi society that caught the attention of the West after September 11. Our conversation at once turned to what he considered the most interesting books—like *Voltaire's Bastards: The Dictatorship of Reason in the West,* by John Ralston Saul, which he sent me a copy of a few days later— to have come out of Britain and the United States in recent years. (Both he and Reem order books by the box from amazon.com, since good bookshops are nonexistent inside the kingdom.) Then talk moved slowly to the fluidity of cultural barriers and their influence on the progress of history.

One of the many legacies of their former king and queen, it was obvious, is the dissenting perspective on life they instilled in whoever was fortunate enough to come under their influence, including Reem and Amr, and in their presence one could not help but feel disheartened that the Al-Faisals have been marginalized so completely from Saudi political life.

Reem's personal love for the Hijaz was obvious. In his columns for *Al-Medina,* Amr too sometimes sounded more like one of the locals than a member of the ruling elite. The domestic issues he addressed ranged from outright mockery of the religious police after they objected to his new company logo because it contained a "+" sign they said too closely resembled a Christian cross (he suggested ironically that all "+" signs in the kingdom's math books should immediately be replaced by "tasteful Islamic" crescents) to criticism of the wealthy Saudis he had encountered while vacationing in the south of France; these men spent tens of million of dollars in the space of a few days despite the fact that hundreds of thousands of ordinary Saudis live in poverty and suffer unemployment back home.

However, when he was told about Angawi's lecture, and I asked him about the increasingly vocal calls for an independent Hijaz, he was contemptuous of the ideas that had been expressed, suggesting that Angawi was perhaps feeding off an American campaign aimed at undermining the kingdom and Islam.

He had faith, he said, in the reformers from within his own Al-Saud family.

"Who doesn't want reforms?" he said dismissively, when I suggested there was too much resistance from conservative royals to get them implemented. "Everyone wants reforms."

As I left, I realized that Amr was fighting a lonely battle as he tried to return to the Arabs a sense of lost pride by stirring their intellectual and cultural roots, all of which—although he would probably not admit it or possibly even accept the argument—had been undermined in the Hijaz, especially by the Wahhabi-Al-Saud hegemony. Conversely, the reformers within the Al-Sudairy branch of the royal family, which held real power—even those from his own generation—seemed to me much weaker than he was willing to admit.

At a private gathering a couple of weeks after our chat, at the house of another big Hijazi family, a third generation prince—known to be reform-minded—from the Al-Sudairy branch of the ruling family was invited to hear the grievances of locals in a majlis, or discussion forum. There it became clear what Amr and Reem were up against as they tried to keep alive the legacy of their grandfather.

In the more than a quarter century since Faisal was assassinated, the merchant families of Jeddah have been marginalized to the extent that they can barely contain their anger. They fired off to the Al-Sudairy prince an endless list of complaints about soaring unemployment, the antics of the religious police, the need for greater press freedom, stifling bureaucracy, and how their status as "Saudis" had plummeted on the world stage. The prince listened patiently, acknowledged many of the points to be valid, but emphasized his belief that the kingdom would marginalize the extremists, as it always had managed to do in the past, and push forward with reforms to overcome its present economic difficulties.

Nevertheless, the guests added in whispers after the prince had left, Jeddah is a city suffering under Wahhabi–Al-Saud colonial occupation. The palaces of the members of the royal family who actually hold power loom along the *corniche*-like vast floodlit garrisons. King Fahd and Crown Prince Abdullah both occupy acres and acres of heavily fortified Hijazi coastline, which forces the locals to follow tedious loops of the coastal road as it diverts away from the sea for miles at a stretch.

Young Saudis in Jeddah say mischievously that they have renamed the fountain on the corniche, the tallest in the world, "King Fahd's bidet." A member of one merchant family, who works for a senior prince, refused to be called "Saudi" by me, preferring "Hijazi." When asked if any of the houses he was building and wanted to rent out might be suitable for a Saudi family, he replied sternly: "I do not make houses for animals." A young member of the Alireza household, who had returned from the United States after September 11, said he had been sent on a three-day assignment to Riyadh, but the same evening he was back in his office in Jeddah. Half an hour of walking through Riyadh—with its aloof Najdi males and completely covered-up females, both closely observed by the hardline religious police— was more than he could bear, and he got on the next flight "home."

These were not isolated comments.

Those from the region who called the Qatar-based Al-Jazeera satellite station to participate in live debates about Saudi Arabia often reacted with fury whenever they were referred to by the host of the show as a "Saudi," insisting instead that they be called "Hijazi." A favorite pseudonym for those who feared giving their real name was "Al-Hijazi Al-Sharif," the latter an honorific given to members of the Hashemite dynasty. A magazine published in London called *The Hijaz,* officially an "orphan," meaning its private backers consider it too risky to be openly associated with, periodically hints at the desirability of independence for the region ruled by an elected government funded by tourism and revenues from the annual Haj.

Mai Yamani, a daughter of former oil minister Sheik Ahmed Zaki Yamani (who steered the kingdom through the oil boom, was for more than a decade the public face of the Al-Saud regime in the West and the most famous Arab in the world, and is himself a Hijazi who has turned on the Al-Saud), claims she was told to stop writing by Interior Minister Prince Naif after publishing a critical book about the kingdom in 2000, and has been living in London ever since. She witnessed Hijazis in Medina, she once said, cheering visiting Hashemite princes from Jordan, declaring them to be their true historic rulers. Undeterred by the subsequent campaign against her, she has published another book, *Cradle of Islam,* that can be interpreted as a manifesto for an independent Hijaz. In newspaper articles she, too, has become a fearless critic of the Al-Saud regime.

If freed from the crushing weight of their portly occupiers, many Hijazis feel, their city could have it all.

The Hijaz has unspoiled coral reefs, beautifully clear water, and the longest pristine coastline anywhere in the region. Over 400 types of sculptures and exhibits are displayed on the *corniche* and throughout Jeddah, even as centerpieces on the roundabouts and median strips. A concrete Arabic engraving of the opening phrase of the Qu'ran ("In the name of God") gives way, as you drive along the coastline, to giant signs of the Zodiac. Their positioning defines a sharp curve in the road and confusingly suggests a tolerance of either non-Islamic or—more accurately—Pagan belief systems. Other sculptures are truly spectacular: a giant bicycle; a flotilla of full-size, ex-navy gunboats, complete with fighter escort; a decommissioned DC-10 airliner; real cars jutting from a vast concrete block; an abstract sculpture created from what remained of a demolished desalination plant. Families idle away the long evenings camped out next to, or underneath, the sculptures, picnicking and smoking water pipes while their children enjoy donkey rides on the beach or navigate the sidewalks away from the coastal roads on little shiny bicycles.

Geographically, Jeddah also has a thousand times more going for it than Dubai and could easily accommodate three times the number of annual tourists as that tiny built-up enclave on the Arabian Gulf. The sense of waste in Jeddah becomes particularly poignant at night, when a drive along the *corniche* can create a powerful illusion that all is well. With large seafood restaurants and hubbly bubbly cafes, their strings of colorful lanterns twinkling over the water, it all suggests at first sight conviviality. However, what looks from a distance like a place where men and women, for instance, could enjoy themselves together, on closer inspection turns out to be—with a few exceptions—yet another manifestation of the Wahhabi insistence that the sexes are not allowed to coexist in Saudi Arabia.

One consequence has been the creation of self-contained island-villages in the north, where the religious police are banned as a result of princely protection and local customs are discarded. On the private beaches, where "beer garden" signs stick out of the sand in an Islamic kingdom where alcohol is officially prohibited, men and women—Saudis and foreigners alike—swim and sunbathe next to one another in skimpy swimwear.

In the winter of 2003, a few months before the start of the U.S.-led war on Iraq, I was invited to a picnic in the desert near Mecca by a 19-year-old nephew of Osama bin Laden, to whom I had been introduced by chance a few weeks earlier by a mutual acquaintance.

Along with a group of their closest teenage friends, both were in the habit of heading to the desert on the weekend, and suggested I should join them. We met up there a few days later with dozens of other young men from Jeddah and Mecca, to drive their four-wheel-drive jeeps up and down massive sand dunes—an improvised recreation activity created in the total absence of anything resembling a youth culture in the kingdom. For a couple of hours, we zoomed up and down, banging our heads on the inside of the roof as the jeep careered over yet another sharply angled peak only to narrowly miss a jeep speeding toward us in the opposite direction.

The patch of desert had carefully—if unofficially—been developed by generations of Hijazi teenagers. Now it stretched over a vast area transformed into a Raleigh course. Each "section" had a different name and number, and the dunes became increasingly difficult to surmount the further into the desert the convoy of drivers progressed—until the last section, Number 5, which only the most experienced drivers in the most powerful jeeps would attempt to surmount, cheered on by crowds of their less-experienced admirers standing by their parked jeeps at the bottom.

All the drivers had CB radios in their jeeps, and long bendy steel aerials swung violently from their roofs. The radios were set to a frequency used only by those who were navigating the course, and everyone who spoke on it seemed to have a nickname or "handle." Such radios were a necessity, of course, in the desert, where drivers found themselves not only mindful of avoiding collisions but also out of range of the mobile phone network, while facing the very real danger of getting stuck in the sand in some out-of-the-way place after taking a wrong turn.

The bin Laden who invited me out that day, and in whose jeep I sat next to, was tall and slim, with short brown hair and a whitish complexion—a handsome, clean-shaven lad who bore a striking resemblance to his uncle Osama (also born and brought up in Jeddah) as a teenager. He spoke English well and was extremely polite: He never did call me anything but "Mr. John," on that or the half dozen or so other occasions we were to meet up. He worked part-time, he said, in the family construction business, and was also studying for his degree (again, as Osama had) at a local college. Every month or so he traveled to a port city known for its liberal environment, ostensibly on business but really, he confided, to take advantage of the whores and alcohol there, both of which were available in that laid-back city's five-star hotels.

After the driving was over, the picnic itself took place—we were as close as was possible, I was told, for an "infidel" such as myself to get to Mecca without violating the city and its environs' strict Muslim-only status. A dozen or so teenagers helped lay out two huge blankets on the sand, which were soon piled high with homemade sandwiches, cakes and dates, and packets of cigarettes. Huge flasks of hot tea were placed next to them, and little Arabian tea cups were handed round. As the only Westerner there, I was first to have my cup filled. Then plate after plate of food was passed over to me by those whose inveterate hospitality meant they could not take anything for themselves until they were certain I, a foreigner and therefore an honored guest, had taken more than enough for myself.

We were briefly joined, half an hour later, by three other members of the bin Laden family. A choking dust storm clouded the picnic area when they arrived in their own speeding convoy of brand new four-wheel drives. One of the three bin Ladens was a brother or a half-brother of Osama (I did not quite catch which during the rapid introductions), and in his thirties. The other two were Osama's nephews, in their early twenties. They, too, were eager to speak in English. But, unlike my bin Laden host, they did so with an exaggerated American accent, which many well-off Hijazis are under the impression is the ultimate in "cool."

The bin Laden family, of course, is in an extraordinarily sensitive position, both inside Saudi Arabia and in the wider international community—and not just because of Osama. It is at the center of a storm of accusations about its connections with the Bush and Saudi royal families, which were explored in Craig Unger's book *House of Bush, House of Saud: The Secret Relationship Between the World's Two Most Powerful Dynasties* and, more noisily, in Michael Moore's documentary *Fahrenheit 9/11*, which drew heavily on Unger's research. Both author and filmmaker traced three decades of allegedly compromising financial ties between the Bush, Al-Saud, and bin Laden families, initiated during the 1970s oil boom when Saudi money poured into the Bush home state of Texas.

Unger and Moore broadly agreed that those ties, and the personal loyalties that were forged with them, undermined the war on terror in the aftermath of the September 11 attacks. The ties also helped to shape the decision, they went on, by the Bush administration to go after Iraq rather than those who were truly responsible for nurturing Islamic terrorism: Bush's friends in the Al-Saud ruling family and their construction business partners, the bin Laden merchant family of the Hijaz.

Both book and documentary hinged on the revelation that 24 members of the bin Laden family, along with hundreds of other senior Saudis, including princes, were allowed to leave the United States within days of the September 11 attacks without being properly interrogated by the FBI and at a time when air transport was restricted even for Dick Cheney and George H. W. Bush.

On the Thursday afternoon early in 2003, when we picnicked in the desert near Mecca, the controversy had yet to become part of the mainstream U.S. media discussion of Saudi Arabia. Details of the infamous flight had been limited to a few newspaper articles that, curiously, few journalists in the United States had initially been willing to pick up on. When he talked about his past, one of the three bin Ladens who had arrived late, a nephew of Osama, talked openly about having taken a flight out of the U.S. immediately after September 11, on which "every other bin Laden" who had been in that country at the time was a fellow passenger.

"Can you imagine how scared we were?" he asked. "Man, we just wanted to get the hell out of there."

His recollection was seconded by another of the bin Ladens present, who readily admitted that he, too, had been on the flight. Both had been students in the United States on the day of the attacks.

So the fact that there was a special flight cannot be in any doubt, despite lingering official denials. But whether it happened when U.S. airspace was closed is still uncertain. Neither of the two bin Ladens that day was specific about the details, and another bin Laden—Yeslam, a Geneva-based businessman—has said that the flight left the United States on September 20, when normal flights had resumed.

The existence of close ties between a leading Texas-based oil family like the Bushes and the Al-Saud family is in itself unremarkable. The fact that the Texas family has produced two U.S. presidents and the Al-Saud family presides over a Middle Eastern dictatorship that rules in partnership with a Wahhabi religious establishment does, though, seriously raise the stakes, especially in the context of the war on terror. Nevertheless, it is still hard to come to clear conclusions about what the effect of those ties has been for the United States and the rest of the world, before or after September 11. The highly politicized debate in the United States has failed to take into account many important facts and details that would undermine deeply entrenched positions. As ever, political pundits are unwilling to entertain contradictions and paradoxes that are an essential and muddying part of the complex historical picture. There is also the problem of a general ignorance in the West about the history of a Hijazi family like the bin Ladens, and its essentially troubled contemporary relationship with the branch of the Al-Saud family—the Al-Sudairys—that now wields all the power in Saudi Arabia.

Like the patriarchs of many other Hijazi merchant families, Mohammed bin Laden, Osama's father, came to Jeddah from the Hadramout region of Yemen. He started his life in the kingdom in the 1930s as a poor laborer but ended up as owner of the kingdom's biggest construction company. During the reign of King Saud (1953–64), Mohammed became very close to the royal family by building the monarch's palaces at cut-rate prices. He also built good relations with other princes, especially Faisal, the pro-Hijazi monarch who would succeed Saud after an intense period of infighting.

After the incompetent Saud was finally forced to abdicate, it was discovered that he had completely emptied the treasury. Mohammed bin Laden helped Faisal get a grip on the economy by paying the kingdom's civil servants' wages for six months, and Faisal then issued a decree that all construction projects should go to bin Laden. For a while, Mohammed was appointed minister for public works. Cementing the Al-Faisal-bin Laden special relationship, the bin Ladens were given the contract to build virtually every road in the country, and in 1973 Faisal contracted them for the grandest project of them all: rebuilding the Islamic holy sites at Mecca and Medina. According to an article in the *New Yorker,* the renovation, which is estimated to have cost $17 billion so far, continues, with no completion date in sight.

This distant history was mistakenly taken by many in the West to indicate that the Al-Saud and the bin Ladens are still the best of friends, with a minority in both the merchant family and the royal family secretly backing Osama and channeling his Al-Qaeda network funds—even after both families publicly disowned him in the early 1990s. This belief logically raised the questionable link between the Al-Saud and the Bush families that had, this argument went, been largely responsible for compromising U.S. policy vis-à-vis Saudi Arabia: Bush was unwilling to address the issue because it would undermine his own family's business interests.

Little of that makes much sense, however, on closer inspection. Leaving the black sheep Osama out of the picture, and the small minority of both princes and bin Ladens who may privately support Al-Qaeda's goals to the extent of secretly funding him, the bin Ladens have long had serious grievances against the current Al-Sudairy branch of the Al-Saud ruling family, while their dealings with the Bush family have always been relatively open and transparent. Their fortune was made, moreover, under King Faisal, and along with the Al-Faisals, the bin Ladens began to be marginalized by the Al-Sudairy princes when the latter took over the reins of power following Faisal's assassination in 1975. Indeed, these days, it is not unusual to hear bin Ladens bad-mouthing the Al-Sudairy princes they work for. They complain especially of late payments for their construction work from the most notorious late-payer of them all: Defense Minister Prince Sultan. Their main gripe, indeed, is that payment for the ongoing renovation of the Islamic sites is constantly delayed. Their employees often receive their salaries two or three months late as a result, according to one I spoke to.

Such intense hostility, bordering on hatred, is mutual. Less than a month after the September 11 attacks, an editorial appeared in *Al-Riyadh,* the capital city's main government-guided newspaper. Written by the editor-in-chief of *Al-Riyadh,* Turki Al-Sudairy, who comes from the same family as the mother of King Fahd and the six other Al-Sudairy princes who presently hold all the key government positions, it sent a very clear signal: The Al-Sudairys were publicly putting as much distance as possible between themselves and the bin Laden family.

Al-Sudairy wrote that the source of the bin Ladens' money "is surrounded by many question marks, as is the case with many contractors"—a clear dig at the Hijazi merchant families generally. Highlighting the bin Laden family's Yemeni origins—implicitly contrasting them to the "true" Saudis of the central Wahhabi bastion of the Al-Najd region, where *Al-Riyadh* is published and the Al-Sudairys hail from—the article stressed that Osama's father, Mohammed, "was not a rich man when he came to the kingdom." Finally, he hit at the family's main source of pride—the expansion of the Mecca and Medina mosques—by writing that Osama's father had not donated any money for the project, but instead merely reaped the rewards from "exaggerated contracts" from "the royal family."

The implication was that the bin Ladens were greedy opportunists seriously lacking in piety, true Arabian character, and love for their fellow Muslims. And they should be reminded how they owe everything they have to their Al-Saud patrons and the kingdom the Al-Saud gave their name to—and to which their errant son Osama had, a month earlier, dealt a devastating blow.

According to the *Wall Street Journal,* which briefly discussed the editorial at the time of its appearance, Turki Al-Sudairy "signaled a shift in government attitudes toward the bin Laden clan." That is far from accurate. It did, how-ever, publicly make apparent for the Western media, at a time when the most powerful faction inside the Al-Saud realized the bin Ladens had become a ter-rible liability, what everyone in Saudi Arabia had been aware of for at least a decade.

Far from breaking new ground, Al-Sudairy was safely roaming in famil-iar territory. Even his criticism of the "royal family" was not as bold as it sounded, since he was directing it not at the Al-Sudairy clan but their main rivals, the Al-Faisals, and the Hijazi merchant families King Faisal had loved and sponsored. The editorial, then, implicitly confirmed the profound mar-ginalization of the Hijazi merchant families inside Saudi Arabia since Faisal's death, effectively becoming the final nail in their coffin—just as Osama's in-famy had confirmed in the eyes of many liberal Hijazis that being associated with "Saudi Arabia" was fast becoming a terrible liability as well.

Given this context, it might be deduced that, since they are so out of favor with their current princely masters, the bin Ladens would have noth-ing to lose by secretly backing their errant son, one of whose main goals is to overthrow the Al-Saud and replace it with a Taliban-style theocracy. But that thesis also falls apart on closer inspection. It ignores the fact of the dev-astating loss of status suffered by the bin Ladens as a result of the Osama connection to September 11. The bin Ladens were, for the most part, well-known before the attacks as free-living liberals, and their main interest was always making money and not funding the global jihad. Now it is difficult to imagine that, after the existing ties between the family business and West-ern companies have run their natural course, anyone from the next genera-tion of business leaders in the West will want to have anything to do with them, any more than the Saudi royal family will.

Just how ashamed most of the bin Ladens are now of Osama, at least publicly, was revealed by my bin Laden acquaintance at the picnic. After a couple of hours, the original group of young Saudis had been largely replaced by newcomers, and a self-styled comedian among them insisted that, since so many people now had no idea who everyone else was, each should introduce himself and say what he does for a living. When it came to bin Laden's turn, he hesitated, and then he gave only his first name followed by "Al-Mudeer"— "the Boss." When pressed, he simply repeated himself, and looked away.

It would be difficult to overstate the significance of a young man in the Hijaz being so ashamed of his family name that he found it too troubling to utter it in public. On the way home, I asked him why he had refused to give his name. He answered only by saying: "We've asked the Al-Saud to change the name bin Laden in our passports, so no-one knows who we are anymore. They've agreed, and God willing we will get our new passports soon."

In late 2003, for the first time in Saudi history, a peaceful "demonstration" went ahead in Jeddah, a miniature version of the state-orchestrated marches in Soviet Russia on May Day. Some 200 students from four National Guard schools carried anti-terror banners and took to the streets. The students, aged between 12 and 18, were dressed in identical sweat pants, white T-shirts, and caps, bearing the words "Together Against Terrorism." The march started at 7 A.M. at the National Guard housing complex on Palestine Street, where the schools are located, and ended 2.5 miles away on the same road. Chanting anti-terror slogans, students held banners aloft that read "Together for the Sake of the Country" and "Hand in Hand Against Terrorism." The march was organized by the student activity committee in the National Guard, the reform-minded crown prince's private army, who wanted to pioneer "a unique, unprecedented student activity in the kingdom" that could be practiced nationwide at some unspecified time in the future.

Earlier in 2003, when an independent peaceful demonstration was planned in Jeddah, not against terrorism but to call for greater democracy, the city became a virtual garrison town overnight. The army closed off whole districts, riot police lined the main streets, special security forces gathered outside the mosques, and the secret police had cameras trained on all and sundry. Hundreds were arrested, many of whom were reportedly sentenced to prison and lashings. As I drove around the city's streets with two young Saudi friends at that time, the sense of just how extreme a police state Saudi Arabia is was manifested as never before. Not even after terrorist bombings were the special forces deployed in such large numbers, and everyone realized that—however much the word "reform" was in the air—anyone who might dare seriously to question the legitimacy of the Al-Saud ruling family's iron grip on power was in for it, big time.

Earlier in the year, there had been a pro-democracy demonstration in Riyadh also organized by supporters of the Saudi exile Saad Al-Faqih, head of a London-based opposition group called The Movement for Islamic Reform in Arabia (MIRA). It too was crushed, with special security forces even firing rubber bullets over the heads of the demonstrators.

A week or so after the earlier demonstration, I got a call from a female friend from the Hashemite dynasty, which still owns most of the property in

Mecca. She said, in an oddly formal manner: "I just want you to know that the Hashemites completely disown the member of our family who has been arrested for demonstrating in Riyadh, and that he does not represent what the family stands for. We are with the Al-Saud."

With that, she hung up.

Later, she explained that, as she knew my mobile was being tapped by the Ministry of Information, she had spoken with a view to passing on those opinions to the relevant authorities.

Among the dozens also arrested in Riyadh had been a prominent young member of the Hashemites. He had apparently been handing out leaflets promoting the goal of an independent Hijaz. This news had sent shock-waves through the elders of the House of Hashem back in Jeddah and Mecca. They convened a meeting, I was told, at which it was decided that the young man in question would be cut off from the trust fund set up by the Hashemites, which still gives an annual payout to every member of the family (the amount determined by the income generated from rents).

Given the long-standing suspicion by the Al-Saud that the Hashemites in Saudi Arabia are a potential fifth column and sympathetic with the ruling Hashemites of Jordan, the measures my friend took were understandable. For it would not have been shocking if at least the immediate family of the "culprit" had been punished, since in Saudi Arabia an individual's behavior is seen as a reflection and the responsibility of his or her family, narrowly or broadly defined. By cutting him off, the family punished him and protected itself, not least by making clear that were he punished by the regime, their honor was no longer at stake. A not-too-subtle play was acted out, all sides knowing what the others were doing, each speaking according to a script defined by living in an authoritarian regime where power is arbitrary and held by men rather than law.

In the seven decades since the Al-Saud had conquered the Hijaz, the uncontrolled urbanization of the oil boom has left Jeddah looking like any other of Saudi Arabia's main cities. Many Saudi royals—like Amr and Reem—have effectively become Hijazi, while many of the Hijazis themselves have thrown their lot in with the Al-Saud. In more recent decades, many other lines have been blurred and many more entanglements have been created. That was shown by the two different demonstrations in Jeddah. There is no doubt that the massive influx of wealth, along with the vagaries of the reliance on oil wealth, means that Hijazis have started to debate more openly the implications of turning their backs on the past to live in an alienating new town which, despite their best efforts, has suffered losses to its culture of diversity and tolerance. For the outsider, such tensions are not easily grasped, because they inevitably revolve around the difference in opinions expressed in public and private.

There is a saying that if in democratic countries everything is permitted except for what is forbidden, in totalitarian countries everything is forbidden except that which is permitted. That is certainly true of Saudi Arabia. To function properly, everything depends on everyone keeping face—on maintaining an image to the outside world and at home of Islamic unity in a manner that can only be described as a kind of higher hypocrisy. Thus my friend from the Hashemite family would talk on the telephone only in a way that was acceptable to the authorities monitoring the call, while the Hashemites themselves panicked in private about what to do about one of their own who had publicly broken ranks.

A rebellion from within the ranks of the Hashemites, backed by local merchant families like the Alirezas (many members of the two families have intermarried), remains the Al-Saud's worst fears for the Hijaz. The "custodianship" of Mecca and Medina has always been exploited to the full as a way of legitimizing its rule both at home and in the wider Islamic world. Such a rebellion is hardly around the corner. But in Jeddah especially, you cannot help but be struck by the remarkable resilience of cultural identities, how they flourish in private and in the local, strongly rooted communities, despite the strange, faceless rule of the Wahhabis over all public life.

Chapter Two

THE DEATH OF THE MAJLIS

On the first floor of the modern Al-Jouf governorate building a dozen or so men of various ages and nationalities were waiting in a small, sparsely furnished room. The Saudis among them were wearing flowing white robes and checkered headscarves. The others, mostly Third World immigrant workers, were in cheap trousers, shirts, and sandals.

Clearly, no one had bothered to get dressed up for the occasion.

Uncomfortable chairs with their straight backs against the walls, endless self-conscious fidgeting, and a nervous sense of anticipation: It could have been a doctor's waiting room in a working-class neighborhood anywhere. But these visitors did not have health complaints needing diagnosis. They were there to present petitions detailing social, political, or personal grievances to their local ruler, Prince Fahd bin Badr. He had been appointed governor of the northern Al-Jouf region in 2002 after serving for two years as vice governor. It was he who had an appointment to keep with them.

The Al-Saud ruling family always recognized the need to try and maintain open, albeit superficial, channels of communication with their subjects. The chosen mechanism was traditionally the majlis, which even reform-minded princes tout as a form of democracy in place of "Western-style" democracy—which, they argue, is "unsuitable" for the desert environment of the Gulf. At such gatherings, the general public meets with the royal governors to present petitions for redress, often against government decisions; to claim justice; to request economic help; or to discuss personal matters.

Scenes of Saudi citizens queuing during a weekly majlis to speak to a governor-prince, or even the monarch, are regularly broadcast on Saudi TV.

In theory, any citizen or foreign resident can attend: from the lowest, desert-dwelling Bedouin to a member of the Bangladeshi immigrant community. Any Saudi citizen can present a petition—of whatever substance—directly to the king himself. The majlis also exists to further the myth of the Al-Saud's benevolence and paternalism, and the arbitrary (because personal) nature of their rule.

Just inside the door to the room where Prince Fahd's majlis was to take place that day in Al-Jouf, four black bodyguards stood to attention in traditional dress. Black leather straps crisscrossed their upper torsos, rifles hung from their shoulders, and Indian swords swung stiffly from belts strapped tightly around their solid waists.

Fahd is a modest man in his late thirties with a gentle voice. He is classic young Al-Saud stock: tall, distinguished looking, and clean shaven but for a trimmed black mustache. He holds his majlis every day, immediately after midday prayers. In addition, he holds a dinner on Sundays at his private residence on the outskirts of town. However, only notable locals who have particularly weighty matters to discuss are invited to the latter.

In the year since being appointed governor, the prince had been away from Al-Jouf—the northernmost Saudi province bordering Iraq—for only three weeks, according to one of his assistants. Even then, he was visiting Jeddah to meet with more senior members of the royal household. Since the parochial capital, Sakaka, amounts to little more than a few streets, and the hostile climate results in 50 degrees Celsius at the height of summer but minus 7 in the dead of winter, the stark fact of a prince's permanent presence is testimony to a serious commitment to meeting the needs of the local population. It certainly contrasts with the behavior of his predecessor, who could not stand to be in the city for more than a few days at a stretch every six months or so.

"Why do you say 'any Saudi'?" his secretary, Zamil Al-Manie, asked in response to a question about whether any Saudi could just turn up to meet the prince any day of the week.

A short man in his fifties, and a brother of the kingdom's health minister, Al-Manie spoke in a cool, matter-of-fact manner, but self-consciously in a way that made him unnecessarily apologize every other sentence for his English. "Anyone of any nationality can come here—Indians, Saudis, Egyptians, even Americans. They all get a fair hearing, and they get a decision the same day," he continued.

The locals' instinctive generosity was very much in evidence during my meeting with Al-Manie. After I went through a metal detector in the lobby of the governorate, a bemused security guard, evidently unused to dealing with Western visitors, showed the way. Realizing I had arrived early, I offered to go back to my hotel for an hour.

"It's only five minutes away," I told Al-Manie.

"Do you have a car?" he asked.

"No," I replied. "But that's not a problem. The hotel is in the next street."

"No, no, you can take mine," he insisted, handing me the key to a Land Rover and pointing out its space in the car park outside.

Two minutes later, driving through Sakaka, I was hardly able to concentrate on the unfamiliar streets, so focused was I on a spontaneous act of kindness which, to its instigator, had been such a natural gesture that it did not warrant a second thought: Even before I left the office, Al-Manie had been busy again sorting through the eternal flow of official paperwork.

At Prince Fahd's majlis that day, among the first to pull up a chair to chat was a pitiful-looking Pakistani in his twenties. His two work companions—also Pakistanis, with equally dirty feet and threadbare clothes—waited on the sidelines. The bolder one explained to the prince, in broken Arabic, that they had all been working for a local company for some time as dishwashers. But, despite promises from the Saudi management that they would be given a residence permit, none of them had yet been issued one. Technically, they were now illegal immigrants, and as such were at risk of being picked up by the local police and being deported.

"Where are the other two?" the prince, clearly annoyed at what he had heard, asked him.

When the three had regrouped, he told all of them to go with one of his assistants.

"Sort this out immediately," he told the latter.

He then invited the youngest of the other visitors—a nervous Saudi boy, about 15 years old—to approach. As on every other occasion, Fahd refused to let the boy kiss his hand, a custom that disgusts the more pious Saudis, including those among the royal household, who believe such veneration should be directed at Allah alone.

In whispers, the boy proceeded to confuse everyone by saying that he had given his petition to the prince's assistants. Then he shyly admitted, after they had flipped twice and then a third time through the bundle of letters but still not found it, that he had in fact not bothered to write one. He spoke in such a whisper that it was not possible to discern what his request was, but he was led off by an assistant who placed a sympathetic hand on his shoulder.

As with the outcomes of officially announced investigations in Saudi Arabia into a whole variety of subjects and issues, it is never made public what kind of follow-through actually takes place after the majlis. But since, after seven decades, they are still packed all over the kingdom on a daily basis, it can be assumed that those who go to them do not think they are completely wasting their time.

However benevolent a governor-prince may himself be, the majlis can no longer take the place of genuine political participation—be it "Western-style" democracy or any other. That is true of small tribal societies like Sakaka, the capital of the Al-Jouf region, where individual sheiks are used to taking care of the problems of the tribe. It is also true of the modern cities like Riyadh, Jeddah, and Dammam, where the majority of Saudis now live and where there has been a breakdown of traditional ways that has undermined those tribal ties as the people adapt to new circumstances.

By constantly delaying meaningful political and social reforms, the patriarchal Al-Saud ruling family has failed to keep pace with the rapid process of urbanization accompanied by unprecedented political and social upheaval. By necessity, such changes warrant a radical restructuring of the mechanisms of governmental rule. Clear and concrete compensation is needed for the erosion of the regime's traditional loyalty system, which effectively means the establishment of civic society. Instead, the Al-Saud have thrown money, when it was available in abundance, at every problem. Or they have employed brute force to stifle dissent. Now that the money they are willing to spend on anything but their own lavish lifestyles (which also comes from the nation's budget) has largely run out, and the population is mushrooming, the regional, tribal, and religious divisions are re-emerging—and nowhere is that fact better illustrated in Saudi Arabia than in Al-Jouf.

Behind Al-Jouf's main Aramco oil terminal, high up on a desolate hillside outside the tiny regional capital Sakaka, lies the Arabian Peninsula's equivalent of Stonehenge. The cluster of sandstone stele, known as Al-Rajajil, has stood there for more than 6,000 years. Most now lean at random angles. All but a few are in a pitiful state of decay. Some have fallen completely to the ground, reduced to rubble by the extremes of scorching summers and freezing winters. A number of the stones are marked with early forms of script. There are crude, comb-like patterns on others. All were brought to the spot for a purpose, but someone has still to give a clear explanation of what that purpose might have been.

In the middle of the field, as the sun slowly sets, extraordinary shadows are thrown around the mysterious rock formations on the Pagan site. Visitors inevitably end up asking themselves: Why did those ancient people, employing what must have been the latest technology of their day, invest so much effort into cutting and erecting these monuments? Why did they drag them, perhaps for miles, to align them in a carefully choreographed formation, the significance of which still baffles even the world's most experienced archaeologists? Archaeology is hardly a top priority in a land that considers anything before the time of the Prophet to be *jahili* (from a period of ignorance), so the existence of excavation sites is proof that, here as in the Hijaz, Wahhabism only managed superficially to impose its ideological extremism.

Al-Jouf is known as the Desert Frontier province of Saudi Arabia. Its capital was moved soon after Saudi Arabia was founded in 1932, away from the historic city of Dumat Al-Jandal to the (now very modern) city of Sakaka, where Prince Fahd's daily majlis takes place. Arar, the kingdom's official border crossing with Iraq, is half an hour's ride to the north.

Contrary to reports by Saudi opposition groups, picked up by the pan-Arab daily *Al-Quds Al-Arabi,* all the main cities within the province, and even the smallest villages, are supplied with electricity. That may not seem like a big deal, unless you know that even in Saudi Arabia's sprawling metropolises power cuts are a fact of life. A sewage system, from which the bigger cities' sewage-drenched streets would also benefit, leads to a man-made lake of purified water in the middle of the desert about halfway between Sakaka and Dumat Al-Jandal. A nearby well is believed to belong to the Nabataeans, a people of ancient Arabia, whose settlements gave the name of Nabatene to the borderland between Syria and Arabia from the Euphrates to the Red Sea.

Local people now say that some areas of Sakaka, as well as the land to the south and east, were once irrigated from this well through underground channels. With only a little planning, the new lake could easily be turned into a recreation and nature resort. Already it attracts local children on summer weekends. Despite having produced the waste that the water was culled from, they find it hard to resist a dip in the cool water. Waterfowl live around the lake's edge. Even herons find enough food in its waters to survive. On weekend evenings, families settle on the lake's banks and picnic.

For thousands of years, some of the finest olives and dates in the world have been grown in Al-Jouf. The local economy still relies heavily on agriculture. Its fertile oases yield fruit, vegetables, and a uniquely flavored olive. Precise lines of carefully tended trees march across sandy hills, watered by the same aquifer that nourished the ancient farms that sustained the region's earliest dwellers. But now, in a vibrant green geometry, circles of modern agriculture also dot the desert. Off the asphalt highways linking the main cities, among palm gardens lush with vegetables and fodder crops, are countless asphalt lanes.

Again, the contrast with the rest of Saudi Arabia is striking. Elsewhere, grand agricultural projects, many of which were designed to encourage Bedouin settlements, were so badly managed that the water resource exploitation grew to alarming levels. As many analysts have pointed out, historically improperly drilled wells reduced their effectiveness by leaching the lands they were meant to irrigate. In the early 1990s, large-scale agricultural projects relied mainly on such underground aquifers, which then provided more than 80 percent of the water for agricultural use. In 1987, about 90 percent of the total water demand in the kingdom was consumed by agriculture. That figure has not changed significantly. There were, however, attempts to cut down on agricultural production, and now production is restricted to domestic consumption.

Until recently, the role Al-Jouf's barren hills and fertile oases played in the history of the Arabian Peninsula was neglected. However, in the mid-1970s the Department of Antiquities and Museums, based in the capital Riyadh, decided to preserve what everyone had at last started to realize was a cradle of Arab civilization. It was part of the same drive to preserve the past that resulted in the historic Al-Balad district in Jeddah being earmarked for renovation. By 1985, serious conservation work had gotten under way. It was not hampered by Wahhabi doctrine, because the influence of the religious zealots had always been limited this far north. The province was too strategically insignificant, and its population too small, to warrant anything other than a permanent royal governor to oversee things.

Even today, the number of outsiders visiting the region remains only a trickle. It is baffling that so few have made the effort to see the historic sites, despite such little effort now being required to get there. Young Saudis in Jeddah say that visiting is "a complete waste of time," because all the locals are "backward." In this sense, Al-Jouf's isolation is testimony to the rigid regionalism that continues to define life in Saudi Arabia, despite the long-established national postal service, airline, road network, universal wearing of the white *thobe,* and media outlets—all of which contributed in their separate ways to the emergence of a national Saudi consciousness among the kingdom's various tribal, regional, and religious factions. But that consciousness is still not ingrained, and the success of the development of any kind of national consciousness is in fact highly questionable.

Fortunately, records of adventurous modern European travelers visiting Al-Jouf go back to 1845, when George A. Wallin wrote down his observations. By 1922, accounts of visits had been published by 18 different Western travelers. As encouragement for the local community to engage with their history, many works by the early travelers are being translated into Arabic by the local library. William Gifford Palgrave, Captain William Shakespeare, and Gertrude Bell, among others, visited, and all wrote studies of the local history. Five such Arabic-language translations have so far appeared locally, and more are said to be on the way. These travelers to Al-Jouf came in the context of European exploration of the Arabian Peninsula as a whole, and those days Al-Jouf was both geographically very difficult to reach and presented great cultural barriers—language, religion, and customs—that were a challenge to overcome. However, all seem to have had some knowledge of Arabic, and according to their writings they were received with hospitality and courtesy. Some came with political aims, some for scientific exploration, others simply as adventurers and eccentrics.

Palgrave arrived in Al-Jouf in June 1862, and was so exhausted from his travels by the time he reached it—following his extended trips throughout Arabia—that he considered it a paradise. Napoleon III sponsored Palgrave's journey, and it is generally accepted that he was a spy sent to assess the political situation. His early summer arrival coincided with the ripening of the first fruits, and he is particularly brilliant in his description of the local landscape. The most distinctive characteristic of the inhabitants was, he observed, their hospitality, and he declared that there was no other area—even in Arabia—where the guest was "better treated, or more cordially invited to become in every way one of themselves."

As the historic crossroad for traders heading into the Arabian Peninsula, Al-Jouf is home to some of the most important archaeological sites in the world. They tell a crucial part of the story of human development in both the pre- and post-Islamic periods. The city of the old capital, Dumat Al-Jandal, was at the center of regional trade and politics for many thousands of years, and Syrian, Roman, and Greek artifacts have all been found there. A large number of Roman coins have also been unearthed, indicating the neighboring limit of the Roman Empire and the commercial activity for which the city was famous when it stood astride trade routes from Syria and Iraq to Yemen.

Many of the coins are now displayed in the Al-Nusl Hotel in the heart of Sakaka, until recently used as the residence of the local governor. It is the most tastefully designed and professionally managed hotel in Saudi Arabia, and doubles as an unofficial museum, the artifacts lining its walls acting as a constant reminder of the rich local cultural inheritance.

Dumat Al-Jandal, the old capital and main oasis in the region, is one of the earliest recorded settlements in Arabia, referred to in the early local literature in which the word "Arab" was coined to identify the local inhabitants. For a long time, it was a center of learning; and it was there that the Arabic language itself, deriving from the Syriac script, was set down. Writing and communicative rock art, too, has a long local history. Over 17,000 separate panels of rock carvings have been located and catalogued, of which some 10 percent are early forms of writing.

Dumat Al-Jandal is home to one of the oldest mosques in the Saudi kingdom, Omar ibn Khattab, built in the seventeenth Hijra year and named after the second leader of Islam, or Caliph, who succeeded the Prophet. Its most striking feature is a 16-yard, cut-stone minaret, which appears to lean slightly to one side because of a raked and curved structure that tapers toward the top. Restoration, alas, has left it looking more modern than the buildings in the new part of town, and it has tacky lighting fixtures and plastic pipes hanging off every wall and ceiling. Worse, the new asphalt car park built for tourists finishes just a meter or so from the mosque's entrance, meaning that the effect of the mosque being built in the middle of the desert is now completely lost.

Nevertheless, climbing the minaret—it is the only mosque in Saudi Arabia that permits entry to non-Muslims—and walking its history-filled interior remains a breathtaking experience. The prayer hall, with three rows of piers, is supported by solid square-cut pillars and arches, the walls of which are set with niches to hold copies of the Qu'ran. Adjacent to the site is Al-Jouf Regional Museum. As you walk its short corridors, the assistant follows you around and provides you with little cups of Arabian coffee, proof that the inveterate hospitality always highlighted by former travelers has remained a defining local characteristic.

During the time of the Prophet, three expeditions came to Al-Jouf. The first was led by the Prophet himself to punish rebellious locals and prevent the area from developing into an independent state. The second was in the form of a successful missionary, when the vast majority of the population embraced Islam (while those who did not were left to follow their own beliefs). The third expedition secured the political borders to the north against the increasing power of the Byzantine Empire. Now, for the modern-day visitor, the close juxtaposition of the mosque, ancient town dwellings, and local castles, all within extensive boundary walls still visible in places, underlines why Dumat Al-Jandal has been so desirable as an addition to successive northern empire builders. The preserved site, now marking the northern boundaries of the third Saudi empire, brings to life a sense of the closeness of the local community.

Since the 1930s, Al-Jouf has benefited in many obvious and dramatic ways from its incorporation into the Saudi state. The populist spirit of Prince Abdul Rahman Al-Sudairy, the local governor for 41 years (1943–1984) and a celebrated poet, continues to define proceedings. By all accounts an extraordinary (but down-to-earth) individual, he personally oversaw the development of the province. Abdul Rahman's mark has literally been left on every street corner of the new capital, Sakaka. There is a world-class library named after him. The four-star, nonprofit hotel was built with money from his Abdul Rahman Al-Sudairy Foundation. His picture hangs on the wall of every official's office, underneath those of the king and princes closest in line to the throne.

The move to preserve the region's unique archaeological treasures was also undertaken under his auspices. During his tenure as governor, the foundation, with funds partly donated by various kings, spent $80 million on public works. One of the most obvious results is the landmark Al-Rahmaniyah Mosque, a sharply delineated geometrical building of glistening marble, two slender minarets, and copper-colored domes. Completed in 1995, the starkly beautiful building has a subtle link with local traditions: The roshan-like stone lattice work that relieves the massive rectangular buttresses on the outer wall, and adds a delicate decoration to the minarets, is actually part of the cooling system of the mosque. Shunning modern air-conditioning, the mosque is the largest building in the world to be cooled by traditional evaporative cooling towers, a respectful nod to the ingenuity of early Arab engineers in adapting to the harsh environment.

The Abdul Rahman Al-Sudairy Foundation also manifested its influence very visibly in the form of the public library and research center opposite the mosque, a meeting place for archaeologists and researchers from around the world. It was started as a public library with 3,000 volumes in 1963. That was a pioneering step in Saudi Arabia at the time, and even now there is no comparable public library in Saudi Arabia. It was greeted with deep suspicion by many local religious leaders in Sakaka. What use, they asked, of books other than the Qu'ran?

Challenging accepted mores while in fundamental ways giving in to them, the building in fact housed—both then and now—two libraries, each a mirror image of the other: one for men and the other for women. Since the foundation had been established by royal decree, and was funded directly from the royal purse, it continued to operate, despite protests. But no one objects any more to the idea of women attending the regular lectures there, so long as there are no men present.

"What started as a library has developed into a major cultural center," Nabil Shabaka, the library director, said as he showed me around.

An Egyptian who has lived in Sakaka for more than two decades, Shabaka was generously proportioned and looked so lacking in confidence that he would need his mother's help to dress himself properly. He was an instantly recognizable type found in offices all over Saudi Arabia that have a royal connection: helpful to the point of being obsequious.

But he was rightly proud of his vast library. Apart form the general services and stock of over 100,000 books, it now acts as a center for the cultural activities of the foundation. "We have an average of 2,000–3,000 readers each month," he said. Up to 3,000 new titles are added to the book stock annually, and the library currently subscribes to 250 international periodicals, journals, and newspapers in English and Arabic.

"Part of the emphasis of the library is on actively providing education, academic and cultural resources for the community," he continued when we sat down again in his small office, near the main (male) entrance to the building.

"We also act as a resource center for academics who visit the area for its archaeology and history, and this has led us to store and display some of the local archaeological finds."

And with that, we were walking together again, so we could have a look at them as well.

No idle public relations exercise, the influence of the foundation continues to manifest itself in the subsidized hotel, clinics, stocks of textbooks for use by local students, and practical skills courses for local women. Complementing a program of public lectures in a 380-capacity lecture theater that would not look out of place at Harvard, the foundation (through the library) publishes the best MA and PhD theses of postgraduate students who have specialized in aspects of the history of Al-Jouf and the wider Arab world. In 1990, it began publishing *Al-Juba,* a semi-annual periodical intended as a forum for discussion of issues of public interest. After 13 issues, the resources were reinvested in a more focused publication, *Adumatu* (an early name for Dumat Al-Jandal), which covers the vast but little-known field of archaeology in the Arab world (again with a particular focus on Al-Jouf). Saudi professors of archaeology are the journal's editors, and the advisory board has a worldwide spread of contributing archeologists.

With the intention of maintaining the flow of interested and qualified contributors to its increasing knowledge base, the foundation finances outstanding students to study at universities with specialized faculties, relevant to the history of the area. At least one student a year is financed, to the sum of $100,000, to cover a course of study that will eventually contribute to one area of the foundation's interest. But funding students for graduate study is the result of a much broader base laid some years previously. After initially setting up kindergarten schools, the foundation decided to open primary schools for boys and girls as well. Rapid enrollment encouraged the building of secondary education facilities and the eventual establishment of the Al-Rahmaniyah schools, which supply a stream of students for higher education elsewhere within the kingdom. Al-Jouf has one of the highest literacy rates in Saudi Arabia.

Less obviously, but perhaps more crucially, the foundation has a network of agricultural and social projects that have helped to shape the community for the last 60 years. A characteristic of the founder's ingenuity at introducing change is that much of it was competed for by the community, rather than benevolently imposed as charity in a way that would merely increase dependence on handouts. When, in the 1960s, the advent of machine-made products threatened the existence of traditional crafts and rendered ancient agricultural practices redundant and noncompetitive, Abdul Rahman organized a camel race and rug exhibition, enlivening traditions that had died out; and he personally funded the prizes.

At the same time, he instituted a farmer's competition, sensing the potential in a relatively water-rich area and hoping to settle the nomadic Bedouin (thus raising living standards for all). The competitions were designed with the principal aim of introducing modern techniques and technology to farmers.

They soon became fierce contests, and companies that serve the farming sector came forward to increase substantially the value of the prizes. Such local competitions, which were the first of their kind in the kingdom, developed into the Al-Jouf Week, which is now an annual event.

The acceptance of technology and the rekindling of a dying craft were the result of a local demand driven by a competitive spirit, underpinned by an understanding (sadly lacking elsewhere in Saudi Arabia) that, however worthy, for an initiative to succeed the people must want to make it a reality. The same idea—development through the encouragement of home-grown effort and competition—led Prince Sultan bin Abdul Rahman Al-Sudairy (Abdul Rahman's son, and immediate successor) to establish a new prize in the name of the founder for exceptional male and female graduates from the schools and institutes of Al-Jouf. This now takes the form of grants for study abroad for male students or, for the best female students, study at one of Saudi Arabia's universities.

The remote, tiny city of Sakaka, with its world-class library, subsidized luxury hotel, student scholarships, and benevolent princely patrons, may seem like the least likely setting possible for the start of a popular, violent revolution against the ruling Al-Saud family. But, from a year before the September 11 attacks until the U.S.-led war on Iraq, when the world was looking elsewhere, Al-Jouf was witness to a level of sustained political protests and terrorist violence perhaps unprecedented in the history of modern Saudi Arabia. Back in August 2000, a prison riot that broke out in Sakaka left a guard and several inmates injured after prisoners took over a prison to protest living conditions. In April 2002, the Saudi army deployed as many as 8,000 soldiers around the nearby town of Tabuk following anti-US riots in Sakaka. Hundreds of young people raised Palestinian flags and shouted anti-Israeli and anti-U.S. slogans. Security forces used force to break up the demonstration.

The deputy governor, Hamad Al-Wardi, was assassinated in a hail of bullets in February 2003 as he drove to his office. Also killed was the police chief, Hamoud Rabih, murdered in his home in a similarly well-planned assassination in April 2003. The region's top religious court judge, Sheikh Abdul Rahman Al-Sahibani, met with the same fate. A soldier was shot dead while on duty. In early 2004, the state Saudi media reported that seven men from the region had been arrested in connection with the assassinations and were being transferred to a Riyadh prison for questioning. Saudi officials admitted that the attacks were linked. The seven alleged killers not only confessed to involvement in all of the crimes, but were said to have been aided by as many as 40 accomplices. Among the seven arrested were two masterminds responsible for organizing the killings, according to official statements.

Prince Naif—infamous for having refused to admit that any of the hijackers on September 11 were Saudi nationals for months after the attacks—characteristically refused to admit that political motives were behind the Al-Jouf assassinations, or that they were in fact in any way linked. But the prince also announced a $150,000 reward for information leading to the arrest of the killers, the kind of incentive offered for information leading to the apprehension of terrorist suspects. In November 2004, four men were sent to trial, but their names were still not released. And now they were also said in reports to have been responsible for "the kidnapping of a foreigner."

Osama bin Laden had mentioned Al-Jouf specifically in one of the lengthy speeches broadcast by Al-Jazeera after the launch of the U.S.-led military action in Afghanistan in 2001. Bin Laden himself lived in Al-Jouf in the late 1960s, after his father died in a helicopter crash. And Mohammed Sadiq Al-Odeh, arrested for the bombings of the U.S. embassies in Nairobi and Dar-es-Salaam in 1998, had also lived in Sakaka.

The latest generation in Al-Jouf has grown up on a diet of satellite TV and the Internet. Inevitably, the slow pace of local life now contrasts in their mind with the bigger, more exciting outside world they would, for the most part, prefer to be a part of. As a result of their higher standard of education, they no longer see farm work as a viable way to spend their life. Their alienation is most obviously manifested in the graffiti that defaces many of the local historic monuments, mostly just kids scribbling their names, but also hostile comments against the Al-Saud. The monuments are also littered with evidence of widespread drug abuse.

The situation worsened in the build-up to the U.S.-led invasion of Iraq, when U.S. troops took control of the airport in the nearby town of Arar, the official border crossing with Iraq. This was deeply resented by most Saudis, but especially by Al-Jouf's residents. They have historic links not only with Syria but also to Iraqis immediately across the border. Many local officers in the Saudi army resigned at the time in protest against being relieved temporarily of their duties by U.S. soldiers. Hundreds, perhaps thousands, of Saudis have sneaked into Iraq via Al-Jouf and other northern regions to join the resistance there to U.S.-led occupation forces.

Four men suspected of having links to Al-Qaeda and involvement in the May 2003 attacks against Western targets in Riyadh chose to take their own lives in Al-Jouf rather than give themselves up to security forces, who had cornered them after hunting them down. They included Saudi Arabia's most-wanted Al-Qaeda suspect at the time, Turki Nasir Mishal Al-Dandani. Security officers raided the residence of an imam, a prayer leader, in the village of Suhair, where the five wanted terrorists were hiding—another indication of local sympathy for anti-Al-Saud agitators.

The imam handed himself over—as did one of the suspected terrorists, Hassan Hadi Al-Dossari. However, the remaining four fled to the imam's nearby mosque, opening fire with machine-guns and lobbing grenades at security forces. During a subsequent gun battle, the group detonated explosives, blowing themselves to smithereens.

So Saudi Arabia's Islamic rebellion has reached even this tiny little outpost. The violence in the city does indeed appear to be political. Although it probably has many other inter-related causes, at its center is the fact that Al-Jouf is the historic power base of the Al-Sudairy branch of the Saudi royal family, which makes all the important economic and political decisions not only in this remote region but throughout the kingdom. Sakaka's streets are now deserted after dusk. According to locals, since the string of assassinations of senior officials of the Al-Sudairy clan have not been able to venture out of their walled villas without an armed guard. The secret police closely watch outsiders allowed past the permanent roadblocks on the approach roads to the city.

Given the influence of a succession of Al-Sudairy governors, business and local government in Al-Jouf have been dominated by the Al-Sudairy clan since the kingdom was founded. In a locally published book, *The Desert Frontier of Saudi Arabia: Al-Jauf through the Ages,* written by Abdul Rahman Al-Sudairy himself, a page displaying the portraits of the eight most important recent community leaders contains no fewer than five photographs of members of the Al-Sudairy clan. Now other local merchant families and tribes, prominent before Al-Jouf was incorporated into the Saudi kingdom, appear to be taking advantage of the vulnerability of a perhaps fatally weakened Saudi ruling family—battling international and domestic pressures after September 11—to reassert historic territorial claims. The rebellion in the once-sleepy Al-Jouf region shows in microcosm what may, one day, be in store for the whole of Saudi Arabia, where the march of progress and modernism, coupled with the population boom and the economic downturn, is proving a potent threat to the social order.

Chapter Three

FLOWER MEN, TRIBAL SHEIKS

In late 2003, when the conservative members of the Al-Saud ruling family were leading a widespread crackdown on both liberal and Islamist reformers, Riyadh-based lawyer Abdul Aziz Al-Tayyar spoke live from his home to Al-Jazeera TV in Qatar about social and economic conditions inside Saudi Arabia.

"All tribesmen are now willing to fight this government—we will protect the rights of our people," he said in impassioned tones over the telephone. "This is not the kingdom of Saudi Arabia any more. It is a jungle full of monsters. The Saudi people are suppressed. They suffer poverty and unemployment."

Minutes later, the Saudi security forces kicked down his front door, and carted Al-Tayyar off to jail.

Many marveled at the efficiency of the internal Saudi security forces, who managed to locate this man—and silence him—almost before he had gotten to the end of his first sentence. That efficiency certainly contrasted with their reaction to Al-Qaeda terrorist cells who, six months later, carried out attacks against mainly Westerners in Yanbu on the Red Sea coast and Khobar in the Eastern Province. On both occasions, it was reported that it took more than an hour and a half for the security forces to engage the terrorists.

Why were the Al-Saud so incensed by what Al-Tayyar was saying?

For one thing, most of the hijackers on September 11 were from prominent Saudi tribes, and those "tribesmen" of whom Al-Tayyar spoke still make up as many as 60 percent of the kingdom's population. By referring to the "tribesmen," Al-Tayyar was referring to the majority of Saudis. Put simply: Whoever has the support of the tribes in Saudi Arabia has control of the kingdom. Al-Tayyar's swift arrest and incarceration was proof that he had touched on a very raw nerve indeed.

In the wake of the two Al-Qaeda bombings in Riyadh in May and November 2003, the ruling family became transparently eager to make a public demonstration of the fact that it had the "full support" of the kingdom's all-important tribal sheikhs. On a daily basis for the whole of November, and on strict orders of the Ministry of Information, the local media carried verbatim statements and photographs from the official Saudi Press Agency showing leaders from the Hijaz and Asir regions meeting Crown Prince Abdullah and Prince Naif in Taif, scene of the Wahhabi massacres in the 1920s. In identical speeches, all pledged their loyalty to the kingdom and its "wise leadership." The speeches were obviously drawn up by the Al-Saud, and the tribal leaders were forced—or at least heavily leaned on—to read them out.

Many outside commentators have incorrectly characterized the 15 Saudi hijackers on September 11 as exclusively the products of the Wahhabi ideology promoted by the kingdom's official religious establishment. According to this theory, it was as though the hijackers had been trained for jihad in a social and historical vacuum, filled only by the powerful calling of jihad screaming from the kingdom's mosques.

However, most of those 15 came from Asir, and the tribal population in that region, like the liberals of the Hijaz and the Shiites of the Eastern Province, have always been reluctant partners in the Saudi state. As with the merchants of the Hijaz and Al-Jouf, the tribes of Asir have never fully embraced Wahhabi doctrine. Periodic local rebellions, and a low-level struggle to keep alive a regional identity, are both testimony to that. The antagonism generated in the Asir for the Al-Saud was reflected, in fact, in the high proportion of terrorists that came from the region.

There are other pockets of less obvious resistance to Wahhabi–Al-Saud hegemony in Asir. The most intriguing are the "flower men" who still populate the mountains of the region: men and boys who wear flowers and herbs in their hair and cultivate a passion for perfume. In Riyadh, where they are occasionally seen amid the glitzy malls, skyscrapers, and women enveloped all in black, they are giggled at, and considered backward. More extremist Wahhabis damn them as infidels and nature worshipers. On trips to Jeddah, they tend to confine themselves to the historic Al-Balad district of the city, where the large numbers of Yemeni inhabitants are more relaxed and welcoming than even liberal Saudis in the north of the city.

In Asir, it is also not unusual to see women driving pick-up trucks, although Wahhabi custom elsewhere means that women are officially banned from driving. Locals, moreover, point the television aerials on their roofs toward Yemen, so they can pick up Yemeni TV. In the mountains they wear *jambayas,* or daggers, in their waistbands, and walk around with kalashnikovs hanging from their shoulders—just as their tribal cousins do in the northern parts of Yemen on the other side of the largely undemarcated border.

Originally a part of Yemen, Asir in the southwest of the kingdom was a small theocracy under the descendants of a Sufi holy man, Ahmed Ibn Idris, who was originally from Morocco but was revered by locals as a saint. But in the 1920s, Ibn Saud sent 6,000 men to punish the Asiris for their resistance to invading Wahhabi forces. Afterward, Asir's incorporation into the Saudi state was achieved mainly by Ibn Saud buying off tribal sheikhs and arranging marriages between the Al-Saud family and the women of various tribes.

Since then, the Asir tribes have generally been superficially loyal, weighing the disadvantages of the gradual erosion of their local customs and traditions and independence against all the advantages—modern schools, hospitals, electricity—that come with being part of a state that sits on more than a quarter of the world's oil reserves. However, there is of course a great difference between loyalty bought and loyalty earned, and the great unanswered question now, when it comes to the Asir region, is what kind of loyalty it is that will characterize the continuing relationship between the tribes and the Al-Saud.

The tribal sheiks in particular have welcomed their own personal empowerment, and would be reluctant to see it undermined. But they and their followers have remained keenly aware that their "loyalty" has not been as well rewarded as it should have been on the national level. That is one reason their loyalty to the state can never fully be taken for granted. For instance, Asiris are rarely considered for the very highest positions in government. And, despite making up as much as 10 percent of the population, they do not have an independent university in their region. Yes, the wonderful views from the tops of mountains have been "ruined" by tall electric and telephone poles, but power cuts are still common in the nearby cities. Corruption among local officials, too, is said to be endemic, with funds for local projects being siphoned off by those who have no accountability to the local population.

Most people of Asir are deeply pious and know by heart a particular Hadith, or saying of the Prophet, to the effect that the final triumph of Islam will be brought about by the people of southern Arabia. However, historically even the stricter preachers among them have not been Wahhabis. The fact that many in Asir followed the local leader, Idris, and revered him as a saint, should in and of itself guard against any such characterization, since of course Wahhabism does not recognize such concepts of sainthood.

The imported Wahhabi ideology that came with the invaders from the Al-Najd region in the 1920s, and which is now widely preached in the mosques and taught in the local schools throughout the cities of Asir, has combined, as in Jeddah and other traditionally anti-Wahhabi regions of Saudi Arabia, with local traditions. The combustible combination ironically fuels both a hatred of the West and local alienation from Al-Najd. The Al-Saud are seen as outsiders imposing their rule, backed by the West, and both are seen as hypocritical—the Al-Saud for claiming purity while living lavishly, the West for espousing human rights while supporting a dictatorial regime that disrespects the customs and beliefs of others.

The entirely negative results have been acknowledged by none other than Prince Khaled Al-Faisal, the falconer, poet, and painter who rules Asir. Khaled has a vision of the southwest as tourism hub. But while the city of Abha is now packed with Gulf tourists in the summer months, who make the most of the amusement parks and concert venues and enjoy the spectacular views from cable cars, this development has in many ways served merely to exacerbate the contrasts between the haves from outside and the have-nots who live there all year round. The prince seems more aware than most of these dangers, posed by the combination of straightened economic circumstances, tribal frustrations, and an influx of radical Wahhabi ideology. In June 2004, he expressed his sense of near-despair in an article for *Al-Watan,* a reformist newspaper he sponsors that is published from the region.

Asiris are full of fun and optimism, he wrote, even when they come to him at the municipality to complain or demand new projects. And always, he added, they begin the discussion with "beautiful tales" about fathers and grandfathers "who took part in the struggles of Ibn Saud" to establish this structure and build this state. That this was a contrived distortion of their historical resistance to the establishment of the state goes without saying, and is par for the course in the tendency by royalty to gloss over reality. But the attempt to create an alternative past had its purposes, not least to hark back to a supposed golden age of cooperation and thus say that things could be like that again, any deviation of the moment being unnatural.

Harking back to the past to speak of a better future was clear when Khaled wrote that the Asiris "are proud of the past and hopeful about the future. When they ask for a new project, they ask in a spirit of optimism, not to reproach because it isn't there."

Having effectively admitted that there are shortcomings now, Khaled proceeded to plaintively wonder why the working relationship had broken down.

"What happened to them?" he asked. "Who scared the children away from laughter, play and joy? Who scared the adults from life? . . . Who convinced our sons and daughters to call their fathers and mothers infidel?"

It takes a moment for the full import of this to sink in. Khaled is admitting, shockingly for an official at his level, a level of despair and alienation that few members of the ruling family would openly accept as reality, and even further that a fundamental aspect of traditional societies, namely respect for parents, has broken down. This is, in short, a society in crisis.

And why?

Khaled continued with more questions that revealed the answer, for he asks: "Who teaches children in orphanages that Saudi Arabia is not their home, that their only home is Islam? That their future vocation is jihad? . . . Who transformed schools and universities into military camps for jihadists? . . . Who convinced Saudi youth that the surest path to Heaven is to blow themselves up and take citizens, foreign residents and security officers with them? Who did this to us?"

Leave aside that to contend that Saudi Arabia is a home equal to Islam is, within the Wahhabi schema, close to blasphemy, as to honor and revere anything other than Allah and Islam is idolatry. For a top official to admit that the jihadis have infiltrated schools and universities is to admit that the vaunted security services have failed to do their job, which itself opens the possibility that they, too, have been infiltrated.

And by whom?

To repeat his question: "Who did this to us?"

Khaled is oblique about the identity of those responsible: "If we look at the books, pamphlets and tapes that have been distributed by the thousands in the schools, universities, mosques and charities over the past 20 years, we will see their names clearly legible in black and white. The websites reveal the rest."

This commentary is extraordinary both for its frankness and, even more so, its implicit revelation of how little control the liberal Al-Faisal branch of the Al-Saud ruling family exerts in Saudi Arabia.

Having been displaced in the late 1970s, the reins of power were taken over by the Al-Sudairy branch of the family, which in turn gave greater importance to the extremists the Al-Faisals clearly hate, but whose ideology they are in many ways subservient to—even in the region they have had continuous control over since the birth of the state. When it comes to trying to limit the influence of the Wahhabis and the Al-Sudairy cousins they rule in partnership with, Khaled is clearly powerless—the universities, charities, schools, orphanages, and print media are all, by his own admission, now in the control of the Wahhabi clerics.

Since he is the governor of Asir, it might have been presumed that he could have done something about the spread of such extremist hatred, at least in his own backyard. But no. Here, as elsewhere in the kingdom, when it comes to the social, cultural, and religious sphere, the liberal Al-Saud princes are, along with the rest of the world and ordinary Saudis themselves, paying the price of the conservative factions of the Al-Saud ruling family having abandoned complete authority to their Wahhabi cohorts in an attempt to maintain an iron grip on dissenting local populations.

While, as Khaled acknowledges, the cities of Asir have been breeding grounds for militants—most of the September 11 hijackers grew up in the region's cities, not in the mountains and countryside—the mountains themselves and their inhabitants, who still lead the simple pastoral existence Khaled movingly evoked, offer a different experience of Saudi Arabia.

The existence of the flower men has been known for many years, and their history over the last half-century—like that of the Hijazi merchant families, and those of Al-Jouf—is a deeply troubled one, and their flower power represents yet another form of resistance to Wahhabi–Al-Saud hegemony. Stumbling upon them while looking for Al-Qaeda, what was most striking was the contrast between the aggression of the terrorists with the passive withdrawal of these flower men—although both movements are (in their own way) equally bold.

Many flower men were forced from their villages, partly because the slow but sure pace of modernization had even there, high in the mountains, eradicated much of the local idiosyncrasies, but also because they were held in such utter contempt by their Wahhabi conquerors for their Pagan ways. The most dramatic episode of their forced expulsion came in the mid-1990s, when a cable car was built to give tourists access to a mountainside village called Habala (meaning "rope" in Arabic; the village called this on account of the fact that in the past the only way to and from it was via a series of rope ladders).

The flower men who lived below, and who had cultivated the land for centuries, initially refused to move to a new, modern village nearby. As a result, once the cable car was working, its first passengers became members of the National Guard. They rounded up the flower men by force, cramming them into this new mode of transportation. No doubt the episode confirmed the estimation of the flower men that the cable car was an instrument of the devil. Eventually, some of the flower men were allowed to return, but only to perform traditional dances for tourists in the summer peak season, which surely only added insult to injury. In lieu of their confiscated homes, they were given free cable car tickets. One opened a tourist restaurant underneath the main cable car station, an indication that they are beginning to adjust to a new reality.

Stumbling on the flower men is not done easily. I took the coastal road south from Jeddah to Jizan, a grimy port city in the southwest that was until recently, like much of the Asir region, claimed by Yemen. Historically, the population along the coastal plain subsisted on a combination of oasis gardening and herding, with some portion being nomadic or seminomadic. Now the drive is through hundreds of miles of featureless, dune-colored desert, undernourished scrub, and the occasional salt pan. Barefoot men and boys dressed in loincloths with loosely wrapped scarves around their heads worked with wicker baskets in the shallow seawater pans, scraping salt up into off-white mounds to dry and then sell.

Even when I was apparently furthest from any sign of habitation, there was someone doing business. Beside a particularly bleak stretch of road stood a pottery seller, far enough south of Jeddah that the work showed the first signs of the characteristic decorative patterns of the south-western region. Crudely made incense burners and somewhat lumpy pots—obviously hand molded, rather than wheel-formed—were decorated with the bright geometric patters of the Asir region. The sales technique was in keeping with the relaxed nature of the region. Patiently sitting and watching, the young man moved only when an item was picked up and examined. There was an awkward moment as he thought about the price he had suggested, as he was a little thrown by the fact that it was agreed to at once, and he quickly added one more item to the stack free of charge.

Moving deeper into the Asir region, the landscape began to change. Large hillocks of gray-brown rock gradually became hills, and then sharply defined escarpments, confining the road to the level sandy coastal strip. Through breaks in the massive walls, cone-shaped heaps of weathered rock offered a bleak prospect. The escarpment was the result of the volcanic activity that accompanied the breaking away of the tectonic plate that separated the Arabian Peninsula from Africa, leaving the chasm of the Red Sea in between. The plate is still moving—at about the same speed that fingernails grow—toward southern Iran and India, pushing the Himalaya mountains minutely higher every year.

A snaking road led from Jizan up to Abha, a climb of 1,860 miles through Mount Souda, the kingdom's highest mountain, dominating the last 80-mile stretch before the inland Asir mountains themselves. It wove its way through a scene of utter devastation. Much of the original concrete roadway, built on massive pillars above flat stream-beds and hugging the walls of the wadi, lay in ruins. Then the major highway became a narrow road, then potholed tarmac, as the climb into the Asir mountains began.

Immediately it became obvious how different the people of the Asir region are in both character and style to those in the rest of Saudi Arabia. In a word, you feel that you are in Yemen. The local mountainous conditions and isolation allowed the traditional mud and stone architecture to survive almost untouched by modernity. This was reflected not only in the elegant tapering rectangles of the mud-brick buildings and the intricately constructed dry-stone defensive towers and houses, but also in the use of vivid colors and patterns as decoration. The dull black of basaltic rocks used in the turrets and mosques that seem to grow out of the hills glistened with imbedded white quartz. The hills were dotted with rectangular and occasionally circular structures of great visual complexity, demonstrating a skill in masonry and an almost obsessive concern with pattern.

Color used for architectural decoration appeared only on the mud-brick constructions, decorating the inner courtyards and interior walls of the houses—all reflecting the patterns favored in the Asir's characteristic woven cloths and blankets. Such decoration extended to the vehicles of the region, where patterns adorned not only the bodywork but also the cage-like containers used to carry goods into the hills. It was almost as if the bodywork's solid color was too heavy for the minutiae of pattern-work, the spidery construction of wire mesh and steel tubing providing a more suitable canvas for the work.

An old map confirmed a track between the last outpost settlement east of Jizan and before Najran, a small city on the Yemeni border with a majority Shiite population. The mountains in between, it seemed, were passable.

Al-Dair, situated along the floor of a steep-sided *wadi,* was the last town before the mettled road, which without warning on a steep slope changed to
roughly graded dirt. From there on it was virgin mountainside, with an ill-
defined goat trail. This was what the map marks as the road to Najran.

At that point, the driving became more interesting: low transfer climbs
up near vertical slopes, pitching over a knife edge ridge and a precipitous
trail on the other side. The quality of the track declined in proportion to the
distance—forty-five degree inclines, loose shale slopes that, at times, were so
narrow that the wheels straddle the entire width.

He was sitting perfectly still on a rock by the road, clad in a shirt and a shin-
length cloth around his waist. And he had a wreath of fresh herbs on his
head. Within moments, another vehicle drew alongside. Three grinning
teenage boys stared through the open window of the jeep, their startlingly
white eyes set in finely chiseled features—all set off by the voluptuous
masses of glossy black curls that framed the faces. They, too, had flowers in
their hair.

Finally, the myth of the "flower men" became a reality—the nadir of a
journey into the least accessible part of the kingdom. Here was living proof
that they had not disappeared altogether from their natural habitat of isolated valleys separated by precipitous slopes and connected by very rough
paths, where locals still survive on goats, small gardens, and abundant water
from the streams that thread through the rocks.

The man wanted to know the reason for the journey. He had seen foreigners in the area in his long life only once before, and claimed not even to
know where Najran was when asked for directions (although he had, he said
proudly, been to Jizan). Once, many years ago, he recalled that a Western
man had visited with some Saudis on an educational trip. They had asked
some questions, and then left. Urbanization, which he evidently wanted little to do with, was another world away. But he did have a shop, and with
the dignified confidence of proprietorship he opened a rusting door to a
barn and looked proudly at a corner where, with complete disregard for display or convenience, was an eclectic mix of goods—from lentils to shirts,
from an old freezer with soft drinks to sharp-looking instruments designed
to perform unspeakable acts on goats.

The three young men, who had stopped to buy something, had a distinct grace to their movement, and over their hair all wore carefully woven

wreaths of dry flowers and herbs, knotted so that the cut stalks formed an upturned peak on the foreheads. Their contents ranged from a simple woven band of thyme, with its silky gray-green leaves worn as a workday tradition, to intricately woven constructions with masses of brilliant seasonal flowers inserted into a band of woven dried grass. The older man had tended toward a less colorful construction of herbs and leaves, whereas the headbands of these faun-like young men were a riot of fresh and dried flowers shouting their vitality and character. Friendly and giggling continuously throughout a brief conversation, they finally scampered away, swinging their thighs and glancing back suggestively over their shoulders.

The old man was as useless as the map for directions, but, after a wrong turn laboring up a tortuous goat track, the jeep pulled into the courtyard of a tiny homestead. With the engine off, the silence of the vast mountains was immense. There was only cool, still air—not a sound but the rushing of blood in the ears.

As if condensing out of the ether, two wide-eyed children appeared from a little brick house perched on the cliff top, silently staring. They, too, had flowers and herbs in their hair, as did their father, who appeared shortly afterward with a warm if nervous greeting.

He proved more than helpful. The road to Najran? Yes, he knew it and was perfectly happy to guide the jeep there with his ancient beige Land Cruiser. It seemed too much to accept, though. As always, it is difficult to tell whether an offer of hospitality in such parts is merely a conformation to local custom or something meant to be accepted. He pointed out the way instead. It seemed that the best "main road" was the one that would lead through to Najran. But far from being a goat track, it was a rock-strewn riverbed, with a one-foot-deep stream still running through it. After a few miles of driving, the goat track itself did at last appear on the bank, signaling the continuation of the route just as the flower man had said it would. It twisted its way through improbably steep hills, looking as if some giant hand had tipped rocks in random piles, to mark the way.

After emerging from the river, underside of the jeep clean, and traveling several miles further into "bandit country," there still were no bandits or hostility; but the scenery was dramatic: harsh, rocky slopes strewn with angular boulders towered over oases of sandy soil that supported clumps of trees and low grass.

The difficulty of patrolling or administering such terrain was strikingly apparent. With few access tracks, and terrain that was extremely difficult to travel over even on foot, it is not surprising that contact with the people who live there is infrequent. It certainly looked like perfect bandit country—but where were they all? On the way, there had only been charming goat herders who, without any hint of hostility, had put themselves out of their way to help give directions or strike up a conversation. But the very challenging topography and its isolation from the mainstream life of the kingdom would make the area a good hiding place.

Eventually, a checkpoint appeared. Little more than a red and white pole and an elderly Land Cruiser on the side of the track, the somnolent Saudi guard asked to see papers, and asked what on earth the destination was. He shook his head on hearing Najran, declining to let the jeep pass, even though the track that led there would reach it within a few miles. The track was very close to the border with Yemen. Indeed, it could already have been Yemeni territory. The old man who owned the shop had said that there was no distinction between the two countries as far as he was concerned, and there were no border markers in the area.

"I could let you through, but I don't want the responsibility of you not arriving on my hands," the guard said patiently. "The bandits out there would love to get hold of a nice new jeep like this."

A U-turn was in order, and if the journey back out was less interesting because through already familiar terrain, that was compensated for by the revelation that if one travels into the Asir mountains to find Al-Qaeda supporters, one ends up encountering men who wear flowers in their hair and cultivate a passion for perfume.

In December 2002, the American Embassy in Riyadh added the inclusion of a tribe's name as part of the procedure for visa applications after it became clear that so many of the Saudi hijackers on September 11 had come from big Hijazi and Asiri tribes. According to one Saudi commentator writing in *Al-Watan* newspaper, this was "clear evidence" that the American authorities had zoomed in, without reason, on the tribal question in response to security concerns gripping the country. The commentator's umbrage was clear as he wrote that "the United States has proved its inability to understand our social fabric and our demographic structure despite its huge intelligence capabilities and cultural influence."

The visa requirement reflected the "mistaken American thinking," rooted in the theory that tribes in Saudi Arabia are "no more than a clan made up of a limited number of individuals who gather in a tent in the evenings." Thus the United States incorrectly reads Saudi Arabia as "Orientalists had misread the Arab world in the nineteenth-century," in the process deluding itself into believing that all those involved in the September 11 attacks who carried tribal names "came out of their tribal chief's tent." The American officials who introduced the new visa rule were unaware, the commentator said, that "none of the hijackers" was born or had even lived in his tribal homeland. Nor were the hijackers themselves aware of the historical and geographical basis of tribal identity. Indeed, thinking about tribes was anachronistic, he argued, as Saudis should be proud that they live in a country stretching from the Arabian Gulf in the east to the Red Sea in the west, as "one nation united in one true and pure faith in a country much larger and more inclusive than any tribal framework. We should not confine ourselves to a narrow geographical space nor shun the larger tent that is this great country and restrict ourselves to an area of a few meters that is the tribe."

Oriental stereotypes do sometimes set the context for discussion by foreign journalists of the complex tribal system in Saudi Arabia. And allegiance to tribe and Islamic heritage in Saudi Arabia did loosen during the 1970s oil boom. During that decade, a new national identity began to emerge. But this identity was weak and in many ways the Al-Saud's strategy of building alliances counteracted, or undermined, attempts to generate a national identity above, or at least alongside, tribal ones. For tribal leaders began to receive more substantial benefits from state agencies, meaning their loyalty could be depended on more than before. But so too was the loyalty of the tribesmen ever more bound to tribal leaders, because it was they who held the benefits. At the same time, the political alliance between tribe and state was reinforced by frequent marriages between tribal women and government officials and Saudi princes. They were encouraged by those same tribal leaders as a means of ensuring continuing access to government leaders.

However, it was in Asir, contrary to the misinformation in the *Al-Watan* article, that many of the families of the 15 Saudi hijackers did in fact live when the attacks took place. A number of the hijackers themselves, among them members of the same tribes, had bonded there in the late 1990s. Many attended the sermons of a radical Wahhabi cleric at the Seqeley mosque in the region's commercial capital, Khamis Mushayt. They pledged to join "the jihad" shortly before they disappeared from Saudi Arabia into the training camps of Afghanistan. No fewer than 12 of the hijackers were from the underdeveloped, highly tribal parts of Hijaz and Asir.

The revelation of that fact, it now seems clear, was part of a deliberate strategy on the part of their recruiter, Osama bin Laden. He knew the area well. Highway 15, which runs from south of Mecca through Taif and Al-Baha province into the mountains of Asir, was built by his father, who died in a 1967 plane crash while surveying it. Bin Laden knew too, of course, that the foundations of the Saudi state had been built on active fault lines and that, sooner or later, a seismic shift was sure to shake that state to the ground. Pulling in one direction is the internal demands of the Wahhabis; pulling in the other is the fundamentally absurd and self-contradictory "special relationship" between the United States and Saudi Arabia that has stood since February 1945, when Ibn Saud met President Roosevelt on the USS *Quincy* in the Suez Canal. That meeting took place three days after the close of the Yalta Conference, where the American president, Winston Churchill, and Joseph Stalin decided the shape of the world after World War II. It sowed the seeds of future instability, with the Al-Saud already torn between a jihad-inspired Wahhabi religious establishment needed to impose order at home and new ties to Western colonial forces—first Britain, then the United States—that were essential to guarantee external security.

With access to cheap oil as the common denominator, the Western powers chose to overlook the fact that their staunch ally, the Al-Saud, was quietly cultivating a Wahhabi religious establishment that placed at the center of its ideology the goal of completely destroying the West. The Wahhabi religious establishment was in an equally untenable position: supporting a corrupt royal regime that took its legitimacy from endorsing the Wahhabi version of Islam while, at the same time, forming such cripplingly dependant relations with foreign "infidel" powers.

There were dissenters on both sides: those in the West who saw through the hypocrisy and warned of the long-term dangers, and those among the Wahhabis who—unlike the official religious establishment—refused to accept such close Al-Saud–U.S. ties. Successive kings backed liberal reforms and embraced Western technology and know-how, but always against the protests of the dissenting Wahhabi hard-liners. The result was periodic crises.

As early as 1929, three years before the Saudi state was formed, Ibn Saud (who had accepted a knighthood from the British) put down a rebellion in the Eastern Province by a group of Wahhabi leaders, who considered him insufficiently Islamic because he had allowed the Shiite minority to practice their rites in private and had signed security pacts with the British. The telegraph, radio, television, satellite TV, and Internet were all subsequently introduced, despite vocal dissent from hard-liners, by Ibn Saud and his successors, as other Western influences transformed the desert kingdom into—in the eyes of those Wahhabi dissenters—a superficial replica of the "decadent" West they despised.

While the official Wahhabi religious establishment itself was largely bought off with perks and power, and the general Saudi population in the region outside Al-Najd never unconditionally embraced Wahhabism, a hard-line Islamist minority periodically rose up during this period of economic growth and cultural transformation, as they had in 1929, to protest both the official Wahhabi establishment and the Al-Saud princes they support.

In 1975, King Faisal was assassinated by a disgruntled nephew—a revenge attack by the brother of one of the king's other nephews who had been killed in a 1965 shootout with demonstrators opposing the introduction of television. In the 1970s, hard-line Sunni Islamic militants believed fundamentalism was not a sufficiently strong force in Saudi Arabia, and these dissidents seized control of the Grand Mosque in Mecca, one of the holiest sites in Islam, in 1979. They charged that the Al-Saud regime had lost its legitimacy due to corruption and its close ties to Western nations, and viewed the official Wahhabi establishment as hopelessly compromised by legitimizing the Al-Saud's rule. The standoff lasted until the Saudi military—backed by French special forces—succeeded in removing the dissidents. More than 200 troops and dissidents were killed at the mosque, and afterward over 60 dissidents were publicly beheaded. In the first terrorist attack against U.S. troops on Saudi soil, five Americans were killed in 1995 when a bomb exploded at a U.S.-operated Saudi National Guard training center in Riyadh. The bombers were said to have been inspired by bin Laden communiqués, which railed against the Al-Saud and its mainstream Wahhabi backers for sanctioning a permanent U.S. military presence inside the kingdom after the 1991 Gulf war to liberate neighboring Kuwait. A large truck bomb devastated the U.S. military residence in Dhahran, Khobar Towers, the following year, killing 19 servicemen. And, after the Al-Saud secretly facilitated the U.S.-led war on Iraq in 2003 to topple Saddam Hussein, Western civilians became the target of a new campaign of Al-Qaeda-inspired violence, terrorism that was again repeatedly condemned by the official Wahhabi clerics. The suicide bombers' videotapes illustrate their martial message with news clips of George W. Bush in cozy chats with Saudi leaders.

This is the context in which to ask why so many young men from the impoverished tribal areas of Asir and the Hijaz were eager recruits to bin

Laden on September 11. Like them and other hard-line Islamic dissenters in the past, bin Laden was always deeply critical of the official Wahhabi religious establishment that rules in partnership with the Al-Saud, which in his view has been co-opted by them. The hijackers also shared his Yemeni-Saudi tribal roots. And, again like him, they resented being ruled by a clan that lives so manifestly by double standards, and by religious sheiks from the central Al-Najd region who give the Al-Saud legitimacy by—as the favorite dissident saying has it—"issuing fatwas for money." So by attacking the U.S. guarantors of Saudi security and survival on September 11, these tribal, hard-line Islamist Saudis were targeting the historic Wahhabi–Al-Saud alliance as much as they were the U.S.-Saudi alliance. The attacks were, in a sense, the seismic shift that became an inevitability as soon as the Saudi-U.S. alliance was cemented back in the 1940s. The only genuinely surprising aspect to the attacks, apart from their horrific scale, was that they had been so long in coming.

The selection of such tribal Saudis by bin Laden was a direct challenge to the Al-Saud regime in other ways, because the question of tribal solidarity is also central to the way the different factions of the Al-Saud ruling family have historically consolidated their power bases. The regular army, which is headed by Defense Minister Prince Sultan, is made up of ordinary people from the cities who have little tribal allegiance, and is trained and funded in a way similar to most other armies in the world. But it has never been trusted by the Al-Saud when it comes to internal security, a fact that is attested to by the presence of the National Guard. The National Guard, which is one of the best-trained and well-equipped armies in the world, is headed by Crown Prince Abdullah, who himself is the son of a tribal mother. The National Guard, in contrast to the army, has institutionalized and cemented tribal, social, and religious ties in the kingdom because it is made up of young men drawn from the various ranks of the Bedu, tribes, and official Wahhabi religious establishment. Commanders, for instance, often head battalions largely made up of their own tribal cousins, which makes the leaders and their followers less susceptible to subversive ideas and outside ideologies. Since they and their families reap all of the benefits of being part of the state apparatus, they are supposed to have a vested interest in maintaining the status quo. By selecting hijackers from among the main tribal groupings in the kingdom, then, bin Laden's message to the Al-Saud and the "bought off" religious establishment was as personal as it was profound: The tribes on whom you all rely to stay in power are siding with me. In the mid-1990s bin Laden had proposed breaking up the Saudi state, suggesting two new countries—Greater Yemen and Greater Hijaz—which could divide the Arabian Peninsula between them.

One Asir tribe, the million-strong Al-Ghamdi, had an especially central role in September 11 and subsequent Al-Qaeda operations in Saudi Arabia, and indeed throughout the world. This is proof that the potential for tribal rebellion in Saudi Arabia, should brother start to join with brother, is greater than has hitherto been acknowledged. Three, possibly four, of the Saudi hijackers were Al-Ghamdis. The cave in Afghanistan where the plan for September 11 was hatched was named the "Al-Ghamdi house." One of three Saudi terrorists jailed in Morocco in February 2003 for planning to attack Western warships was an Al-Ghamdi. A leader of Arab fighters in Chechnya killed in April 2004 was a Saudi called Abu Al-Waleed Al-Ghamdi. When bin Laden wrote a poem praising the tribes of Asir, he made special mention of the Al-Ghamdis. At least two, and possibly three, of the Al-Qaeda cell members who carried out the May 12, 2003, attacks in Riyadh were Al-Ghamdis. They included the alleged mastermind of the attacks, Ali Abdul Rahman Al-Faqaasi Al-Ghamdi. However, when his capture was announced by the state-run Saudi Press Agency, Ali Al-Ghamdi's tribal name was left out. Following protocol, none of the Saudi newspapers therefore carried it the next day. That was an indication, along with the meetings between senior princes and tribal leaders in Taif in November 2003, that the Al-Saud recognized, and was deeply troubled by, the threat posed by tribalism in general, and the Al-Ghamdi tribe in particular. During the meetings with Saudi princes, the Al-Ghamdi tribal sheik was among the first to declare his loyalty to the regime.

One reason the Al-Saud ruling family was able to secure the support of the various tribal groupings during the formation of the state is that it itself was not perceived to be a tribe but a family, which does not have any overt tribal allegiances. Indeed, one reason they have denied tribal leaders the highest positions in government is because, should there be any serious disagreements, it would mean facing down not just one man but his millions of tribal cousins as well.

Among tribal members, allegiances are still strongly expressed even by the young who have grown up in the new urban centers throughout the kingdom and have little direct experience of tribal customs and traditions. That is especially true with the Al-Ghamdis, who are historically based in the Asiri city of Al-Baha, but includes among its members those who have never been to Asir. The son of a senior London-based Saudi diplomat, who is an Al-Ghamdi but who has spent almost none of his life in Saudi Arabia and speaks poor Arabic, spent an evening with me in Jeddah, for instance, talking about how he was proud of his Al-Ghamdi tribal characteristics: generosity, loyalty, a refusal to judge anyone on any basis other than their merits, even if he comes from the same tribe. Another Al-Ghamdi, who again has never been to Asir, told me that on September 11 he had heard about his "cousins" holding celebratory dinner parties across Al-Baha. He was acutely aware of the role the Al-Ghamdi tribe had played in various conflicts and attacks the world over, and he beamed with pride as he listed them, one by one. "Look what we managed to do with just a few of our members on September 11," he declared on one occasion. "Imagine what we could do if a million of us rose up together!"

Chapter Four

SHIA FEAR

Located in the southwest of Saudi Arabia near the border with Yemen, the city of Najran is populated by tribes whose members also straddle both Saudi Arabia and Yemen. The city is one of the most fascinating, but least visited, in the kingdom. Its green farms contrast with the desolate sands of the surrounding Empty Quarter to the east and the dark, shattered basalt of the surrounding mountains to the west. In the past, when approached from the Empty Quarter by travelers on camel or on foot, the oasis must have seemed an earthly paradise. Its architectural beauty remains a wonder to behold, even if you arrive in a four-wheel jeep: the date palms, vegetable gardens, and dull, rectangular mud-brick houses still have towers and castellated ramparts, the upper surfaces of which are painted white or a brilliant sky blue. Najran is famous, too, for its mud-brick castles, palaces, and ancient watchtowers, which form one of the most significant pieces of architectural inheritance in the Arabian Peninsula.

The city's history incorporates periods of Jewish, Christian, and Islamic dominance. Most famously, Najran is home to a trench—Al-Akhdood—which is said in the Qu'ran to contain the bodies of Christians and Jews, burnt for their faith in the sixth century by the local Pagan king.

The locals, alas, are still persecuted; but these days they are the kingdom's Ismaeli "sevener" Shiites. Ismaili Shiites hold that the seventh Imam, or religious leader, was rightfully Ismail (hence the name) rather than his brother, and his descendants are still represented today in an official called the Aga Khan (currently the forty-ninth Imam, Prince Karim Aga Khan IV, who became Imam at the age of 20 in 1957). They make up the majority of the local Najran population, and represent an offshoot of "twelver" Shiite Islam, which is dominant in Iran. The sect has about 100,000 adherents in Saudi Arabia, and 50,000 in Yemen. And they are now the main victims of the official policy of religious and ethnic discrimination in Saudi Arabia.

The Ismaelis, most of whom are members of the Yam tribe that also encompasses several neighboring communities in Yemen, have considerable armed strength. And they are highly concentrated geographically. Like their tribal brothers in Asir, they obtain weapons and other forms of assistance from across the border. Many consider themselves to be "Saudi" only in the limited sense that they happen to hold Saudi passports. Their history in Najran long predates the Al-Saud conquest of the city. In fact, they trace their origins in terms of tribe, not nation, and in particular to the tribes that fought alongside the first Shiite Imam.

According to Said K. Aburish, Najran was the setting for one of the estimated 26 anti-Al-Saud tribal and other rebellions that took place between 1916 and 1928 in what is now the kingdom of Saudi Arabia, each of which was brutally suppressed by the Wahhabi forces backing Ibn Saud. It was an orgy of mass killing of mostly innocent victims, women and children. A staggering 7,000 people in Najran alone may have been put to the sword. The brutal Wahhabi massacres in the formation of the Saudi state continue to reverberate in Najran, as they do in the Hijaz and Asir, and they form the historical context for the eruption of violence between Saudi security forces and armed Ismaeli tribesmen in Najran in April 2000. It was an indication that the rule of the Al-Saud regime in the southwestern tribal region could quickly become vulnerable if instability on a national scale were to occur.

The April 2000 disturbances began when government-backed religious police stormed a major Ismaeli mosque, seized many of its religious texts, and arrested three clerics. Local Ismaelis, who openly bear arms, reacted by firing on the security forces and torching some of their vehicles. In the resulting clashes, as many as 40 people were killed, and scores were injured. Reenforcements from the army were rushed to the scene, and Saudi soldiers began a sweep of the area. They made numerous arrests. In response, hundreds of Ismaelis marched to the palace of Prince Mish'al bin Saud, the local governor responsible for giving orders for the mosque to be closed. Fearing for his life, the prince fled to a nearby hotel. He ordered the army to surround it for his protection with their American-made Bradley armored fighting vehicles.

The clashes came after local Ismaelis decided, for the first time in many years, to openly celebrate Ashura. That Shiite holiday commemorates the death of Imam Hussein, grandson of the Prophet, whose murder in Karbala in the seventh century had given birth to the Shia sect. Shiites generally are extremely active, holding prayers and religious ceremonies, during the first 10 days of the Islamic month of Muharram, which is when Ashura takes place. The tenth day of Muharram is the most revered, but also the most agonizing, as it marks the anniversary of Hussein's martyrdom.

The decision by the Ismaelis to flex their muscles was influenced in part by an Amnesty International campaign aimed at publicizing the lack of religious freedom and other human rights abuses inside Saudi Arabia. Past improvements in religious rights for Saudi Shiites in the oil-rich Eastern Province had come about partly as a result of such external pressure. The Ismaelis had hoped they could wrangle similar concessions. Consistent with their strategy of buying loyalty, the Al-Saud regime had been successful during the several years leading to the violence in diminishing the potential for religious incitement against the government by providing minorities like the Shiites with generous amounts of financial subsidies for local services. However, the funds earmarked specifically for the Ismaelis were distributed through one Sheik Ali bin Musallam, a leading member of the Yam tribe and a cabinet minister related by marriage to Defense Minister Prince Sultan. Shiite dissidents claim he pocketed most of it.

The persecution of the Ismaelis had increased sharply after the arrival of Prince Mish'al in 1997. Since then, officials have embarked on a campaign of eradicating the Ismaeli heritage and other expressions of the "infidel" faith. Several officials publicly stated their plans to convert all Ismaelis to Wahhabism. Sheik Ali Khursan was one such official, and he declared that Ismaelis are infidels because they do not follow the Sunna (the tradition of the Prophet), they do not believe that the Qu'ran is complete, and moreover they hate Sunnis. The antagonism was clear when he continued: "We don't eat their food, we don't intermarry with them, we should not pray for their dead or allow them to be buried in our cemeteries."

The director of the Ministry of Islamic Affairs announced that a new ministry office in Najran had been opened solely to propagate Wahhabi doctrine. Even before the end of Ramadan in 1997, Prince Mish'al had got the process of Wahhabization under way. He dispatched police to prevent

Ismaelis from performing prayers during the Islamic festival known as Eid Al-Fitr, which takes place at the end of Ramadan. Afterward, Ismaelis were instructed by their leader to perform their prayers at home. Nevertheless, the leader's subsequent arrest, officially on charges of "sorcery," sparked the rebellion, after the locals had once again emerged from their homes to mark the religious ritual.

The government had initiated in the meantime a project to build nine new Wahhabi mosques in Najran. At least $11 million was earmarked for the task. Anti-Ismaeli campaigns resulted in many arrests and floggings. Land confiscation also became commonplace. The government even attempted forcefully to change the demographic make-up of the city. Two Sunni-majority Yemeni tribes were given Saudi citizenship, and were allocated land and offered jobs in Najran—a city where unemployment among Saudis is running at about 40 percent. The Yemeni tribes had lived in Najran as refugees since the 1960s, after fleeing the communist control of South Yemen. The area where they now live as Saudi citizens is named after the governor-prince.

Meanwhile, thousands of the Ismaelis themselves were demoted, fired, or transferred from Najran after the April 2000 mosque attack. Hundreds of Ismaeli interior ministry employees were sent packing to other parts of the kingdom. In August 2000, many teachers were transferred to Al-Jouf—in other words, from the southern-most point of the kingdom to its northern-most province. Suddenly, no Ismaeli students were being accepted at military colleges either, in contrast to previous academic years. The army stayed one week in Najran, and was responsible for most of the arrests and beatings.

Four Ismaeli high school students were soon afterward flogged for fighting with a Wahhabi teacher, who openly insulted their religious beliefs in front of other students in the classroom. They were sentenced to two to four years in prison, and 500 to 800 lashes. The majority of prisoners held in Saudi Arabia now on political or religious grounds are Ismaelis, according to Shiite exiles, although the U.S. State Department has said all Ismaeli prisoners involved in the disturbances and arrested have since been pardoned.

The Al-Saud's repression of the Ismaelis carries a number of dangers, not least how it will affect the long antagonism between the governments of Saudi Arabia and Yemen. But such dangers pale in comparison to those posed by the anger and alienation Saudi repression creates in the all-important oil-producing Eastern Province.

The lights were dim in the sparsely furnished room in the nondescript terraced house in the heart of Dammam, the regional capital of the Eastern Province that is its longest settled and largest town—a run-down urban center compared to its modern twin sister, Khobar, and a place where Westerners are rarely seen. The majority of the Muslim population—Saudi and expatriate alike—in the oil-rich region are from the persecuted Shiite sect. That evening, during Ashura in 2002, about 20 Shiite expatriates, mainly Indians and Pakistanis, had gathered soon after sunset. They had the air of a group of men about to undertake a highly dangerous, clandestine operation. But it was not a secret political gathering. Nor were they a group of terrorists plotting a mission. Rather, they had simply come together to mourn the martyrdom of Hussein.

Shiites are a liberal people, except in their faith, in which they are self-professed fanatics. The host of the gathering that day, an Indian and a friend of a trusted friend, explained that, despite the Wahhabi establishment's strict ban on their religious rituals, thousands of Shiites all over the kingdom continued to mourn the tragedy of Karbala. It is so central to their identity as to be something they cannot live without, he added. But there was little need for such commentary.

The reality of what he was trying to explain quickly became evident in the room itself. After the final guests arrived, one of the group started to recite verses from the Qu'ran in Urdu. Soon, everyone was weeping and moaning; tears freely flowed from their eyes. It was as though they were no longer in this world, but back in the seventh century in Karbala, personally witnessing the slaughter of Hussein and his family and friends.

Shiites—both Saudis and immigrants, such as the people who had gathered together that evening—have always observed the annual Ashura ritual in the Eastern Province. But, until very recently, they did so only in secret and in genuine fear of arrest—even if they were inside their homes with the doors locked and the curtains drawn. The expatriate Shiites in the Eastern Province, the host told me, typically split into small groups, with no single group exceeding 50 or so in number. In the past, hundreds were "caught" observing such religious rites, he said. They were arrested, and the foreigners among them were deported while Saudi Shiites faced jail terms and torture.

The authorities continue to increase the frequency of police patrols in Shiite neighborhoods during the ritual period. However, orders in recent years have been to ease off engaging in mass arrests. Instead, the police seal off Shia districts, a move aimed mainly at thwarting possible terrorist attacks by Wahhabis. The latter are incensed with the "infidels" in their midst, whom they detest with a passion that words cannot describe. For the Wahhabis, the Shiites are daring to profess what, to them, is anathema to every truth revealed by Allah to the Muslim faithful.

Some towns and cities in the Eastern Province—such as Qatif, Sihat, Tarout, and Safwa—have 100 percent Shiite populations. Historically, they have been silently contemptuous of the Al-Saud ruling family and the Wahhabi religious establishment, which was given free rein to propagate anti-Shiite hatred. Neighboring countries, too, have majority Shiite populations, including Bahrain, which is nearly 65 percent Shiite but also ruled by Sunnis, and Iraq, which is 60 percent Shiite and was, until the fall of Saddam, similarly ruled by a hostile Sunni minority.

In the Eastern Province generally, according to often-quoted but ultimately unreliable figures, Shiites constitute 55 percent of the population. Huge oil reserves in the region, which the local population would have benefited from in the normal course of events, became a major contributor to the Shiites' persecution. It became imperative for the Al-Saud and the Wahhabi religious establishment to suppress them, both politically and economically, lest they establish a power base that might one day rival that of the Al-Saud and Wahhabis in the heart of the petrochemical industry. That huge oil wealth led to an unprecedented development program elsewhere; but areas dominated by Shiites initially remained neglected, showing no outward signs of the prosperity transforming the rest of the kingdom on an almost daily basis. In these areas, there remained poverty, hunger, and beggary. The fact that most local Shiites were traditionally farmers, a profession held in low status in Arabia, added to their lot of being at the bottom of the pecking order.

Throughout the Al-Saud's various defeats and victories and alignments and re-alignments with tribal chieftains, Bedouin clans, and sedentary peoples, there remained one constant: outright hostility from the Wahhabis to the Shiite sect. And that hostility was mutual. In Shiism, there is no provision for rule by monarchy, meaning the sect's followers naturally resist being governed by the Al-Saud. And it followed that, since Wahhabism was supporting the imperialist designs of the Al-Saud family, that ideology, to the mind of the Shiites (and for that matter most Sunnis), violated the basic teachings of Islam and the traditions of the Prophet. The fact that the Shiites also invest their religious leaders, who are in theory direct descendants of Ali, with supreme spiritual authority further complicates the loyalty issue when it comes to the Saudi state. Then there is the added factor that the only difference between a Sunni and Shiite Muslim is a state of mind that differentiates their privately held beliefs, meaning Shiites can easily pass themselves off publicly as Sunnis. This increases the paranoia of hard-line Wahhabis, who fear that subversives have secretly infiltrated their ranks.

In the 1950s, unemployment and discontent among the Shiites became so potentially destabilizing that American executives of the then Arab American Oil Company (Aramco), now called the Saudi Arabian Oil Company (Saudi Aramco), feared an uprising by Shiite youth. The Aramco compound, walled and gated, served to highlight the poverty that surrounded its interior, while American expatriates who lived inside it enjoyed all the luxuries of a model American suburb. All that, warned Aramco executives, could have an adverse effect on oil production. They successfully lobbied the Al-Saud into allowing the hiring of Shiites from Qatif and Sihat, but initially only in menial jobs. Slowly, however, the Shiites rose through the ranks. Now there are many leading Shiite businessmen and executives throughout the Eastern Province.

After Shiites eventually comprised as many as half of the labor force of Saudi Aramco, the Al-Saud regime flip-flopped, and grew to consider their presence in the company as a new security problem. At the same time, Shiites remained banned from taking up positions in other professions, such as the army and educational institutions. In most other respects, their lot—albeit with exceptions—did not improve. Even in their strongholds they were not allowed to practice their faith—or, when they were, the "privilege" was granted not because of a new-found, genuine respect for their beliefs but rather as a result of a need by the Al-Saud regime to respond to international condemnation of the lack of religious freedom in their Wahhabi kingdom.

In September 2004, the U.S. State Department finally added Saudi Arabia to its "countries of particular concern" when it comes to the issue of the lack of religious freedom, stating simply that freedom of religious expression in the kingdom does not exist.

At first glance, Qatif resembles most other major Saudi cities. An oasis city north of Dammam on the coast, it is the center of one of the most important fishing and agricultural areas in the kingdom. Its inhabitants are mainly fishermen, farmers, businessmen, and government employees. The Qatif area contains a population of 300,000 people, who are scattered over distinct regions.

There exists a slum in the city, however, made up of semiconcrete houses, which are inhabited by the poorest of the poor Shiites. The area resembles the worst slums of Bombay. The Shiites in this police no-go area remain outcasts, even to their own wider community. They must resort to beggary to survive. Girls and women sometimes resort to prostitution. These Shiites, too, long each year for Ashura, but not only to commemorate the martyrdom of Hussein. During the ritual, the more prosperous Shiites from outside shower them with charity. At other times, a single Shia-run NGO, which officially does not exist, does what it can to give assistance. According to a local Shiite, there are neither schools nor clean water. They have to survive without electricity and medical facilities.

There is, however, a brand new, multimillion-dollar Sunni mosque in the center of the modern town. The money wasted on that could have been spent renovating the slum. It could also have provided an education for its children. But reinforcing eternal Wahhabi supremacy and Shiite humiliation took precedence. Of course, the mosque remains empty even during prayer times. Locals defiantly shuffle right past it, on their way to their own rundown Shiite places of worship.

It would, in any event, take more than genuine investment in Shiite communities and an official end to discrimination to rid young Sunnis of the inveterate distrust they have of Shiites as a consequence of being brainwashed about the Shiite "enemy" for generations. A decades-long campaign by the Wahhabi religious leaders, fully endorsed by the Al-Saud, has embedded in the minds of young Saudis stereotypes prevalent among many Sunnis elsewhere. Shiites, they were told, are not in fact real Muslims, and as such are a constant subversive threat to the well-being of the nation. The misinformation campaign alleged, falsely, that the Shiites believe Ali was a prophet (a total negation of Islam, which says that Muhammad is the last Prophet). It was also propagated that Shiites do not believe in the universally accepted version of the Qu'ran, because they have secretly added chapters of their own. Meat slaughtered by Shiite butchers is not fit for consumption, it was claimed. Sunni Muslims were even encouraged to shun Shiites socially, with warnings like "Shiites will spit in cups of water before they hand them over to Sunnis" and "an inherent tenet of Shiite belief is the absolute necessity of betraying Sunnis."

Even under King Faisal—the most progressive, clear-headed, and best-educated of Saudi Arabia's kings—a series of fatwas, or religious edicts, were issued that blindly condemned Shiites as heretics (although during his rein Faisal personally removed many restrictions against the Shiites and enabled them to benefit from state educational and health services). Even today many local schools continue to teach Shiite children that their sect is an apostasy from Islam, and even part of a Jewish plot to sabotage the Muslim nation. In order to pass certain examinations, they must damn themselves as infidels in the answers they give to questions.

In 1979, when the Iranian revolution brought Ayatollah Khomeini to power, Saudi Arabia's Shiites got a shot in the arm. Until then, they had had little choice but to tolerate passively all the humiliation, exploitation, and repression that came with living in Saudi Arabia. Iran's revolution, however, promoted political Shiism as a potential force for revolutionary change and empowerment, not only in Saudi Arabia but throughout the rest of the Arabian Gulf.

As a result, there were uprisings in neighboring Kuwait, where Shiites were also a persecuted minority, and Shiites elsewhere started to call for their rights. The Al-Saud had never before had to resort to force to suppress the kingdom's Shiites, as the latter had neither asserted themselves collectively on the political level nor launched campaigns of mass civil disobedience. All that changed, however, when Khomeini called for the export of his Islamic revolution. The Al-Saud viewed the local Shiites as inevitable allies of Khomeini, and therefore representing the kind of internal threat to the state the Wahhabi religious establishment had always warned about when it came to the question of Shiite loyalty.

The late 1970s and early 1980s witnessed the worst repression of Shiites in the Eastern Province in the kingdom's history, aside from when, during the first Saudi empire (1744–1818), the Wahhabis invaded Qatif and destroyed the city's Shiite shrines. In 1979 in Qatif, it was Shiite demonstrators who took to the streets, responding to calls by Khomeini. In response, the Al-Saud deployed its tribal National Guard and savagely dispersed them: another example of Saudi-Wahhabi history repeating itself. The following year, Shiites in Qatif were strafed by helicopter gunships during Ashura, which they had defiantly decided to mark in public for the first time. Many were killed and injured. Meanwhile, hundreds of Shiite religious leaders were jailed, while many more went into self-imposed exile, where they established opposition groups.

The Al-Saud now faced a dilemma: How to deal with the Shiites who had become completely alienated from the national mainstream? Overnight, blueprints were drawn up for underdeveloped areas inhabited by the Shiites, and initiatives were taken to bring Shiites closer to the national mainstream. Despite massive resistance from the Wahhabi religious establishment, the Al-Saud tamed the campaigns that had damned Shiites as un-Islamic. More employment sectors were opened up to Shiites, and a Shiite bureaucrat was even appointed as an advisor to the king. The death of Khomeini in 1989, meanwhile, resulted in the taming of the aggressive, expansionist nature of the Iranian revolution.

During the Iran-Iraq war of the 1980s, Saudi Arabia had been allied with Saddam Hussein. It did so in the hope that—when seen along with its own limited domestic reform initiative—a weakened Iran would dampen unrest among its own Shiite population. During Iraq's invasion of Kuwait in 1990, the invading Iraqi army reached as far as Khafji, the Saudi town on the Kuwait border. Saddam had made clear his intention of entering Saudi Arabia if it continued its support for Kuwait. The Shiites of Kuwait, until then persecuted by the ruling Al-Sabah family and charged with numerous acts of sabotage and treason, formed much of the resistance inside occupied Kuwait. Suddenly, they won huge sympathy and support from the Sunnis in Kuwait, as well as Saudi Arabia. In the same way, the Shiites of southern Iraq would become heroes—for a few weeks—to the Middle East's Sunni majority during their resistance at the beginning of the U.S.-led war on that country in 2003.

After the 1991 Gulf war ended, the Al-Saud regime started indirect negotiations with Iran, and soon afterward there was a noticeable thaw in relations between the two countries. Feelers were also sent out to Shiite dissidents, both those within the kingdom and those who had been forced into exile, with the Al-Saud promising to guarantee their safety if they dropped opposition to its rule. The initiative was openly endorsed by Iran. In 1993, the Al-Saud finally announced a general amnesty and, as a result, various Shiite leaders were released from jail, and those who had gone into exile returned. Hundreds of young Shiites were provided with jobs in the governmental and private sectors.

The subsequent appeasement of Shiites, as well as their Iranian sponsors, even resulted in the sacking of the Imam of the Prophet's Mosque in Medina. He had attacked Shiism in a Friday sermon in the presence of Ayatollah Akbar Hashemi Rafsanjani. Crown Prince Abdullah, who by then had become the kingdom's de facto leader and was known to have a certain sympathy for the Shiite communities in the kingdom, publicly apologized to the Iranian leader for the Imam's "irresponsible remark," and afterward the crown prince visited Shiite-dominated areas in the Eastern Province. He ordered a number of religious places there that had been closed by the authorities decades earlier to be re-opened.

The question everyone was asking, after the fall of Saddam in 2003, was: What would stop the Shiites of the Eastern Province, who have little incentive to support the regime that oppresses them and damns them as infidels, from welcoming U.S. forces if they rolled into the Eastern Province to "liberate" Saudi Arabia's oil fields? They would certainly be seen as liberators in the dingy back streets of Qatif, and perhaps initially even in the other Shiite-majority town in the Eastern Province.

After the fall of Baghdad, the powerful images of more than a million Shiites in the streets of Iraq for the Ashura commemoration, banned under Saddam, was not lost on Saudi Arabia's Shiites. Nor was it lost on the Saudi authorities. Saudi Shiites traditionally have strong links across the border. A leading Saudi Shiite cleric said that Shiites in Saudi Arabia were hopeful that the defeat of Saddam would help their cause in the kingdom. At the same time, the fear that Shiites could align themselves with outside forces led the Al-Saud regime once again to speed up an ongoing process of granting them greater religious freedoms and human rights. In a sense, the pattern of superficial appeasement after the 1991 Gulf war is now being repeated. The kingdom's senior religious leader, Sheik Abdul Aziz bin Abdullah Al-Asheik, suddenly declared that charging other Muslims with disbelief—essentially, the official attitude toward Shiites until then—was wrong. "Charging other Muslims with whom one may differ as disbelievers results in murdering innocent people, destroying facilities, disorder and instability," he added for good measure.

Other, subtler historic tensions were also brought to the surface. In 1802, Wahhabis supported by the Al-Saud penetrated Karbala in Iraq and destroyed the mausoleum of Hussein. With that attack on the tombs of Hussein and his followers in Karbala, the Wahhabi movement and the Al-Saud had declared their open opposition and hostility to the Shiite sect. After the fall of Saddam, during the first Ashura three massive car combs exploded in Karbala, killing hundreds and maiming many more. Locals instinctively blamed Wahhabis, meaning Saudi jihadis who had sneaked across the border. It was as though history was repeating itself.

In late 2003, leaders of Saudi Arabia's Shiite Muslim minority handed over a petition to Crown Prince Abdullah demanding a greater say in the affairs of the Sunni-ruled kingdom. The move came just after authorities announced an investigation into a number of Shiite mosques in the Eastern Province set ablaze in apparent arson attacks. The Al-Saud regime was, of course, closely watching the resurgence of the Shiite majority in neighboring Iraq. The petition sought for the right for Shiites to be referred to their own religious courts, as Sunni courts do not recognize testimonies by Shiites.

Shiite activist Jaffar Al-Shayeb, who was among the delegation that met with Prince Abdullah and coauthored the petition signed by 450 Shiite academics, businessmen, writers, and women, played his cards close to his chest. Yes, he told me, the Shiites have "raised their voices in unison to demand reform," and the 30-minute meeting focused on the "constant trouble the Shiites face in Saudi Arabia." The petition asked for the kingdom to accept all Islamic sects, he said. There had to be a group or body that represented the Shiites to push for equal opportunities, especially in the areas of education and employment. The petition further asked for the annulment of laws that prohibit the formation of lobby groups, such as those that would promote the rights of Shiites. And it demanded the introduction of new laws that would both protect individual rights and combat all kinds of religious discrimination. One result of the meeting was the establishment of a religious forum, set up so the Sunnis and Shiites in Saudi Arabia could better understand one another.

Al-Shayeb flatly dismissed my suggestion that the Shiite community in Saudi Arabia has a common agenda with outside groups.

"We have no alliance with anyone outside the country, and want to resolve this issue so that it doesn't leave any space for outsiders to exploit," he insisted.

"This petition goes hand in hand with the reformist document also submitted to Prince Abdullah earlier this year," he added, referring to a group of mostly Sunni intellectuals who called for elections, freedom of speech, and other reforms.

Like the earlier petition, his was couched carefully in the language of national unity and the ultimate legitimacy of the ruling Al-Saud family.

Thousands of Shiites had taken to the streets of the Eastern Province two months before the petition was presented, to mark Ashura with unprecedented freedom. In the town of Seihat, close to Dhahran, several thousand Shiites beat their chests in a night-time Ashura procession. Similar marches took place in six or seven other towns. It was the first year there were so many people. Police and residents had cooperated to seal off parts of the mainly Shiite town for the religious ceremony. Red, green, and black Shiite flags decked a central Seihat square, where a reconstruction of the death of Hussein and an art exhibition depicting his suffering stoked Shiite grief. Police had set up security road blocks on the approaches to the town to thwart any potential attacks.

But the backlash was already underway. Three Shiite places of worship in Tarut Island, in the Eastern Province, had been torched by unknown assailants as the Shiite delegation was meeting Crown Prince Abdullah. The historical Prophet Al-Khoder Mosque was the first to be torched, then the Sheikh Alaa Mosque and Al-Saif Hussainya. A local reported that the fires were started after gasoline had been poured on the doors and windows of the mosques. There were other reports of sectarian strife. Four Shiite students from Al-Qudaih were permanently expelled from Jubail Industrial College, also in the Eastern Province, following a fight with several Sunni students who assaulted them and attacked their Shiite religious practices. A Shiite cemetery in Anaak had been desecrated two months earlier.

Deep loathing of Shiites, an ingrained habit of associating them with hostile external and internal powers, and fears about the future position of Wahhabi clerics in a more accomodating political system all continue to feed anti-Shiite sentiment in Saudi Arabia. In a region obsessed with conspiracy theories, many Saudis, both Sunni and Shiite, think that Washington has plans to split off the Eastern Province into a separate entity and seize control of its oil reserves after Iraq has stabilized. No amount of appeasement from the Al-Saud is in the meantime going to pacify extremist Wahhabi elements—or, for that matter, the majority of the Shiites in the Eastern Province, who, not satisfied with token gestures, seem certain to exploit their ambiguous position when it comes to the issue of loyalty to the Saudi state in the wake of Saddam's fall to push even more strongly for greater freedoms and rights.

Chapter Five

TICKING TIME BOMBS: SAUDI YOUTH

On the second anniversary of the September 11 attacks on the United States, Al-Jazeera aired a two-part documentary on the complex series of events that had culminated in the terror attacks that left the Twin Towers wholly, and the Pentagon partly, destroyed. The focus of the documentary was on the lives, and the ideals, of the 19 hijackers, who had mostly come from Saudi Arabia. Everything was shown from the terrorists' point of view, complete with dramatic reconstructions of their last weeks and days. The docudrama that was supposed to pass for verisimilitude in fact bordered on hagiography, as the hijackers and their beliefs were not simply explained but in effect praised. Their hatred for the West was taken as given, in classic, tabloid-style Al-Jazeera, playing cleverly to shallow Arab sentiment. The subtle presentation of the legitimacy of their reasons—hatred of the West, anger at Arab regimes, loathing of Israel—aimed only to reach for the lowest common emotional denominator that binds the Arabs, however superficially, throughout the Middle East.

The documentary's main purpose was not to examine complex and contradictory subject matter, but to elicit a wholly approving reaction from as large an Arab audience as possible by presenting the attack as a "martyrdom operation," pure and simple. Unanswered were the complex questions of why young men would be so full of hatred and despair as to plot resolutely and act against the tenets of Islam, whether in terms of joining in

the decadence of the West while under cover, in terms of targeting inno-
cents, or in terms of deliberately killing themselves. And left unanswered,
too, was the most troubling question, and thus the one least likely to have
been asked, namely what is it about Saudi society that breeds and raises
such men and, further, seems to hold them in some esteem.

I watched the second of the two-part series in Riyadh with a 19-year-old
Saudi friend, Mohammed. I had met him a year earlier in Jeddah, but that
summer he had moved back to the capital after completing a diploma in engineering, and he had since started a degree at one of the capital's main universities. Since his life—like that of all middle-class Saudi youths—was lived
almost exclusively locked away inside a bedroom isolated even from what
went on in the rest of the family villa (which was itself isolated from the local
community by a huge surrounding wall), it did not really matter too much
which Saudi city he lived in. His room, which is to say the center of his entire existence, had an en-suit bathroom, and was equipped with all the latest Western technology: widescreen television, DVD player, computer,
satellite TV, Internet connection. There was no music system, though, in
keeping with his aversion, on religious grounds, to listening to music. And
there were only two books. One, it goes almost without saying, was the
Qu'ran. But the other—which he kept under his bed because, he said, it was
banned in the kingdom—was on magic and the Islamic interpretation of
dreams. This book was kept hidden, almost like pornographic magazines are
by many Western youths, because its non-Wahhabi discussion made it dangerous and contraband.

The only magazine Mohammed ever bought, meanwhile, was the London-based political weekly *Al-Majalla,* the most respected publication of its
kind in the Arab world—and, considering that it is funded by the Al-Saud, ad-
mirably bold in its treatment of the diverse range of Arab and especially Gulf
issues it covers, to the extent that it has frequently been censored back inside
the kingdom itself. He only bought it, however, because it regularly published
e-mails it claimed were from leading Al-Qaeda operatives, which typically de-
tailed their strategies, gave warnings of further attacks, or just ranted in order
to play up or legitimize their call for a global jihad. Whether or not the letters
were really from Al-Qaeda mattered little; the friction, the excitement of the
forbidden, was a selling point, and the kingdom's youth were hooked.

Nor was this the only form of their addiction. Mohammed and his
friends were avid readers of Islamist websites sympathetic to the goals of Al-
Qaeda. Although most web sites that criticized the Al-Saud specifically were
blocked inside Saudi Arabia, remarkably Al-Qaeda's home page was not,

even after the terror organization had fixed the royals themselves squarely in their sights. And they enthusiastically participated in chat rooms where a cyber war raged between extremist Jews and Muslims on the issue of the Is-raeli-Palestinian conflict. In a sense, one had to respect the devotion and dedication, not to mention the strong need for participation and activism, however misplaced it might have been. So concerned had Mohammed's rela-tives in Jeddah become at his Internet addiction that they had finally cut off the phone connection in his room to prevent him from surfing the web al-together. "My life is meaningless," he lamented, glancing every few seconds at the lifeless computer screen.

As we watched the Al-Jazeera documentary on the September 11 at-tacks, Mohammed told his driver to bring for us the only thing he ever ate: American junk food. Soon wrappers of burgers and fries from Hardee's, and empty Coca Cola cans, littered the floor. They added to an increasingly sur-real occasion. He became engrossed in the anti-Western documentary while sitting with a British friend, as we chain smoked American cigarettes and spoke only in English (a language he loved and was desperate to improve his proficiency in).

Toward the end of the documentary, an Imam was shown reciting the line from the Qu'ran that the lead hijacker, Egyptian Mohammed Atta, had reprinted on the cover of his doctoral thesis in Hamburg: "Say. My prayer and my sacrifice and my life and my death are [all] for Allah, the Lord of the worlds." The Imam's voice grew ever-more emotional, hysterical even, as images of the two planes crashing into the Twin Towers were relayed in slow motion, followed by terrifying shots of men and women jumping from the windows of the burning buildings.

Mohammed was fighting back tears. "They had everything and they gave it all up for Allah," he said quietly, in reference to the fact that the hi-jackers had, like him, mostly benefited from relatively privileged back-grounds and a good education. "Look at me! I haven't sacrificed anything at all. I'm ashamed."

In Riyadh, he was connected again to the Internet. He pulled himself together, and after logging on he entered straight away a chat site for Ameri-can lesbians, and asked me what he should say to get them "hot."

When they lived in Florida preparing their attack, some of the Saudi hi-jackers had draped a cloth over a framed print of a woman in their room, their Wahhabi upbringing making them despise this image of the human form. They also frequently hung out on the balcony overlooking their apartment pool, eyeing up the sunbathing girls in bikinis. Other of the hijackers frequented strip clubs in Boston, made phone calls to escort services, and paid prostitutes for sex.

For most observers, such behavior was inconsistent. But it is not all that different from Mohammed's regret, one moment, that he had not partaken in the attacks, and his request, the next, for advice on how to get American lesbians "hot" on the Internet. The roots of the bifurcation and the alienation it results from lie within the clash between traditional Saudi societal attitudes and the increasing rootlessness of Saudi youth exposed to the opportunities and freedoms—even licentiousness—of the West while devoid of structures or values that are constructive in dealing with the modern world. The result is something bordering on schizophrenia.

For seven decades, generation after generation of Saudis has grown up being told at school by Wahhabi-inspired teachers that the West is the source of all evil. At the same time, they have been forced to accept, also without question, that the very survival of the kingdom's ruling elite—and the development of its infrastructure—is entirely dependant on its intimate cooperation with the West. How to reconcile the pride, even arrogance of the former with the at least implicit admission of weakness of the latter? Saudi youths partake in the bounty of the West, are able to buy the latest consumer goods, which exposes them all the more easily to its temptations. My friend Mohammed would not listen to music, because it is forbidden, but he would look at pornography, which is equally so. That is understandable in a way, given that adolescent boys are told they can never meet girls because Islam forbids sex before marriage, and that the purity of females would be defiled merely by being gazed at. But it goes deeper than that. They are told, after all, that their king is the "custodian of the two holy mosques," but have also heard reports that he spent much of his time, before being incapacitated in 1995 by a stroke, gambling and whoring in Monte Carlo. One year the official government mouthpiece Saudi TV tells them that the campaign against Russia in Chechnya is legitimate jihad, but a few years later they watch Crown Prince Abdullah, on a visit to Russia, meeting the Russian-appointed head of Chechnya, while promising to crack down on Saudi funding for the Chechen "terrorists" fighting their separatist campaign.

It would be tempting, but false, to believe that with the increase in communications and availability of information there would be a breakdown in divisions. But just as some research in the United States indicates that the diversity of views on the web results in further entrenchment of opinion as people only read more avidly what they already agree with, so the wider range of opinions and cultures available due to the sudden introduction of satellite TV and the Internet has exacerbated, in all the most dangerous ways imaginable, Saudi convictions. The images of Israeli soldiers abusing and murdering Palestinians—plastered over the front pages of all the region's newspapers and broadcast daily by Al-Jazeera and the other Arabic language satellite channels—only further enrages Saudi youth aware of their own safety, indulgence, indolence, and impotence. For the Palestinians, by contrast, are poor, oppressed, and brave—and manly. That many Palestinians are youths only heightens the self-indictment of the Saudis.

Trashy American movies and music, pornography and sex scandals: this is all such media offers young Saudis, or at least all they choose to take from it. As pious Muslims, it repulses them, reinforcing negative stereotypes—rampant crime, promiscuity, the complete absence of ethical and religious codes and standards—that their Wahhabi leaders have always warned them constitutes the hell on earth that is life in the infidel West. However, since they are young men fired up with testosterone, they are also drawn, like moths to a flame, to the constant bombardment of sexually stimulating images and narratives. Repulsed and yet attracted, they are tossed and turned, with few navigational guides.

In the past, families were the guides—and the most direct enforcers of cultural and societal rules and traditions. Respect for one's elders was a pillar of social maintenance. Family honor was a centerpiece, and offending it brought punishment from the family that could be more fearsome than from the state. Honor killings—murders—of women, including married women whose sexual activities offended family honor, were, and are, carried out by the woman's family. A somewhat distinct example of the rules of the game came after Saddam Hussein's brothers-in-law defected from Iraq, spilled secrets about weapons of mass destruction, and then, amazingly, returned to the country and were murdered. Traitors of course get killed, but in this case it was their families that killed them, rather than Saddam's regime. The point was not that Saddam was too afraid to kill them. Rather, it was that family honor had to be maintained, and so the action became the families' responsibility.

Fear of punishment can be an effective form of social control, one arguably necessary for adolescents in any society. But that threat, which imposes and teaches limits of acceptable behavior, is rapidly disappearing in

Saudi Arabia. For one of the main, but largely overlooked, reasons for the emotional and religious vacuum young Saudis face is the presence of so many foreign maids and drivers in the kingdom. Their numbers mushroomed during the oil-boom years, and their influence has led to a distancing of parents and children, since the servants were expected to act as surrogate parents. Most of the domestic servants are non-Muslims and non-Arabs, meaning the results have been doubly negative: They lack the authority—and presumably, since they themselves are treated by many employers as little more than errant children, also the inclination—to discipline those in their care, while being unable to pass down by example the core Islamic values and traditions that have always formed the bedrock of Saudi society.

If absence of authority is one side of the equation, the other is the feeling of entitlement among so many youths in Saudi Arabia. The growing legions of middle-class teenage Saudis—perhaps the majority—are now like my friend Mohammed, able to obtain anything by simply shouting at the top of their lungs. A few seconds later—whatever the time of day or night—a Filipino maid is knocking gently at the bedroom door. Coddled by servants, ignored by parents, aware of the limitations of their own education and abilities to succeed in the wider world that attracts and repels them, taught that they are deserving and should be served rather than that they need, and should, work to obtain goals, Saudi youth have no guides, which leads some to wantonness and others to the straight and narrow of fundamentalism.

What did Mohammed want from his life? The answer depended entirely on his mood, which had a tendency to swing rather sharply. In one mood, he wanted to join the ranks of Al-Qaeda, to act, to rebel, to lead a life with meaning and worthy of praise, even if the former was short and the latter provided over his grave. In another, he only wanted to get out of Saudi Arabia forever, travel to southern Spain and marry a Catholic girl, and forget about politics altogether. And in yet another, he despaired of the consequences of perhaps having to spend the rest of his life inside the kingdom, cursing the outside world for assuming that he was a potential terrorist just because he was a Saudi. Somewhat typical adolescent angst, one might say, the desire to escape and fear of the future combining in daydreams. Except for him, and others, those daydreams include the exploding two towers. One of the tragedies of September 11 is that the deadly proficiency of the terrorists on that day was, in a very real sense, a rare validation of Arab strategic planning, which is better known for the devastating defeat in the war against Israel in 1967 and, as such, an indictment of the Arab status quo. That Al-Qaeda explicitly framed its message and justification both in the grievances of the Muslim world and in the framework of Islam helps explain why it resonates.

Young Saudis are, to all intents and purposes, devout and believing. This is what Saudi society demands of them, at least superficially, from the moment they can walk and talk, and so they do not know how to behave in any other way. Dissent on the issue of religious belief is out of the question and punishable by public beheading. So appearances must be maintained. The result is that they dwell psychologically in a series of logic-tight compartments that touch each other but never overlap, and that often relate only to the snapshots of the various competing cultures they are exposed to through the media and the mosques. To an outsider, the ability to hold manifestly inconsistent views—to cover the picture of a woman but ogle real women sunbathing; to not listen to music but to seek to make lesbians "hot"—may seem like outright hypocrisy. But Saudis' thinking patterns revolve around a series of rituals, obsessions, and categories that are self-contained. On the one hand, devoutly religious and strictly so; on the other, prone to folk beliefs akin to magic and superstition, including which foot to step first into the bathroom with, or urinating on the wheel of a new car to ward off the evil eye. Their behavior does not reach the self-conscious level of hypocrisy, of believing one thing and doing another, for it is a set of dissonant beliefs that they do not even recognize coexist at the same time.

In *Seven Pillars of Wisdom* (1926), T. E. Lawrence wrote of the Arabs he encountered:

> At the very outset, at the first meeting with them, was found a universal clearness or hardness of belief, almost mathematical in its limitation, and repellent in its unsympathetic form. Semites had no half-tones in their register of vision. They were a people of primary colors, or rather of black and white, who saw the world always in contour. They were a dogmatic people, despising doubt, our modern crown of thorns. They did not understand our metaphysical difficulties, our introspective questionings. They knew only truth and untruth, belief and unbelief, without our hesitating retinue of finer shades. This people was black and white, not only in vision, but by inmost furnishing: black and white not merely in clarity, but in apposition. Their thoughts were at ease only in extremes. They inhabited superlatives by choice.

This is, of course, a simplification and a generalization, as critics of Lawrence and other "Orientalist" writers argue. But it likely contained an important truth then, and it certainly does now. For the absence of doubt and "introspective questionings," what exists are certainties that compete with each other—which one is acted on, or held at a given moment, being a reflection of moods like those of my friend Mohammed. And there is little reason for these beliefs to be shaken, as the signals sent and received simply reinforce set beliefs.

The Al-Jazeera documentary was thus typical, unsurprisingly so since it was produced and presented exclusively by Arabs. It argued that the September 11 hijackers visited prostitutes to provide a cover for the terrorist operation. In short, even engaging in sex was portrayed as a sacrifice, a burden rather than a pleasure. The possibility that these "martyrs" had visited the prostitutes because they wanted to have sex with them, period, would have been harder for the audience to understand or accept. After all, these were devout young men, pure of heart and purpose as evidenced in the hardness of heart that led them to kill almost 3,000 innocent men and women and legitimize it because the latter represented the "decadent," exploitative West that, with its satellite TV and pro-Israel foreign policy, was threatening to undermine the very foundations of Islamic society. For them to have willingly partaken in the decadence they condemned would have been inconsistence itself, and also because then they would in effect have been no different than the Saudi princes doing the same—Saudi princes who had been their indirect target that day. But then again, there is one other way out of this impasse: Young Saudis are given to saying that screwing Western women is not religiously forbidden in Islam, because, since they are "infidels," they do not come into the moral scheme of things.

In the past, when wealthy young Saudi teenagers went abroad, it was implicitly accepted that many of them would—like upper-class Protestant Englishmen opting for the Grand Tour in "decadent" Catholic Europe in the eighteenth century—let their hair down and generally get up to no good, but then quietly return (with no questions asked) to the family bosom and the rigid Puritanism of old (in this case Wahhabism) they had only briefly decided to leave behind. The problem facing such young Saudis these days are twofold. Traveling in the "decadent" West since September 11 has ceased to be an easy option because of new visa restrictions and the Osama bin Laden/Saudi hijackers connection. And they are increasingly not being handed down core Islamic values to begin with during their formative years by their appointed role models.

In theory, those who got to travel did, like their eighteenth-century English counterparts, have the opportunity to expand their intellectual horizons, as well as sow their seed. But all the evidence suggests, alas, that most opted only for the latter at the complete expense of the former. One young Saudi I knew in such a situation was typical of many others I encountered, in the sense that for all he gained from the experience of travel he may as well have stayed at home. He was from the holy city of Medina, and had spent more than five years in the United States. Like so many of the famously hospitable inhabitants of Medina I met, he was an extremely likeable and kind individual. But, despite his prolonged presence in American culture, during a general conversation to do with his time there he did not even have a clue what I was talking about when I mentioned the magazine *Cosmopolitan,* and had no opinion to speak of when I asked him about leading American politicians and the issues they represented. His English, meanwhile, was painfully flawed. Like so many young Saudis who go abroad, often for education, he had shown little inclination to learn much, either from his studies or from the culture surrounding him. Rather, the time in the West is purely functional: Get a degree, exploit the sexual opportunities, stock up on consumer goods. Why learn, why develop skills, why open oneself to differing perspectives, why question when one is going to return to the perfect society blessed with oil wealth and a paternalistic state? The exceptions, predictably, are the sons of the more enlightened members of the royal family, and the big merchant families of Riyadh and Jeddah. The latter, though, are no more "Saudi" in their lifestyles and beliefs to begin with than is the average Jordanian. Their grandfathers had already become men of the world, part of the global network of trade and commerce, by the turn of the twentieth century, and their own upbringing has more often than not been couched in subtle anti-Wahhabi rhetoric. For such people, interacting with the world is considered normal and beneficial, in addition to being necessary.

Because of the complete lack of any kind of youth culture, young Saudis who do not have the means or desire to travel abroad remain, by and large, locked away with their frustration in their bedrooms, watching satellite TV, surfing the web, and contemplating an increasingly difficult life in a kingdom full of unemployment, poverty, repression, and nepotism. That, of course, is great news for radical Islamists, ever-eager to recruit to their ranks young men who have few critical faculties and a crudely simplistic world outlook. With so many youngsters wandering aimlessly into adulthood with increasingly few prospects of a decent job, ruled by a corrupt elite closely aligned to an America the young are told to hate and hold responsible for Israel's ruthless suppression of the Palestinians, the call of the Islamists is not falling on deaf ears. Young Saudis' essentially shallow understanding of Islam, taught by hard-line Wahhabi teachers and clerics, sits in their minds like a highly combustible tinder box, just waiting for a loose spark to set it alight. And the collapse of the paternalistic state could well provide it. At such a time, Islam will provide young Saudis with a deep and profound sense of security and unity, a stable set of beliefs from which to judge an ever-changing home country and hostile outside world, and a meaningful link back to the time of parents and grandparents.

Shocking evidence for just how combustible that tinder box is came in early 2002, when the first Al-Qaeda-related arrests in Mecca were announced. Those apprehended were—according to the Ministry of Interior—mostly schoolboys. It became still more apparent after members of the main Al-Qaeda–affiliated gangs had been arrested or killed in the wake of the 2003 bombings that those who were taking their place were increasingly in their teens or early twenties. All that is proof of nothing more, perhaps, than that there is only one thing worse in Saudi Arabia than leaving schoolboys to the exclusive care of non-Muslim domestic servants, and that is having those servants send their charges off to schools and mosques run by radical Wahhabi teachers and clerics, who teach them not about Islam as it would be recognized by the vast majority of the world's Muslims, but rather Islam as defined as an extension of the Saudi state ideology, Wahhabism, which is based on fundamental hatred not only of Jews and Christians, but even of non-Wahhabi Muslims.

These anti-Semitic and jihadist foundations have, since September 11, thankfully become known to the whole world. What is painfully and continuously made obvious from living among them is that Saudis are seeped in a culture of profound anti-Semitism. That is not to be confused, as apologists might indicate, with anti-Israeli criticism, although the two inevitably feed off one another. This was made clear in September 2004, when the government was supposed to be leading a crackdown on extremists, after thousands of clerics had reportedly been sent for retraining, and after all the senior princes in government had given repeated lectures to the young about how they should follow moderate Islamic teachings, the official Saudi IQRA TV channel aired a program in which young Saudi men and women were asked a number of questions about "the Jews."

"Would you, as a human being, be willing to shake hands with a Jew, and why?"

"Of course I wouldn't be willing to shake hands with a Jew, for religious reasons and because of what is happening now in Palestine, and for many reasons that don't allow me to shake a Jew's hand," was the first answer, given by a clean-shaven young man in his early twenties wearing Western clothes.

"No. Because the Jews are eternal enemies. The murderous Jews violate all agreements. I can't shake hands with someone who I know is full of hatred towards me," came the second, from another young man also in Western attire.

Others were asked what they would tell a child if they were asked by him: "Who are the Jews?"

"The enemies of Allah and His Prophet. The murderers of prophets."

"Our eternal enemies, of course. Allah's wrath is upon them, as the Qu'ran says."

"Allah's wrath is upon them and they all stray from the path of righteousness. They are the filthiest people on the face of this earth because they care only about themselves—not the Christians, not the Muslims, nor any other religion."

And on and on and on it went, with not a single dissenting voice of reason. The level of intolerance, indeed hatred, toward non-Muslims in the Saudi education system, directed especially but not exclusively against Jews, was made apparent to me one evening in Jeddah when Fahd, one of my students in his late teens (I taught English part-time at a local college in the mornings), in a gesture of hospitality invited me to his house. As we settled into the inevitable routine of watching satellite TV and talking about politics in his bedroom, we were disturbed by a great commotion on the landing outside, banging on the door, and the screams of excited kids.

"Do you have brothers and sisters?" I asked.

"Yes, two brothers and a sister," he said.

"What do they want?"

"They heard from the maid that I have a Western guest, and they want to come in and say hello. Maybe practice their English."

"Then let them in."

"No way."

"Why not? Don't worry, I love kids, they're not going to bother me."

"If I let them in," he said, "they will tell their friends at school tomorrow that they met a Westerner, and if the teacher hears this they will be in big trouble. He will tell them never to speak to infidels, and use them as a bad example for the other children. And then the other children will make fun of them."

"And what do you think of that?"

"Of course, I think it's stupid. But what can I do?"

"You can invite them in and try to make them understand that their teacher is an idiot! You have a duty to challenge such terrible attitudes."

"I cannot go against what their teachers say and what they say in the mosques and what their friends say! It will make their lives very bad. It will make them different from everyone else."

He got up, opened the door a fraction, and shouted at them. They ran away.

Maybe Fahd simply did not want to impose on his guest. Or perhaps he was embarrassed, as so many older brothers are, of his younger siblings. But his explanation cum excuse was mind-boggling—and he was not even aware of how so. That it was an indictment of the Saudi schools almost goes without saying. One only mentions in passing the indictment of a society in which meeting a Westerner is cause for teasing from other children. And all this in supposedly liberal Jeddah. It was difficult not to be insulted, for was not the implication that I, and others like me, are dirty, dangerous, contagious, unsafe? But it was impossible, at the same time, not to be sad at his profound need to fit in, conform, and shield himself from different perspectives.

In Riyadh, I had translated the word "contradiction" for Mohammed, after challenging him to reconcile his apparently inconsistent views of the September 11 hijackers and the purity of their example, on the one hand, and of his puerile and prurient interest in lesbians, on the other. When at last he grasped the point in Arabic, it elicited from him a mere shrug of the shoulders: He could not see the point of discussing the issue. For him, there was no contradiction.

On another occasion, I lost my temper during one of his outbursts on the need to "kill all the infidels," asking how he could claim to be a friend of mine—even buying me a Christmas present—and yet engage in such vile talk. Was I not in fact among those infidels who should all be killed? He backed down and qualified his statement with the absurd concession that I was "different." This expressed desire to kill all the infidels may have been exaggeration, or I somehow was an exception, perhaps as a useful guest or even as a protected subordinate, the traditional and historical place of Christian and Jewish *dhimmi* within the Muslim world. I even thought that maybe he was beginning to recognize, the first step toward reconsidering, his bigotry—after all, it is easier to hate "that kind" (put in your favorite groups subject to discrimination: blacks, gays, Jews, etc.) in the abstract, and more difficult when one gets to know some of them. But, a few days later, he told me, again quite casually, that he had explained our tempestuous friendship to his friends, who had apparently criticized him for hanging out with an "infidel," by saying: "By talking to him I get to know our enemy better."

It was nice to know who I was, at least in Mohammed's eyes, and those of his friends who were even more closed minded. But who is Mohammed, who are they, the youth of Saudi Arabia? The difficulty of those questions became clear a few weeks before I left the kingdom. A young Jeddah resident I knew recalled an encounter he had with a policeman at a checkpoint, where he had been pulled over as part of routine inspection.

"Are you a Saudi?" he was asked.

"No," he replied.

The cop then demanded his identification card, which in fact revealed him to be a Saudi. The cop was puzzled and asked my friend why he answered "no" when he obviously is a Saudi.

My friend recalled that he had responded rather rashly, by saying: "Am I a member of the Al-Saud family? No. Then I am not a Saudi!"

To be a Saudi literally means to be a follower of the Al-Saud ruling family, and the conflation of the subjects, for they are not citizens with rights, with the ruling family speaks the truth often elided: "Kingdom of Saudi Arabia" means that it is the Al-Saud who own it, and its residents are their vassals. So, my friend's refusal to identify with the ruling family had a certain logic, albeit a risky one.

"You can go to jail for saying things like that," he said the policeman had replied, smirking as he handed the card back and waiving him on his way.

My friend drove off, thrilled with the excitement of bucking authority and thus presumably rather less stunned than was I, upon hearing the story, at the cop's inactivity. For my friend had obviously engaged, consciously or not, in a profoundly subversive act. The cop had, too, by refusing to impose his authority and punish the culprit. The breakdown in legitimacy and authority in this complicity was complete.

So, if that young Jeddah resident is not a Saudi, what is he?

That the question so rarely gets asked, and that the answer is so unclear, is an indictment of the failure of the system the Al-Saud have created and ruled for the past 70 years. Generally unprepared to take the initiative, often actively dissuaded from doing so, the lot of many Saudi youth is to suffer the immense boredom that hangs over Saudi Arabia like a great toxic cloud, stagnation that contrasts in their mind with the general excitement and stimulation of life in the West, whatever hostility as Saudis and Muslims they may have encountered there, and however hostile to it they have been taught to be at home. And having been taught at school only to listen, respect authority figures, learn by rote, and then forget everything they were told as soon as the final examinations were over, they are mentally ill-equipped to internalize and rationalize new experiences. Given no values except those of a rigid Wahhabism clearly out of step with the twenty-first century, their morality is simply self-serving, a total negation of the communal values, including respect for elders, that they are taught to venerate, and a massive burden in a world of ever-more rapid integration and globalization. Do the young even know this, while realizing, too, that if anything is to change for the better it will be only because they themselves have changed?

The great unanswered question is: Who will the young, who make up 60 percent of the population, side with? The Al-Saud as it tries slowly to reform, the radicals intent on overthrowing the Al-Saud, or the limited number of liberals seeking to reform the kingdom more quickly than the royals will allow, to create the political and social space the young need to express themselves and develop their ideas? For too many youth the answer is not clear. Even more frightening, it is clear that too many are likely to choose the side of the radicals.

For its part, the Al-Saud can no longer perform its historic role of providing cradle-to-grave support to its subjects, and third-generation princes are beginning to wake up to the consequences of their elders having bought, rather than earned, the loyalty of the people. Their subjects no longer enjoy the benefits—excellent health care, free education, rapidly developing infrastructure, guaranteed employment—they did in the oil-boom years, meaning the continued indulgence of the senior Al-Saud princes is distancing the two groups as never before. The younger members of the ruling family in government who are not corrupt, and who are eager to introduce some kind of system of checks and balances, are for the most part still bankrupt ideologically, insisting while they call for change that absolutely *everything* must *always* revolve around themselves and their arbitrary decisions, even when it comes to issues where they have absolutely no expertise. The liberals, in their turn, are tarred by their association with the West, with its often crude anti-Saudi propaganda in the U.S. media especially that damns all Saudis as extremists, blindly equates Islam with terror, labels the kingdom the "kernel of evil," and endorses plans for an imperial-like U.S. invasion to take control of the oil fields and divide its regions along historic lines. In such a political environment, the Al-Saud appear, in their continued reliance on the West, to be colonial puppets, caught between a rock and a hard place and exposed for the double game they have played with both their people and the United States for decades. Backed into a corner and under attack is hardly when people of any religion or culture are likely to open up, and Saudi Arabia appears to be entering a renewed period of fundamentalism.

PART TWO

Chapter Six

EXPATRIATE LIFE (AND DEATH)

Concrete barriers, striped an alarming red and white in the otherwise desert-yellow monotone of the street, block the straight approach from the main road. A roundabout drive leads to more concrete barriers, which ring high concrete walls topped by barbed wire. An armored truck with mounted machineguns guards the only breach in the fortification, and a man in the uniform of the National Guard demands that the car be parked outside and credentials shown. At the gate, a security guard asks to see more papers. After inspecting them closely, he waves toward the reinforced steel gates, a narrow, short opening that has to be ducked through.

This was not a nuclear weapons research installation or a military headquarters in a country at war. It was a residential compound for Western expatriates, in November 2003, in the once laid-back city of Jeddah. The residents were mostly British and American citizens, who worked as dentists, engineers, teachers, and IT specialists. They came to earn generous salaries, with free housing and a months' annual leave, and to enjoy the guaranteed sunshine.

The compounds were always meant to keep the reality of Saudi Arabia out—as much to shield Westerners from the alien customs of a strictly segregated tribal society as to guard that society and its hard-line interpretation of Islam from the perceived threat of Western "decadence."

Earlier in 2003, if you had driven your car into the same compound, the bored guard at the gate would not have given you as much as a second glance. At that time, the compounds really were all-year-round holiday resorts. The families of working expatriates sunned themselves by the pool in skimpy swimwear. Alcohol flowed during the frequent parties. But, by the end of the year, not a sound could be heard over the compound walls. The residents did their shopping in the city early in the morning, when there were fewer people in the supermarkets. They slunk in and out of their heavily guarded walls, like thieves in the night.

Why Western expatriates progressed from largely self-imposed segregation to frightened, paranoid isolation is very easy to explain: there had been terrorist attacks targeting them in their compounds.

In the past, the obvious foreignness of these Westerners was hardly a great burden. It even proved on occasion to be an advantage—marking them, for instance, for swift processing at airports, and opening jobs for them that were closed to both Saudis and other foreigners (and would in fact have mostly been closed to the Westerners themselves at home). Then, when the rhetoric of Osama bin Laden and his spiritual brethren, highlighting how the foreigners undermine and are a threat to the purity of Islam in the religion's heartland, was given renewed impetus by the Al-Saud-assisted, U.S.-led invasion of Iraq to topple Saddam Hussein, every Western man walking in public who wore anything other than traditional Saudi garb was only drawing attention to himself. A suit and tie marked one out as a target.

The threat of terrorism, however, only intensified what has been a bizarre reality since the foundation of Saudi Arabia: that one of the most closed and xenophobic societies in the world relies for its economic survival on the presence of some nine million foreigners. In other words, a society that at least on the surface looks uniquely homogeneous manages to wall itself off from, or wall in, an extraordinarily multicultural minority—from both the West and from various Third World countries, especially South Asia—making up as much as a third of all the people who live there.

For many ordinary Saudis, the compound walls are a necessary barrier to keep foreigners at bay because polluting influences could threaten the very fabric of the Wahhabi kingdom. But with the emergence, since the September 11 attacks, of stronger home-grown militant Islamist factions inside Saudi Arabia, in some ways linked to Al-Qaeda, the extremists are already one step nearer their goal of total segregation of everyone—men from women, foreigners from Saudis, Muslims from infidels, neighbors from neighbors.

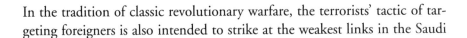

In the tradition of classic revolutionary warfare, the terrorists' tactic of targeting foreigners is also intended to strike at the weakest links in the Saudi economy: its heavy reliance on Westerners to keep the oil pumping and the infrastructure operating, given the near-total failure of the Saudi regime to train and educate its subjects—combined, it has to be admitted, with the general laziness and arrogance of those subjects brought about by an over-generous welfare state and the religious-nationalistic propaganda of the Saudi rulers.

That is not to say that the Western expatriates had not willingly colluded in the segregation effort. When the Saudis asked American oil firms to help tap their newly discovered oil in the 1940s, the oil firms agreed only on condition that compounds be erected to allow their employees a semblance of a Western lifestyle in the middle of an alien culture. The reasons were entirely pragmatic: Western experts would have to be paid massive salaries just for agreeing to work somewhere as remote and climatically hostile, from their point of view, as Saudi Arabia. If they were on top of that expected to comply with local Islamic customs, which even other Muslims in the world considered extreme and bizarre, the compensation they would demand would become unaffordable.

Of course, the Al-Saud was not unhappy with the arrangement, helping as it did to preserve in its Wahhabi partners' eyes the all-important "purity" of the young kingdom.

Western compounds were designed to provide maximum comfort for the expatriate far from home—a little bit of England or New England for the wife and children, complete with school and swimming pool. The Western rules that govern life inside the compounds mean that the inconvenience of strict Islamic regulations, which set the slow, strict pace of life outside them, can be sidestepped. Shops do not close for 30 minutes for prayers five times a day, as they do in real Saudi cities. Women do not have to wear the all-enveloping abeyya. In the evenings, mothers and fathers can relax by the pool, keeping an eye on the children.

The only way in or out is through the heavily manned security gate. If you do not live there, or have a friend who does, you can no longer get in—unless you are armed, that is, and desperate to kill an infidel.

All the pleasures and viciousness found in small communities were repeated in the hothouse atmosphere of the high-walled compounds: illicit relationships causing tension between families, barking dogs, noisy neighbors, and all the false jollity of a holiday camp under pressure of a foreign culture.

I always lived in the local community, mainly in working-class neighborhoods. My apartment buildings had running water most of the time, it is true, but raw sewage often bubbled out of the manholes outside. When I lived in Jeddah's old town, my neighbors in the same building were Saudi and Pakistani families, and both welcomed me graciously when I first moved in, and shyly made conversation when we bumped into one another in the elevator or at the door. Those who lived in the nearby streets looked at me with some curiosity when I walked past on my way to work, but I did not get the impression that they resented my being there.

Across the road lived Somalis and Yemenis, some legally, some not, and while they would occasionally shout their hellos, they generally left me to my own devices—less because they resented my presence, I assumed, than because they would have thought it intrusive to approach me. I bought most of my provisions in the local market where, despite the fact that I was the only Western face around, I attracted little comment. And I felt safe walking around. While garbage would occasionally pile up in the streets, and most of the cars in the neighborhood had a broken-down, much-repaired aspect to them, I felt as if I were participating in such life as the essentially Third World city of Jeddah had to offer, rather than retreating from it whenever I went home. What I am trying to say is that the extremists were obviously a minority.

Until the 1970s, Saudis and Westerners up to a point did mix. Many Saudis—especially in the Hijaz, Asir, and the Eastern Province—were willing to entertain foreigners, within certain contexts, because as Arabs they had a long tradition of hospitality that transcended the narrow Wahhabi reform movement they themselves were having to endure as a new reality. In their turn, some of the Westerners learned Arabic and attempted to learn about the kingdom's history and culture. While it stopped far short of a genuine cultural exchange, and was limited to an elite on both sides, it nonetheless was a healthier form of coexistence—akin, perhaps, to the way Westerners are accommodated these days in Southeast Asian societies.

Then the first batch of highly skilled and well-educated Westerners—who, along with the Saudis, helped build the kingdom's infrastructure—mostly left, their job done. In their place came the general flood, many to earn a quick buck, and among them those who just help keep the cogs oiled and turning, those in need of a second chance far away from home, teachers of English as a foreign language, and others who were simply adventurers and eccentrics only at home in an extreme social environment.

These newcomers often displayed an infuriating air of superiority, perhaps because of insecurities of their own. Compound life became more entrenched. Segregation deepened. The new batch of Westerners often had neither the desire nor the inclination to find out about the kingdom or abandon the prejudices of their—more often than not—lower-middle-class backgrounds. In the compounds, their simple needs were satisfied, and a group mentality took hold. Expats started to do everything together.

After the Al-Qaeda bombings, some Saudi commentators woke up to the fact that the compounds, and the people who live on them, had always represented a problem for the Saudis surrounding them.

"The expats who live in those compounds live an artificial life," Dr. Mohammed T. Al-Rasheed, an outspoken Jeddah-based columnist, has written. "They meet only vetted and semi-Westernised locals, they ooze a sense of condescension that rubs the nerves of the local population, and they seem to tell everyone that they are better, smarter and make more money."

At the same time, they appeared to contribute to a Westernization—a whiting—of Saudi society, which many of the wealthy who have spent time in the West readily embrace but that ordinary Saudis, with declining incomes and consequently less access to its pleasures, increasingly resent seeing in their midst.

There were, though, also Saudis—and not a few of them—who themselves moved into compounds, happy to abide by rules that banned local dress on the premises, and often convinced that they were moving in a more sophisticated atmosphere as a result. They, too, looked down on their more traditional cousins outside the walls, and predictably they were resented by them in turn.

All this is vaguely akin to what developed in the British Raj, where the early British (despite essentially being crude colonizers) melded with the locals, absorbing their cultures, learning their languages and generally welcoming—almost incidentally—the richness of the experience. Many "went native," married locals, and became to a significant extent Indian. But in their wake, a new set of Britishers arrived, fanatical in their sense of superiority and puritanical in their Western beliefs—and with them came white women shipped out to snare white men, and with them a deepening of an ideology that saw the natives as inferior and beyond the pale as marriage partners. The consequence was entrenched divisions. Finally, there was total resentment at the arrogance of the British.

During my first visit to a compound with mostly Britons and Americans, I had a taste of what it was like to live behind walls.

We sat on the terrace looking out toward the swimming pool in the failing light as a Filipino watered the landscaped garden. We sat outside because their unit itself, with its overstuffed furniture, wall-to-wall carpeting, and tiny windows, felt uncomfortably close despite the fact that it cost a good five times as much as what I was paying for my spacious rooms downtown.

In the course of our conversation, it became clear that these Westerners, highly educated though they in principle were, had brought with them a mentality that fitted in perfectly with their physical situation. They were university graduates—some doctors and engineers, others English teachers, who in the kingdom are often required to hold at least a Master's degree. But their conversation was essentially gossip about other members of their tiny closed community.

Among them was a middle-aged Englishwoman who held a fairly senior position at a local hospital and, it soon became clear, spent much of her free time looking for erotic adventure within the narrow circle assembled on that terrace. We could have been in any lower-middle-class neighborhood in Britain or the United States, although the slightly superannuated appearance and leathery tans suggested more specifically a timeshare community in the Canary Islands.

What struck me most was that all these compound inmates had to say about the kingdom, from their first word to their last, was that Saudi Arabia was awful; that Saudis were awful; that they missed "real beer" (as opposed to the home-brew they made in their cellars and that we were to varying degrees "enjoying" that evening), and that they missed all those other representations of their truly magnificent Western culture.

They did not miss, it seemed, access to the West's rich literary culture, its arts and music—which censors and zealous customs officials in the kingdom do manage to keep away from them much more successfully than they do alcohol (the Internet and occasionally successful deliveries from amazon.com notwithstanding). Instead, they missed nights down at the bar with their friends; they missed vomiting in the gutter come closing time; they missed brawls in the street. It is difficult to see what many of them could have to offer a Saudi host foolish enough to have invited them to their house.

There was among them, that is to say, little recognition that living in the kingdom could present them with the opportunity to reassess their narrow values, to seek out new experiences, to challenge their preconceptions about Arabs and Islam. To the extent that they were willing or forced to engage with the locals, they were instead keen to bring some of the blessings of their home countries to Saudi Arabia.

"I think of myself as a father to my students," one South African English teacher told me earnestly, before proceeding to describe ways in which he attempted to broaden his students' minds.

He was genuinely unaware that a cultural exchange must work both ways if it is to go beyond the proselytizing of a secular missionary. He liked to ask, he told me, uncomfortable questions to challenge his students' certainties—and, to be sure, many of the certainties of Saudi students are well worth challenging, among them the notion that all Westerners' minds turn obsessively on thoughts of alcohol and sex. But these were hardly the people to challenge that particular misconception.

There were honorable exceptions, undeniably. Keith Birmingham, though coming from the same lower-middle-class background in provincial England as many of those who shared his compound, was one of them. An engineer by training, he learned passable Arabic and conceived such a passion for carpets that Jeddah's chaotic Afghan souk, where Afghans and others sell the carpets of their homeland, that it became almost his second home, so much time did he spend there with his wife Tina and son Brandon learning everything there was to learn about all manner of woven fabrics. So knowledgeable did he become, indeed, that when after more than a decade and a half he returned to Britain he did not stay in engineering but instead opened a business importing Afghan carpets. Moreover, he was genuinely sad to leave the kingdom and the friends he had made there, if not among the Saudis then at least among other Arabs and Afghans.

Alas, Al-Qaeda's kidnapping and beheading in June 2004 of American Paul Johnson was tragic in a way quite apart from the barbaric murder itself: Johnson, unlike a surprisingly large number of other U.S. defense contractors, had chosen not to live in a compound but instead rented a villa in a middle-class district in Riyadh. The attack on him, as well as on his fellow countryman Robert Jordan the same day, who lived in another villa and was reportedly like Keith keenly interested in Islam and Arab culture, reinforced the sense that guarded and fortified compounds were the only places where Westerners could now hope to find a modicum of safety.

In the 1970s, Saudis acquired the infrastructure, and believed they had learned the skills needed, to run things successfully on their own—erroneous though that belief may be beyond the (again walled) confines of Saudi Aramco, an island of Saudi professionalism in the Eastern Province in a desert of otherwise staggering incompetence and inefficiency.

Above all, in the wake of the oil boom Saudis had money, and it is perhaps a commonplace that nothing makes a person more narrow-minded and defensive than the sudden acquisition of wealth from nothing. As a consequence Saudis, too, drew back—the oil boom appeared to validate them in their Saudi-ness. They believed that they deserved their windfall, that the treasure the kingdom sits on is in some ways a gift from God, a reward for having spread the message of Islam from a land that had hitherto seemed barren in every aspect. The sudden oil wealth entrenched a sense of self-righteousness and arrogance among many Saudis, appeared to vindicate them in their separateness from other cultures and religions. In the process, it reconfirmed the belief that the greater the Western presence, the greater the potential threat to everything they held dear.

At the same time, the Wahhabi elements of the state increased their iron grip on the kingdom after the death of the cautiously liberal King Faisal. Afterward, the rulers sought both to appease the hard-liners and consolidate their own hold on a mushrooming population by becoming more extreme themselves, giving, for instance, freer rein to the prowling religious police, who cracked down, often violently, on any mingling of the sexes in restaurants and other public places. This in turn gave expatriates another reason to retreat into their compounds.

The divisions deepened, until it was almost a self-fulfilling prophecy when, after all the embassy warnings and nervous dinner-table speculations, what every Westerner in Saudi Arabia knew in his heart was sure to happen sooner or later finally did.

In May 2003, Al-Qaeda attacked three residential compounds in Riyadh by driving trucks loaded with explosives through the gates and detonating them in their most densely populated parts. Some 26 people died, some of them Westerners, but many Saudis and Arabs who also lived there. For the small number of radical Saudis who had always reviled the presence of Westerners, who had never accepted the compromise of close cooperation with the West that even the Wahhabi religious establishment had been forced to swallow as reality, there could not have been a better target, or one that appeared more just. The fact that foreign Arabs, who had been housed there by the companies that employed them, made up a significant minority of the residents would not, of course, have bothered the extremists. Even if they were Muslims, by choosing to live among the "infidels" they had, in the view of the extremists, dug their own grave.

Moreover, residents in one of the compounds worked for Vinnell Corp., as did some of Al-Qaeda's later victims. Vinnell is a U.S. defense contractor developing weapons systems for the Saudi government and involved in training its security forces. It therefore represented everything that is loathsome to Osama bin Laden—and not a few others—about the deep historical entanglement between the Al-Saud and the United States.

There was an even more worrying dimension to the May 2003 bomb-ings: they depended on a significant level of insider knowledge of the three compounds hit, almost certainly provided by those "defending" them.

The suicide bombers detonated their vehicle inside Vinnell's strongly walled compound right outside the main housing block, which it took them less than a minute to get to from the gate. They had to know where the switches were to operate the gates, after attacking the guards; and they had to know exactly where the main housing block was located, as they drove at breakneck speed with a bomb weighing nearly 200 kilograms to the most densely inhabited part of the complex.

When another attack on a compound, again in Riyadh, occurred in No-vember of the same year, the implications of that attack were equally dis-turbing. Those targeted were apparently for the most part Muslims. But the official Saudi account of what happened stretched credulity beyond the breaking point, even by the fictitious (and often preposterous) precedents set by the official Saudi Press Agency. According to the official line, suicide bombers drove into the compound and blew themselves up, targeting a compound of minor importance housing mostly Arabs because all the West-ern compounds were too well guarded. But too many details of what actu-ally happened did not add up to that reality.

For example, it had become the norm after such incidents for Interior Minister Prince Naif to visit the families of victims among the security forces at their homes. He righteously declared that those who died "de-fending the kingdom and the faith" are officially recognized as martyrs, and handed out cash to their near and dear. Saudi television typically carried the spectacle live.

However, not only were there apparently no visits that time, there was not even an initial announcement that members of the security forces had died in the attack, despite reported gun battles, both before and after the ex-plosion or series of explosions, between the Saudi and private security forces defending the compound and those terrorists determined to destroy it. Of course, no deaths means no visits. But why no reported death or injuries among the security forces, given the exchange of gunfire reported?

Saudi opposition figures, who are often right about these things because they have excellent sources among disgruntled members of the security forces and the government, presented their own, more credible, version of what happened. They said that the attackers did not blow themselves up but instead they detonated the car bomb by remote control, after retreating to a safe distance. All of them, according to the same sources, got away. That would explain why the Interior Ministry identified none of the "suicide bombers," although in September 2004 an Al-Qaeda website claimed that the one suicide bomber who (in their version of events) did die had been a member of the National Guard, meaning that the infiltration of security forces by Al-Qaeda had reached the point of them being able to secure close cooperation in actually carrying out the attacks. And while it was reported that the "suicide bombers" were driving a regular police car, in fact it was a car belonging to the Saudi special security forces.

All this, it should be clear, was both surreal and frightening to Westerners, who were increasingly going to sleep at night wondering whether a few hours later they might be woken up by shattered glass and a collapsing roof. It was these special security forces, after all, who were supposedly not only protecting them, but also actively engaged in hunting down Al-Qaeda cells. That they were doing so with little initial success, or seriousness, might be explained by incompetence, a theory that has some credibility. But more disturbing was the possibility that even if the top officials were serious, the implementation was not—because the campaign against Al-Qaeda was being conducted against the will of the rank and file, many of whom sympathized with Al-Qaeda's goals.

The government admitted that the attackers were all dressed as policemen, which is bad enough, but not overly surprising given the incompetence of the Saudi police. No one, though, has yet given a credible explanation how they managed to get hold of a security forces vehicle. It is certainly not the kind of car that can be stolen from outside a sleeping policeman's home in Riyadh in the early hours of the morning.

So, it dawned on Western expatriates, there were attackers dressed as policemen, driving a special security forces car, taking care not to kill any of those defending the compound, and apparently not themselves being fired upon with any degree of accuracy. There could not be greater evidence, if even only half of that proved true, that Al-Qaeda had infiltrated Saudi Arabia's military and security forces, including those entrusted with the protection of residential compounds.

Moreover, the foreigners who lived in the mainly Arab residential compound devastated by the November bombing say they were visited three months earlier by the Saudi religious police, who put them on notice that their Westernized lifestyle was under scrutiny—a rare intrusion into the refuge from Saudi morality that the compounds are supposed to provide. When the religious police conduct their raids, they are always accompanied by regular police officers, who in turn cooperate closely with

Saudi special security forces. The religious police have been under intense pressure since the May attacks, as liberal Saudi writers accused them of promoting the kind of extremist environment that encourages Islamist terrorism. It is an open secret that many of them, if not the vast majority, support Osama bin Laden.

So, rather than the residential compound having been selected by mistake, as Saudi officials in Washington insisted after officials in Riyadh played up the idea that "Arabs and Muslims" were targeted, the cell that carried out the attack may have believed it to be a "legitimate" target. The reason is that their friends among the regular police could have told them, based on information passed on from the religious police, that it housed not only Muslims who had "deviated" from the true path, but also Arab Christians.

A year later, the ever publicity conscious attackers became more sophisticated in their choice of victims.

In the Eastern oil city of Khobar in May 2004, the killers went from house to house, first separating Muslim from non-Muslim, then coolly debating whose life they should spare and whose life they should take. They had started by attacking the offices of a petrochemical company early that morning, tying the body of one Western victim to their car and dragging him for several hundred meters along the highway before dumping him by the side of the road. Then, engaged by police, they apparently turned back and drove into the residential compound, where they took their hostages and occupied a building.

Witnesses recalled that when the four young Saudi gunmen encountered Muslims, they exhorted them to wear Islamic dress and moved on, asking where Westerners could be found. After the gunmen had completed their "tour of duty" in the early hours of the morning, 22 people, mostly foreigners, were dead, many with their throats slit. Then the security forces sent to kill them, who had been surrounding the compound all day and night, apparently let three of them escape through the tight cordon, to fight another day.

The Saturday before, Islamic radicals had attacked a petrochemical plant in Yanbu on the Red Sea coast, killing five Westerners. There were disturbing similarities in the Yanbu and Khobar attacks. In both, Saudi security forces took more than 90 minutes to engage each Al-Qaeda cell after the shooting began, by which time both had dragged the body of a Westerner through the streets from the back of cars. After the two attacks, there were unconfirmed reports of mass resignations from energy giant Saudi Aramco, where Americans make up the bulk of the remaining 10,000 Westerners whose expertise the kingdom relies on to run its most vital economic sector.

One of five Westerners shot in the Yanbu attack was a Muslim. Michael Hardy was a Briton in his sixties who had changed his name to Michael Muhammed after he converted to Islam. He had been about to return to the Indonesian island of Batam to start an idyllic retirement. Hardy was helping to upgrade the oilfields, which remain remarkably vulnerable to a major terrorist assault. More than 10,000 miles of pipeline crisscross Saudi Arabia, an oil web more than double the size of Iraq's, where since the U.S.-led occupation of that country insurgents have repeatedly sabotaged lines, despite the massive U.S. military presence.

Batam is a 45-minute ferry ride from Singapore, where I happened to be at the time of the Yanbu attack. I took a ferry over to the grim industrial island and met his grieving wife, Teti, and his closest British friend, Roger Smith. Hardy, who was an only son, died alongside three of his Western colleagues and a Saudi when the Muslim militants opened fire on oil contractor ABB Lummus Global Inc.'s main office. "He was doing a last stint in the Gulf so he had enough money to take retirement and enjoy a quiet life in Batam with his beloved wife," Smith said, fighting back tears.

"Michael had just finished building a house here, and he said that he intended to spend the rest of his life on the island with his wife and their eight-year-old adopted son, Nico Andrea."

Smith, who had been best man at Hardy's wedding in Batam in 2001, is also a Muslim convert.

"He was a very gentle man who kept himself to himself. He said in his e-mail that he stuck to a quiet daily routine in Yanbu. He went to the office, then went home and watched some TV before going to bed. He was just counting the days before he could be back with his wife."

Hardy had been scheduled to return to his island home that same weekend. He had met Teti, a 34-year-old Indonesian, in Batam after he moved to the island on a contract with a local engineering company. Hardy dressed in local costume for the couple's traditional Indonesian marriage ceremony, which was attended by the bride's family. The local Muslim community in Batam held nightly prayers for him at a mosque near his family home after news of his death broke, and people there were said to be outraged that Hardy was apparently killed because the fanatics thought he was an "infidel."

Hardy's wife was still too distraught to talk about the murder. "My mother is sleeping with me because I can't spend time on my own," she said.

"I've spoken to Michael's mother in England and all his friends have called me to offer their condolences. All my own family and everyone who knew Michael in Batam are devastated."

It was a glimpse into the intensely personal suffering of those left behind when people are randomly mowed down inside the kingdom, only to become statistics in headlines in the following days and then forgotten as some new atrocity elsewhere dominates instead the news agenda.

Not long after Hardy's death, U.S. and Saudi authorities in Riyadh were desperately trying to trace the kidnapped American Paul Johnson after Al-Qaeda threatened to execute him within 72 hours.

Johnson, like Hardy, was building a home for himself in Southeast Asia when he fell into the hands of the group. He had married a Thai woman on one of his frequent trips to Bangkok, and, as friends and family hoped against hope for news of his release, yellow ribbons were strung out along a major road in the Thai capital as well as in the New Jersey town he had left behind. Johnson, who was seconded—from Vinnell, again—to work on Apache helicopter security systems for the Saudi government, was first shown on an Al-Qaeda website blindfolded and sitting in a chair with a sleeve of his orange uniform ripped off, showing a tattoo. An accompanying statement said: "If the tyrants in the Saudi government want to secure the release of the American hostage, they must release our mujahideen held hostage in its jails. They have 72 hours from today or else we will sacrifice him."

The threat to "sacrifice" him had chilling echoes of the videotaped beheading of Nicholas Berg, an American businessman kidnapped in Iraq in April that year. Three days later, Johnson was dead, as gruesome online pictures of his severed head placed on the small of his back testified.

The ensuing hunt for his remains was one of the more undignified episodes of the kingdom's war on terror. It was not until weeks later that Johnson's head was recovered during a raid of a terrorist hideout in Riyadh—in the freezer, where his abductors had apparently kept it as a souvenir of a successful operation.

The killing of the other American, Robert Jordan, happened outside his Riyadh home on the day Jordan was abducted. Jordan was gunned down as he was parking his car outside his home, and a video of that event was also posted on an Al-Qaeda website. There on the soundtrack, for all to hear once an Islamic marching song had faded out, was a recording of Jordan's last words—"No, no, please, please"—as three men in Western clothes calmly advanced to finish him off with more bullets and then apparently sawed off his head with a long knife.

With fears of a mass exodus of Westerners growing, Prince Naif announced that expatriates in the kingdom would be allowed to carry guns.

"In principle, a citizen has the right to carry a licensed weapon, and so does the resident," he said. "If he senses danger, he can carry a personal weapon as he does in his country"—an odd misconception of what is allowed in Western countries.

One Arabic-language newspaper later published pictures of Westerners at target practice at a shooting range, though it never became clear what conditions would have to be fulfilled if the foreigners were in reality, rather than principle, to arm themselves. Like so many policy announcements in Saudi Arabia—from grand educational projects to road improvements— that one too seems to have fizzled quickly into nothing.

The hunt for Paul Johnson's corpse meanwhile became significant in another respect. Only hours after Johnson's killing, Saudi security forces gunned down a man believed to be the Al-Qaeda leader in Saudi Arabia, Abdul Aziz Al-Muqrin, in an ambush at a petrol station in the capital. He and several of his followers were caught, the Saudis claimed, in the attempt to dispose of Johnson's corpse. Yet the next day, Johnson's corpse, it transpired, had not in fact been found, and as of early 2005 it still had to be located, with the U.S. Embassy announcing the search for it had been abandoned.

Despite the Saudi government's attempts to link Al-Muqrin to the abduction, this was probably the one atrocity he was innocent of, though he had a long and bloody history, from fighting in Chechnya to apparently planning the attacks on the Riyadh compounds. The authorities had launched a massive manhunt for Johnson that, Saudi spokesmen repeated mournfully in Riyadh and Washington, had narrowly missed saving him, but at least brought rough justice to his abductors shortly after the deed. But despite the misty-eyed sincerity of the spokesmen's manner, this turned out to be but another example of rhetoric replacing reality. Instead, the indications are that Al-Muqrin was lured into a trap independent, and planned well ahead of, the Johnson case, and that it was another terrorist leader, Saleh Al-Oufi—later named Al-Muqrin's successor—who had carried out the abduction. For when the head was recovered a month later, it was in the freezer of a safe house used by Al-Oufi.

That is the context of suspicion and deliberate misinformation in which we must look at reports that three of the four members of the Al-Qaeda cell in Khobar were allowed to go free by the security forces, apparently wearing military uniforms given to them to facilitate their flight. The promise of a safe getaway for the gunmen had evidently been given to save further lives, according to widely quoted "Saudi experts" claiming inside knowledge. However, it would have been easy enough for the authorities to renege on the promise of a safe getaway and simply shoot the terrorists after they emerged from their hideout.

That they did not gives rise to all kinds of speculation among Westerners: Were the security forces afraid that to renege would leave them, and the Al-Saud ruling family, fearing for their lives in revenge attacks? Did they not see much wrong with slitting the throats of "infidels"?

They had certainly taken their time in coming to their aid.

The new fear and insecurity the Westerners were experiencing, however, was nothing compared to what lay in store for the millions of immigrant workers in Saudi Arabia who are not white, terrorist attacks or no terrorist attacks. The Westerners, after all, were for the most part in a position to pack their bags and leave, and their "plight" was given maximum exposure in the Western media, with the concomitant pressure on the Saudis to do what they could do ensure their safety. That most of those who died in the Khobar attack—non-Muslims though they may have been—were from the Indian subcontinent made few headlines. It also raised mainly shrugs among many of their compatriots from India and Sri Lanka, for whom such vicissitudes were nothing out of the ordinary. They are, after all, quite used to the petty harassment from the security forces and the ongoing insecurity that is part and parcel of exploitation. One South Indian, for instance, was caught in the crossfire between security forces and terrorists in Khobar, a man who was simply in the way. Among the hostages killed, many Indians and Sri Lankans had been too frightened to lie about their religion, or had hesitated for just a fraction of a second before the terrorists finished them off without a second thought. Little publicity was given to these deaths in the international media because the attackers had also killed two Westerners.

Prior to September 11, there were nearly 50,000 Americans, 35,000 Britons, as well as smaller numbers of French, Germans, Italians, and other Europeans in Saudi Arabia. These numbers have, however, dropped drastically since then. It is estimated that at present there are approximately 27,000 Americans, most of them in Saudi Aramco or other oil-related industries, and 25,000 Britons, most of them in British Aerospace and Aramco. But Saudi Arabia's labor minister announced in 2004 that there were between eight and nine million foreign workers in the country—a much higher figure than previous estimates. And of these, 1.6 million or more are Indians, followed by at least one million Pakistanis and Egyptians each, 800,000 Filipinos and 600,000 Bangladeshis. The rest include workers from other Asian countries, like Sri Lanka, Nepal, Afghanistan, and China, and the Middle East, like Lebanon, Palestine, Jordan, Syria, Iraq, and Turkey.

In the pecking order of immigrant workers, the Westerners clearly sit at the top, as their salaries and living conditions attest. Although Saudi Arabia was never itself colonized, perhaps it is a hangover from colonial days that, as many believe, Saudi businesses like to have a white man at least in nominal charge. Americans especially have always enjoyed a special status in the Saudi labor market. Despite their social and religious prejudices, Saudis tend to treat Americans preferentially. Their pay scale is different and many rules do not apply to them.

From the mid-1970s to the late 1990s, Americans were called first-class nationals (FCNs); Saudis, Britons, other Europeans and Arabs were called second-class nationals (SCNs); and Asians third-class nationals (TCNs). Of course, this was not an official segregation, but it was widely used and reflected the psyche of the Saudi manpower sector. Even non-Saudi Arabs are subtly graded from, say, Jordanians and Syrians down to Egyptians and Yemenis. But it is clear that Filipinos, Indonesians, Pakistanis, Sri Lankans, and Bangladeshis are at the very bottom of the scale. Out of nearly 5 million Asian workers, more than 75 percent are blue-collar workers like unskilled laborers, farm laborers, construction workers, plumbers, welders, electricians, carpenters, masons, drivers, maids, counter salesmen, butchers, vegetable vendors, and maintenance workers.

In the ostensibly Western-style cafes in north Jeddah's upmarket Al-Hamra district, wealthy Saudi youngsters, who have often spent time abroad and are dressed in expensive foreign labels, go to drink coffee and smoke hubbly bubbly, reclining in upholstered wicker chairs while a wide-screen television flashes images of skimpily dressed Lebanese and Egyptian pop stars into the night and their shiny Western luxury cars sit just beyond a curtain of potted palms. The proximity of a Westerner will immediately cause them to break into a localized version of American English as they declare their love of hip-hop or clubbing. They are never prouder than when showing off their purchased and superficial "Westernness," certainly prouder than when they talk about their own country and culture. In doing so they manifest, of course, precisely the dangers of intoxification, alienation, and corruption that bin Laden and his supporters rail against.

But as they mimic the worst of the West, they also demonstrate the haughtiness and arrogance of the newly rich who—as a wit said about America—have passed from barbarism to decadence without the intervening stage of civilization. For those same youngsters snip their fingers and bark their orders at the Asian waiters like minor potentates of a bygone age. Through their impatience and frustration, fueled by countless cups of coffee and the all-male environment they are forced to exist in, they display an almost joyous contempt of those whose misfortune it is to serve them, taking relish in calling them back for one petty complaint or another. The waiters, Filipinos and Indians, take the abuse with equanimity. They appear, if not unperturbed, then at least numb to the shouting, and do as they are told without, it appears, a second thought: it is all part of their job.

Indians, and some Pakistanis and Filipinos, are making considerable inroads into white-collar jobs in a changing Saudi Arabia, through sheer skill and hard work, but also because they are cheaper than their Western counterparts. Still, the rule remains that it is Indians, Pakistanis, and Bangladeshis who clean the streets in the 40-degree Celsius heat, wearing orange uniforms reminiscent of nothing so much as the jumpsuits of the Guantanamo prisoners, earning a pittance and often living in conditions that would shame a Third World jail. They sleep six or more to a tiny, ramshackle room; they are often supplied only with some blankets to sleep on the raw concrete floor, a single window that provides the only access for a cooling breeze, if it ever comes, and a toilet and bathroom to share with countless others.

Many Asian countries like India, Bangladesh, and the Philippines have agreements with Saudi Arabia that stipulate minimum wages for their respective laborers. But hardly any company follows the minimum wages rule, and most pay their Asian menial workers such a low salary that it is humanly impossible to survive. As a result, these workers moonlight, particularly washing cars or running errands, and are therefore constantly harassed by the police as well as their managers and employers.

Maintenance workers are the worst off among menial workers, but their ordeal is representative of many others. There are more than 200,000 maintenance company workers in the kingdom who draw a monthly salary of about $65. These workers are employed by maintenance companies with cleaning contracts from the municipalities of big cities like Jeddah, Riyadh, Dammam, Medina, Mecca, and Jubail. The housing is provided by the company they work for, but there is no food allowance or other benefits. They are entitled to a vacation after two years, but most of them have not been back to their country for several years, since a trip home would cost more than they manage to save.

A report by the New York–based Human Rights Watch in 2004 cataloged abuses suffered by a predominantly Asian labor force. "Migrant workers in the purportedly modern society that the kingdom has become continue to suffer extreme forms of labour exploitation that sometimes rise to slavery-like conditions," it said. It described the case of 300 women from India, Sri Lanka, and the Philippines who cleaned hospitals in Jeddah. They worked 12-hour shifts, 6 days a week, and at night were locked in crowded dormitory-style accommodation where 14 women shared one small room. Human Rights Watch said abuses of women are particularly disturbing. "Some women workers that we interviewed were still traumatized from rape and sexual abuse at the hands of Saudi male employers," the report said. There have been cases where the families of immigrant workers executed for some crime in the kingdom—often drug-related—were not told until the expatriate had been beheaded.

It would be easy—perhaps too easy—to single out Saudi Arabia as unique in exploiting foreign workers, and it should be pointed out that this is a universal phenomenon. For instance, forced labor, often bordering on slavery, is an American problem, too, according to a report in September 2004 from the Human Rights Center at UC Berkeley and the Washington-based Free the Slaves, an advocacy group focusing on slavery worldwide. The report found that at any one time some 10,000 people are working as forced laborers across the United States. California is one of a handful of states where forced labor operations tend to thrive, and immigrants—both legal and illegal—are frequently the victims.

Enticed by the promise of a job, they arrive only to find themselves trapped in an exploitative relationship they cannot escape. Instead of living the American dream, they are living the American nightmare. One of the cases highlighted in the report is that of Lakireddy Bali Reddy, who lured young girls from his native village in India to work in his restaurants and apartment buildings in Berkeley and is now serving an eight-year prison sentence after pleading guilty to foreign transport of minors for sexual activity, immigration fraud, and tax evasion.

But Reddy is in jail, and that is where the difference lies.

Saudi authorities often protest that the Labor Law offers comprehensive protection against such abuses, but as in so many other ways, the difference between rhetoric and reality is vast. For example, 160 Egyptian and Asian employees went on strike at a factory in Jeddah in 2002. They had the law of the land on their side, and the Labor Office ruled in their favor. However, six months after their industrial action began—undertaken in protest of the company's failure to pay outstanding salaries totaling millions of riyals—their plight was still far from being resolved. They then launched a last-ditch appeal to the Court of Cassation because their salaries had not been paid for seven months. Many of their residence permits, or "iqamas," which all foreigners in Saudi Arabia are required to carry about their person at all times or risk arrest and imprisonment, had in the meantime expired, meaning they had now become illegal "overstayers."

The experience of being in such legal limbo was already familiar to many of their colleagues, who claimed—when I interviewed them for an article for *Arab News*—that the company had previously failed to renew 120 of their residence permits. Now they were living hand-to-mouth, many doing odd jobs to sustain themselves.

The stress was greatest on the Asian (mainly Indian) workers. Unlike their Egyptian colleagues, they did not speak Arabic and found themselves in an alien culture. Neither group, however, had anything but token support from their consulates. A complaint from the Egyptian Consulate in Jeddah that Egyptian workers were caught up in the labor dispute at the factories was acknowledged by the Foreign Ministry's office in the Mecca region, but that was the extent of their involvement.

The Indian Consul for Labor, when I asked him about the case, was not even aware that it had moved to the Court of Cassation, despite the fact that it had been prominently reported in the press some time before; and, when pressed, he could think of only two ways in which he had offered the Indian workers assistance: providing a single translator and agreeing to send a "reminder" to the court. Despite being left largely to their own fate, the workers followed the correct legal channels by filing a complaint at the Labor Office. It found in their favor, ordered the owner of the company to pay outstanding back pay in full, fined him $1,000, and recorded his specific violation—issuing dud checks—at the Jeddah Chamber of Commerce and Industry. The consequence of that verdict was that the employer disappeared.

Judging by the accounts of those who tried to make a living at one of his factories, such deception was his chief characteristic. Under this employer's "sponsorship," the workers were denied their annual leave, meaning in many instances that they had been separated from their loved ones at home since they arrived in the kingdom years earlier. They endured recurrent power cuts in the substandard accommodation provided by the company. They did not get the medical benefits they were entitled to. And those who left the kingdom on exit-only visas were routinely owed months of back pay and end-of-service benefits, which did not subsequently materialize. The company initially claimed that the factory stopped issuing salary checks for "only a few months," due to market depression and the late collection of sales returns from its distribution centers. It further claimed that the delay in renewing residence permits was caused by the employees themselves, who failed to submit them on time. The employees, it continued, subsequently linked the renewal of residence permits with the payment of salary arrears.

However, according to a statement by the finance manager of the company, the truth is that the workers at the factory had not been paid for a much longer period than a few months: some 13 months, meaning they were now owed in excess of half a million dollars. Moreover, the salary arrears and end-of-service benefits still outstanding for those who left the kingdom on exit visas exceeded $750,000. The finance manager attributed the company's failure to pay the workers to a virtual halt to production, which resulted in severe financial losses.

The workers welcomed reports that the Ministry of Industry and Electricity was setting up a committee to discuss possible ways of resolving their situation—but, as anywhere else, committees in Saudi Arabia are set up as much to bury an issue as to resolve it. The workers could at least take small comfort in the fact that, unlike the many thousands of other workers in the kingdom facing similar difficulties, their plight became a focus for the national media—and as such also shone a light, albeit dimly, on the Kafkaesque conditions they live in and that too often are taken for granted.

The sad fact is that there is hardly anything right about labor conditions for Asians in Saudi Arabia. Domestic labor laws and international labor norms are rarely followed. The existing Labor Law was enacted in the 1960s and since then the entire business environment not only in the kingdom but the world over has undergone drastic changes. The existing law ostensibly defends the rights of the workers, but in implementation—as the factory strike in Jeddah revealed—it often becomes yet another tool in the hands of Saudi employers to exploit the foreign workers.

The system of sponsorship requires that every foreign worker is under the patronage of a Saudi sponsor, who in theory takes responsibility for him, providing the necessary visa and the all-important iqama and standing as legal guarantor in the worker's relationship with the Saudi state. It is an inherent part of the Saudi labor law governing foreign workers, formulated to provide a kind of security to the expatriate workers. The sponsor of an employee was meant to defend the rights of the workers. But in effect, it became a means by which the employer or sponsor had complete control over his expatriate employees. Most of the blue-collar workers have the status of bonded laborers rather than bona fide employees—beginning with the fact that workers are expected to hand their passports for safekeeping to their employers in return for their residence permit.

Sometimes employers simply take the passports and then refuse to hand over the work permits, even if they have procured them, leaving their employees extremely vulnerable. In one reported swoop, the Passport Department arrested several Bangladeshis for not carrying their residence permit. However, each of them had a letter from their company saying that their permit had gone for processing to the Passport Department. All these workers were released after a day or two, once a company representative presented the document to the relevant authorities. The story should end here. But the company deducted their wages for the days they were in detention, and so they could not report for work.

"Tell me, what was our fault?" asked an Indian worker. He said there had been many instances where the Passport Department fined immigrant workers for not carrying their permit and the company deducted that amount from the salary of the worker, as well. These particular workers' sponsor denied the allegations and said the iqamas of the employees had gone for processing to the Passport Department but he was not aware of salary deductions. He promised to "look into the matter."

The workers said that this was not the first incident and in all cases fines were deducted from the arrested employees' wages. "Our supervisor and manager blame us for the arrests, saying we must have gone to work elsewhere and got arrested in the process. Don't we have freedom to move?" asked one.

The answer, of course, is no.

Freedom does not suit the interests of employers, who prefer a vulnerable and dependent group of employees beholden to the company not only for their wages but in effect for their lives. Their managers tell the workers that they will not give them their permit—despite also holding their passports—because in the past there were incidents where workers fled and took up jobs elsewhere. "To prevent this, we keep the permits with us," a supervisor told a Bangladeshi employee of the company.

Additionally, the companies incur very little cost for noncompliant employees, because they can always dock their pay and fine them for the disruption caused by their absence. But paying their employees such minimal wages simply forces workers to seek odd jobs elsewhere. "I work as a part-time house boy at a couple of households and clean half a dozen cars every day to supplement my income," another Bangladeshi worker told me. "Can anyone really survive with $60 a month, leave aside sending money back home for the family?"

One of the households where he worked, incidentally, was mine.

A small, neat man, he attacked the dust that would blow in through the windows with a systematic dedication I have rarely seen anywhere else, and which I myself would have certainly been incapable of.

If Western expatriates are paid high salaries as enticement to live and work in Saudi Arabia, their Third World counterparts are so desperate that they are often ready to believe the false promises of recruiters and pay to come work in Saudi Arabia. To get the job, this Bangladeshi had to pay nearly $2,000 to a recruitment agent in Bangladesh. "We sell our land, our wives' jewelry, and take out loans to get the job. There we are told a different, much higher salary and different work with so many promised benefits. But here what we get is $60, harassments, and pain," he said.

At least these are the workers who are paid their salaries regularly and can leave the country after giving appropriate notice. There are thousands all over the kingdom who are not paid for a long period of time, again as a security measure to stop them from running away from their abusive employers. One contracting company in Jubail can stand for many in its gross violation of the labor rules. The company has more than 130 employees, and in the summer of 2004 some of them had not been paid for nine months, others for more than one year. All the 130 employees were technically illegal overstayers because their general manager ran away from the company with their passports. By then, all their residence permits had expired, and many were frequently arrested by the Passport Department.

The owner of what was essentially a labor camp where the workers were housed meanwhile threatened to evict them because the company failed to pay the rent. Many of the workers resorted to beggary for their survival. Their embassies said they did take up the issue with local authorities as well as the governor of the Eastern Province, Prince Muhammad bin Fahd, a son of King Fahd, but it was not until late September 2004 that the prince finally ordered the release or repatriation of those workers still in jail—he left the choice up to them—though, it appears, without making provisions for them to receive the pay they were owed.

Many companies, even those considered reputable in the international market, have created their own rules in contravention of the Saudi Labor

Law. Such companies issue "edicts" that no new laborer should be paid for the first three months (in some cases seven months) as a security that he will stay with the company and as indemnity against any future losses incurred by him. How, then, are the workers supposed to survive? The ingenious solution is that management will introduce the workers to a nearby general store and make arrangements for the store to give goods to these workers on credit, with the company standing as guarantor. The worker thus becomes indebted to the store, which is paid directly by the company, and the worker thus gets no wages. Even when the store is not directly linked to the company, the possibilities for corruption are clear.

"I promised that as soon as I got to Saudi Arabia I would start sending money," said Mustapha, a Pakistani who works for a large contracting company who became indebted to a local store. "It's been six months since I came here and I have not been paid. I know how much harassment from the recruitment agent and other creditors my wife and children must be facing." The practice is common mainly to contracting and maintenance companies, according to a lawyer who deals in labor cases. "But the problem is that the laborers are scared to go to Labor Court, and they do not have the resources either."

Some laborers with a maintenance company in Dammam decided to cut their losses and asked their company to send them back home on an exit-only visa. "But this too did not happen. My supervisor told me that I am bound to complete the two-year contract," said Sahul, a wiry south Indian laborer.

Needless to say, all these workers were expected to pay for their own residence permits and were told that they and not the company would also pay for exit and re-entry visa fees. The Saudi Labor Law clearly stipulates that all the costs of the residence permit and other legal documents pertaining to the stay of the foreign worker will be borne by the sponsor. Nor are private companies unique in this: Many government institutions also follow their "own rules," which contradict the law—hospitals run by the Saudi Ministry of Health are particularly persistent offenders in this regard. Newly recruited doctors in such hospitals are not paid for the first three months, with the employing hospitals invariably saying that the delay is "due to processing."

According to a report issued by a group of NGOs, there are an estimated 5,000 agricultural laborers in the rural areas of the Eastern Province, and they too are essentially prisoners of their sponsors. Many of them were not paid for more than two years. The survey revealed that more than 2,000 Indians had not seen their country for the past five years because their employers did not have any intention to allow them to go home for their statutory annual vacation. Few of the workers have ever seen their residence permit and doubt that their employers ever applied for one. Their employers meanwhile refuse to let them travel to their consulates in Dammam or Riyadh to renew their passports.

Embassies and consulates of the workers are overworked and mostly apathetic to the workers' conditions. They have their hands full, for example, with the mysterious phenomenon of the disappearing maids. Domestic staff in the kingdom come from India, Sri Lanka, Bangladesh, the Philippines, and Indonesia. There have been endless reports of sexual harassment, beating, torture, rape, and forced abortions, and there are almost weekly stories of suicides. According to survey conducted by the Manpower Council—the body tasked with coordinating employment matters in the kingdom—every third Saudi household in cities like Jeddah, Riyadh, and Dammam, and every fourth household in small cities like Mecca, Medina, Jubail, and Yanbu, has at least one maid. Maids are cheap—with salaries ranging between $150 and $200 a month without benefits, insurance, or medical allowance—and they are often kept around the clock behind the high walls of their employer's home.

The Saudi Labor Law does not define any rights and duties of the employer of domestic staff, who are in effect his slaves. Of course, not all employers are deliberately cruel or abusive. Many are merely casually so. They believe what they have been told for decades: that theirs is a perfect society and that they, as a consequence, are more completely civilized than anyone else. Quite innocently, they regard their maids and drivers as lesser humans, born in filth and ignorance, who should be grateful for the opportunity to serve them. Children in such matters tend to take their cues from their parents. Small wonder then that sexual abuse of maids is common at the hands of adolescent boys, some of them following in their fathers' footsteps, some simply acting within the general climate of contempt for Third World nationals that pervades the kingdom. The maids are uniquely cut off from the contact with their community that sustains many other foreign laborers. Kept prisoners in the home, they are more likely to resort to desperate measures than others. Hence the suicides, which many maids attempt by jumping from balconies. Others run away. Each Indonesian and Sri Lankan embassy and consulate reports scores of escapes every month. They have set up shelters for the "runaway maids," as they are known, where the often young women can be accommodated while their government attempts to settle the Byzantine paperwork necessary to repatriate them.

It is only to be expected that where there is so much real abuse and legitimate flight, an industry has also arisen from the phenomenon of the disappearing maids. There are recruitment agents, according to reports, who
will encourage maids they have supplied to run away only days after their
probation period—usually three months—is over. In that event, the employer, not the agent, becomes liable for all costs—visa, work permit, and
recruitment fee—and the agent can reassign the maids somewhere else and
collect another fee. To the maids, it usually matters little where they work,
as one employer is pretty much as bad as another, though of course there are
also maids who are treated well and with respect and stay with the same employer sometimes for decades. There are others who are resigned to the fact
that their job involves some form of prostitution, and they make extra
money on the side by meeting the neighbors for assignments. Saudis, after
all, are among the world's most enthusiastic clients of prostitutes abroad,
and anecdotal evidence as well as frequent press reports suggest that there is
a thriving underground industry in prostitution inside the kingdom, usually
taking the form of informal brothels staffed by Asian and African women.

With their numbers making up what would amount to the population of a
small country by themselves, competition among Asian immigrant workers is
fierce, and it would be naive to overlook the many ways in which they themselves contribute—however unwittingly—to a situation where some can abuse
them with impunity. In a legal vacuum, where only the harsh laws of the market hold any sway, it is natural that Asians undercut one another in their hunt
for jobs, or in their desire to stay in them. There are many reasons for this.

Many Asians in Saudi Arabia, for instance, find themselves in a world
where there is very little entertainment, and nothing for even those who
bring their families with them to do except procreate or pray; a steady income also encourages them to have more children, whom many still see as
an insurance in their old age. Taking their cue from their Saudi neighbors,
they have much larger numbers of children than they would at home—in
India, for example, government policy actively discourages people from having too many children.

It was not unusual for Indians of my acquaintance to have up to eight
children, the oldest already at high school or college back in India, the
youngest barely more than a toddler, others in between attending the kingdom's massive Indian schools. More children meant ever-growing financial

pressures, and these parents needed to be assured of a steady job on the relatively high (compared to what they could earn in their home countries) Saudi-style salaries. That meant that in many cases they put up with anything, not merely abuses at the hands of their employer but also a system that on all sides encouraged corruption, such as the buying of visas, the bribing of officials, and the trading of favors for favors that is as common a currency in Saudi Arabia as it is in the rest of the Arab world and beyond.

This is not helped by the fact that they often come from countries where corruption is equally endemic: Bangladesh is, after all, regularly confirmed as the most corrupt country on earth. When Asians find that corruption in Saudi Arabia is merely an extension of the corruption at home, they are often only too eager to play the game. While it may be fair to say that a majority of foreign workers in the kingdom experience some form of, if not outright abuse, or at least treatment that is not entirely aboveboard, it is also fair to say that many have long become used to the system and learned to make it work to their advantage—be it by cutting corners themselves, working several jobs, or doing any of the myriad of underhand deals that corrupt systems based on the giving and taking of favors encourage. The possibilities are endless.

For many, then, Saudi Arabia remains a land of opportunity. Rafiq Hariri, Lebanon's prime minister for most of the last decade, assassinated in 2005, was perhaps the most glaring example of a man who became rich beyond his wildest expectations as an expatriate in the kingdom. His billions were made in Saudi Arabia beginning in the 1970s, mostly from construction and publishing, as he ingratiated himself with the royal family. The ostensible piety of certain foreign staff at my own newspaper, meanwhile, had opened for them a lucrative field of translating Islamic literature—read Wahhabi propaganda—into English. That included on one occasion the rewriting of a badly translated "encyclopedia" of religions—in fact a propaganda tract condemning everything other than strict Wahhabi doctrine as deviant or "disgusting"—by an infamous extremist group. The project would net the translator several thousand dollars and a useful connection for any further pamphlets, leaflets, and other flotsam in the endless stream of proselytizing literature emerging from that organization and many others like it. Stories like these abound.

Some in Saudi Arabia feel that taxi drivers are among the most abused foreign workers, or perhaps simply the most blatant victims of unfettered capitalism at work. But they are often also the pluckiest and smartest at playing a system that denies them any rights or job security. Mainly Bangladeshis, Indians, and Pakistanis, they buy their jobs for $1,600 or more after an assurance from the recruiting agents in their home countries that they will be paid a salary of not less than $400 a month and receive accommodation and free medical and food allowance. They are also assured of huge overtime payments. On their arrival, they find that all the promises were empty and that there is no salary at all.

The most common practice in the taxi business is that drivers pay a daily rent on their cars and, once that is paid, work on a commission basis per fare. Saudi taxis are in principle metered, but the fare is so inflated that nobody uses the meter. Under the system, a taxi company gives a car to the newly recruited driver and asks him to earn a minimum of $40 per day. Anything above that is their money. If they fail to earn the minimum, the target for the next day goes up. In addition to paying $40, the drivers are to pay for the fuel and maintenance of the vehicle as well. On average, each driver works for more than 17 hours per day. As a result, there are endless accidents on the roads involving taxi drivers, many of them fatal. The drivers also pay for their resident permits and all other paperwork.

After repeated stories in local newspapers about the plight of drivers, the Transport Ministry made it mandatory for the employers to pay a minimum salary of $134 a month. However, not a single taxi company paid any salary to the drivers. Instead, the companies asked drivers to sign salary vouchers to satisfy their legal obligation; the form rather than the substance of the law was thus maintained. Meanwhile, the massive failure of the government's attempts to cut reliance on foreigners and create jobs for Saudis is nowhere more obvious than in the taxi sector, which was officially fully staffed by Saudis by 2002. In all my time in the kingdom I had two Saudi taxi drivers, one of whom—to judge by his accent—may have been a disguised Egyptian. This is but one indication of the extent to which the kingdom depends on foreign workers. Quite simply, taxi companies were unable to find more than a minute number of Saudis to drive taxis for their compatriots, as Saudis are generally unwilling to undertake what they consider demeaning work.

Not that the government has not sought to encourage Saudis to take on such jobs. Whether because it is afraid of creating a literate middle class or despairs of ever doing so, the Saudi government decided in the 1990s to squeeze out foreigners and replace them with Saudis—to "Saudize" the kingdom—from the bottom up. First came the vegetable market, then the taxi drivers, the checkouts in supermarkets, then the gold souk, then travel agencies, then a multitude of sales jobs. In all these sectors, salaries are low and staff work long hours—conditions likely to put off Saudi applicants used to handouts and superiority over foreigners.

Notwithstanding the government's push for Saudization, most workers in these fields remain foreigners. This is not surprising, given that surveys consistently show that young Saudis want administrative jobs in the government, hardly taxing occupations, or at a stretch managerial positions in private businesses, but definitely not jobs that involve manual work. In sector after sector, therefore, Saudization has failed. Some companies keep phantom Saudi staff on their rolls, others keep a bona fide Saudi at the door while an expatriate does the work for a fraction of the money. Still others simply defy the regulations openly and pay the necessary bribes to keep doing so with impunity. Yet there can be no doubt that Saudi Arabia must Saudize if it is to survive, as there is no other way to address the massive poverty, youth unemployment, and government revenues overly reliant on the fickle price of oil.

So the failed education policy, lack of motivation, and a neverending flood of Asians willing to brave the abuse and grueling work conditions mean that the prospects of a Saudi one day picking up the garbage other Saudis have so liberally left behind them are slim. Notwithstanding their pretensions, there are few Saudis moreover yet qualified to take on top managerial and technical positions, and few Saudis being trained to do so.

One result is a continued reliance on foreign experts who live in the high-profile compounds, and who then become targets of bin Laden and his sympathizers. Another result is a massive group of underemployed, increasingly impoverished Saudis who envy the West as much as they despise it, and whose vague grudges are gradually fermenting into something more dangerous.

"There is a market illusion how much the kingdom is affected by foreign workers," Oil Minister Ali Al-Naimi said after the Khobar attacks. "It is part of the market illusion that if 10 foreign workers leave, the kingdom's production is affected."

Analysts confirm that the minister is correct, at least in the short term—but only where Western expatriate workers are concerned. Americans, Britons, and other Europeans in the kingdom, who only number in the tens of thousands compared to the eight million Asian and Arab immigrant workers, are mostly employed in the oil and finance sectors. Even if the Westerners left at once, which is highly unlikely, Saudi Arabia could, as it already is doing, turn to skilled Asians.

Despite a certain hysteria in the international press, it is another of Saudi Arabia's myriad paradoxes, then, that an exodus of the most valued and respected expatriates would not make much of a dent in its prosperity.

If, on the other hand, the despised Asian blue-collar workers left en masse, the country would collapse overnight. Garbage would pile high in the streets, families would go hungry, restaurants would close, goods would remain undelivered and rot, and the water supply would stop. There would be no more farming the desert, no transport, no fixing and filling the all-important cars, no air-conditioning, no lighting the streets, no repairing of roads. There would be no trade in anything but sheep and camels, and the wind would whistle through deserted markets. And the sick, injured, and dying would pile up in the corridors of hospitals, if they somehow managed to make it there.

Chapter Seven

URBAN CRIME WAVE

For a square mile the Saudi traffic cops, sitting at junctions in groups of three or four on their parked motorcycles, were communicating with each other via walkie-talkies. Half an hour earlier, they had closed off the flow of traffic from all the side streets in the district. On the main stretch of the now deserted Medina Road, the main artery in Jeddah usually chockablock with traffic and that leads directly to chop-chop square, all the traffic lights were permanently set to green. At the bottom of the road, next to the square itself, dozens of cars had been parked randomly, sometimes four or five deep, making it nearly impossible to navigate the adjoining roundabout. Their owners had abandoned them, despite the protests of a solitary traffic policeman blowing his whistle and shouting abuse at them for doing so, because of their eagerness to get a glimpse of the only form of public entertainment in Saudi Arabia that exists, apart from soccer matches: a beheading.

Since they are not announced in advance—even to the man or woman selected for execution—and can take place on any day of the week, those who get to see beheadings in Saudi Arabia do so by chance. Hence the last-minute commotion. Those who happened to be passing by that day were especially lucky, it turned out, for what was planned was an even rarer event: a double beheading.

Hundreds had formed a ring around the chopping block. Hundreds more spanned out over the main road and the surrounding open space. Perched on walls or clinging to the sides of a clock tower in the middle of Medina Road, all were happily suffering the intense discomfort of direct and prolonged exposure to the desert sun in the middle of a blisteringly hot summer's day.

In the square, which doubled as a parking lot, armed cops were stationed every 10 yards, their backs turned to the block and their eyes fixed sternly on the crowd. They were there in case the relatives of the men to be slain tried to sabotage the executions at the last minute. It was also their job to make sure no one took any photographs or video footage. Such material, very occasionally shot clandestinely in the past, had proven highly effective propaganda in the West for those opposed to the Al-Saud regime, ever determined as they are to provide evidence of the "barbaric Wahhabi culture" the ruling family presides over.

There were both men and women in the closely observed crowd, standing side by side, taking advantage of an unusual relaxation of the rules governing the strict segregation of the sexes in public. The majority of the men were Third World immigrants. Since the women were covered from head to toe in black, they could have been from anywhere, although most of the excited chatter coming from beneath the veils of those near me was in Arabic.

The executioner himself, Muhammad Saad Al-Beshi, was recognizable from a photograph that had been published a few weeks earlier in *Arab News,* in which he had given a rare interview. Saudi Arabia's leading executioner had talked calmly and proudly of how he had executed numerous women and men. A huge black man with piercing eyes and massive hands, he professed his hatred of violence against women, but added that—when it comes to God's will—he had no choice but to cut off their head or shoot them in the back of it if the Sharia court so deemed it necessary. He expressed indifference, too, on the subject of the number of beheadings he was required to carry out on each occasion. It does not matter—two, four, ten—as long, he repeated, as he was doing God's will.

That morning, he walked around the chopping block in a studied manner, his eyes firmly fixed on the ground. He was dressed in an immaculate white robe and a red checkered headscarf. He gripped his beloved sword firmly in his hand, clearly wallowing in the extraordinary solemnity of the occasion.

The sound of police sirens could at last be heard, and soon afterward two police cars, lights flashing, sped into the square. Behind them came two police vans, followed by three more police cars. From the back of each of the vans emerged a man, blindfolded and with his hands tied behind his back. Each was escorted to the block by a policeman. They were obviously drugged. So sluggish were they, indeed, that they needed the support of the policemen to walk the short distance.

They were made to kneel on the block and were fixed in place, with their heads slightly bowed. Their nationalities (Pakistani), ages (both in their thirties), and crimes (smuggling heroin into the kingdom) were broadcast over loudspeakers.

A verse from the Qu'ran was recited.

The executioner leaned over to the Pakistani nearest to him, and whispered into his ear that he should say the *shahada,* the Muslim declaration of faith. There was no indication that the man could even comprehend what was being said, let alone the nightmare his short life had culminated in.

The executioner stepped back, raised the sword, and with a precise but powerless swing managed to sever half of the man's head from his body. His suddenly lifeless torso fell, as if in slow motion, toward his compatriot awaiting the same fate. Then it tumbled completely off the block. The executioner took the man's head by its hair, and hacked two or three times at the skin and muscle still attached—all with the cool, matter-of-fact diligence of an expert butcher.

After wiping the blood from the sword with a white cloth, he dealt the same fate to the second Pakistani. For all of his talk in the *Arab News* interview about the years of practice it takes to get to his position as chief executioner, he botched the job again, failing to sever the head completely from the body, necessitating once again a bout of follow-up, close-quarter hacking.

An ambulance pulled up. Both heads and bodies were put on separate stretchers. As the blood was hosed down with a powerful jet of water by the local fire brigade, the loudspeakers were already urging the crowd to disperse, to the inevitable chants of "Allau Akbar" (God is greatest).

In May 2004, less than a year after that double execution, a son of Interior Minister Prince Naif, who had been found guilty of killing a 15-year-old boy after an "argument," was saved from beheading when the father of his victim forgave him at the last minute.

Prince Fahd bin Naif, who was 19, gunned down Mundir Al-Qadi two years earlier. Fahd, too, was brought blindfolded to a public square. But, as the executioner prepared his sword, the young prince shouted: "For the sake of God, please spare my life." Suleiman Al-Qadi, Mundir's father, was standing in the crowd of spectators, and he relented when he heard the plea.

"It was a big shock," a Saudi justice official, Ibrahim Al-Shathry, told reporters afterward, "since Al-Qadi and his brothers had told the officials to make sure the execution was carried out."

In Saudi Arabia, a crime victim's family does have the power to pardon the accused. The judge dutifully signed the pardon document—which demanded that Fahd learn the Qu'ran entirely by heart. Then Fahd went to the office of his uncle, Riyadh governor Prince Salman, who is a brother of the king, who is said to have given him a big hug.

Was it, as the official claimed, "a big shock" that the father of the victim spared Fahd? Almost certainly not. The episode smacks of having been stage managed, a transparent attempt to demonstrate that the Al-Saud would apparently be willing to let one of their own face the consequences of his criminal activity. It is difficult to believe that the father of the murdered boy would have been able to live a free and fulfilling life had he not pardoned Fahd at the last minute. The only thing that was remarkable about the whole charade was that Fahd had been charged at all.

In January 2002 four other young princes were among some 300 youths arrested for causing disturbances during Eid Al-Fitr on Jeddah's corniche, where thousands of families and picnickers had gathered to celebrate the Islamic holiday marking the end of Ramadan. The four princes were said to have been among the young men who blocked the main road and harassed families, ignoring orders from the cops to disperse. "The youths went berserk on the beach, sowing chaos and confusion in the crowd. Eyewitnesses said they put on masks to frighten women and children. The unruly crowd also attacked a patrol team and damaged their cars," a report in *Al-Watan* the following day said. On various Arabic-language websites it was further claimed that the princes, in particular, had tried to drag some young girls away from their families to force them to have sex, although those allegations could not be independently confirmed.

Other newspapers, emboldened by a domestic debate about the future of the kingdom in the wake of the September 11 attacks four months earlier, also took the unusual step of reporting that the four princes had been among those arrested. That prompted an equally unusual statement from Mecca's governor, Prince Abdul Majeed, to the effect that "no one is above the law." A week later, however, when Abdul Majeed indicated to reporters that the princes would be prosecuted along with the other youths, he oddly spoke about there having been "two" of them, and that figure was dutifully reprinted in subsequent discussions of the case in the official media. Then, just as it was beginning to seem like justice might be seen to be done in a case involving a member of the royal family for the first time in the history of the kingdom, the episode—as with the Fahd beheading charade—culminated in an anticlimax: Orders came through to editors in chief from the Ministry of Information that nothing more about the subject was to be printed. So the matter was closed, and all four of the princes got off scot-free.

Such crude protection of alleged criminals sometimes extends to those who, although not themselves members of the royal family, are close to an influential prince. In July 2004, for instance, a Saudi man working at the Saudi Arabian embassy in London was questioned in Britain about a sexual assault he was alleged to have carried out on an 11-year-old girl, but he was immediately released after claiming diplomatic immunity. Scotland Yard said police were left with no choice but to take "no further action," yet it did report the matter to the Foreign Office. One officer, however, was apparently so outraged that he leaked the incident to the local press. The 41-year-old Saudi, it transpired, had been arrested on suspicion of indecently assaulting the girl in west London after an official complaint was received; and a Foreign Office spokesman told reporters at the time that it was highly usual in such cases for there to be a request to waive diplomatic immunity. For its part, the Saudi Arabian Embassy in London said it was "fully aware" of the case (the story had led the TV news bulletins and newspaper front pages for three straight days, so it could hardly not have been) and was conducting an "inquiry." The Saudi ambassador himself, Prince Turki Al-Faisal, complained—after the outcry in the British tabloids had reached fever pitch—that the Saudi diplomat was undergoing "trial by media" over the allegations. The case had meanwhile prompted children's rights campaigners and even a member of Parliament to call directly on the Saudi government to waive the man's immunity, an act for which there are many precedents from other embassies in Britain. Turki, though, just reiterated that the man had been treated unfairly, adding that the embassy was "co-operating" with police. "There are issues about this situation where he is being tried in the media, and we think that that is unfair," Turki told the BBC. Trial by media is indeed a sad phenomenon in Britain, as in many other parts of the world; such a complaint would be fair comment coming from anyone else, at least until the facts were established and the actual trial was over. But, considering that the Al-Saud is infamous the world over for using its own state-controlled media to launch smear campaigns against its opponents, Turki only ended up sounding like a first-rate hypocrite, confirming in the process all the stereotypes many in the West have about how the Al-Saud royal family will go to whatever lengths are deemed necessary to protect their own, and at any cost. In the BBC interview, Turki would not even comment on the question of whether he was prepared for the diplomat to be further questioned by police, nor whether he was in fact considering waiving the man's diplomatic immunity. As with the Jeddah corniche incident involving the four young tear-away princes, the matter was to all appearances swept under the carpet.

One of Turki's fellow princes had earlier escaped justice after being indicted in the United States and France for allegedly running a successful cocaine smuggling operation—with the help of Saudi diplomatic passports and a royal family Boeing 727 jet. On an ABC news special aired in October 2004, Tom Raffanello, a Drug Enforcement Agency veteran investigator based in Miami, identified the prince as Naif bin Fawwaz Al-Shalaan. According to Raffanello, Naif has been the key player in the drug ring's activities, including the transport—by royal family jet—of about two tons of cocaine from Colombia to France. "He's the straw that stirs the drink, he made it happen," Raffanello was quoted as saying. "No plane, no dope. Dope stays in Colombia." In an Arabic-language newspaper, the prince has protested that he travels internationally to enlist investors for a plastic pipe business, not to smuggle drugs, and that he has been absolved of any wrongdoing by Saudi authorities. In the ABC documentary, Raffanello was having none of that, complaining that the prince, safe inside Saudi Arabia—which has no extradition treaty with the United States—is outside the reach of American law and remains "a fugitive in violation of federal narcotics law." Furthermore, according to the DEA, the prince is a fugitive from an earlier U.S. drug case as well (dating back to 1984), and Raffanello told ABC that at least some of the drug ring profits have been used to fund terrorism. The ABC report also featured claims by a former French police investigator, Fabrice Monti, that Interior Minister Prince Naif used threats to French business interests in an effort to persuade the authorities to drop their investigation: "The Saudi government acted as one," said Monti, "to set up a protective barrier between the prince and French justice and threatened to not sign a very important and lucrative contract in the works for a very long time."

That same tactic was employed, according to an article in the London *Times* in November 2004, against Britain's defense industry, which the newspaper said could lose billions of pounds worth of work if the Saudi royal family suffered embarrassment by an ongoing Serious Fraud Office investigation into a slush fund allegedly maintained by BAE Systems, the UK's largest defense contractor. According to the *Sunday Times* report, the Saudi government threatened to cut British arms dealers out of all future contracts—including over $8 billion in pending deals involving combat aircraft for the Saudi air force—if the BAE investigation focused unwelcome attention on any member of the royal family. In fact, a central figure in the investigation is Prince Turki bin Nasser, the Saudis' principal contact with the British defense industry, who allegedly received about $32 million worth of luxury benefits paid for by BAE, including private-jet transport and lavish suites in five-star hotels. The *Times* quoted an unnamed source in the defense industry, who confirmed that the Saudis were in an uproar about being tainted by involvement in such a scandal. "They are very proper, they are very private," he said. "They feel very offended. The constant implication that these people take bribes is obviously offensive to them."

What seems peculiar, in retrospect, is that the Al-Saud believed they had some kind of reputation to protect. After all, there is probably nobody in the world who would not think the allegations pointed to anything but what was routine in how Saudi princes behave abroad and do business. Nevertheless, the details were riveting. The alleged BAE slush fund was uncovered by the BBC's highly respected weekly news magazine *The Money Programme* in October 2004. The BBC's main source was travel-agency owner Peter Gardiner, who revealed how he used BAE money to heap luxury on Prince Turki bin Nasser for over a decade, beginning back in 1988. According to Gardiner, BAE channeled over $13 million a year through his small travel agency, enough to provide Prince Turki and his entourage with the most lavish hotel accommodations, chartered jets to exotic holiday locations, limousines, bodyguards, and the other trappings of a lifestyle "way beyond" that of most movie stars. Among the items enjoyed by Turki and his family at BAE's expense, as reported by the BBC, were a three-month summer vacation ($3.7 million), a ski trip to Colorado for the prince's son ($187,000), a wedding video for the prince's daughter (almost $380,000), and a Rolls-Royce for the prince's wife on her birthday ($320,000), not to mention cash payments—about $100,000 at a time—to pay off the prince's credit card bills.

The BBC program also featured an interview with Edward Cunningham, another BAE insider, who was in charge of making sure that lower-level Saudi officials received their share of the BAE perks. According to Cunningham, officials at the Saudi embassy in London were offered canteens of gold or silver cutlery worth nearly $2,000 each but "wouldn't take the silver ones." He was "inundated by everyone who was of any standing in the embassy," Cunningham told the BBC. "They all wanted gold." Cunningham also reported that he had to set young Saudi pilots up with prostitutes, pay off gambling bills, and arrange for lavish evenings on the town for Saudis visiting London.

Attempts at reforming the Saudi "justice system," a term that even Europe in the Dark Ages would have been more accurate in using, will continue to be radically undermined by its fundamental flaw of leaving Al-Saud princes like Fahd completely above the law, while setting an example of impoverished Third World immigrants who do not have the right to be represented by a lawyer and who, for that matter, frequently remain unaware of the charges leveled against them—to the moment their heads are inexpertly separated from their bodies.

What cannot be in doubt is the need for widespread reforms, both in the way crimes are prevented and criminals are dealt with, because a population boom, rapid social change, and massive unemployment are bringing a new and frightening social reality to Saudi Arabia.

The statistics available are breathtaking. A 2003 report by the Saudi Arabian Monetary Agency, for example, said that crime among young jobless Saudis rose 320 percent between 1990 and 1996, and is expected to increase an additional 136 percent by 2005. More than 60 percent of Saudis are under the age of 21, and the kingdom's population growth rate is roughly 4 percent—one of the highest in the world. Urbanization is the one physical development above all others that has changed the face of Saudi society in the last 50 years, and the capital Riyadh is well on its way to becoming the first megacity of the Gulf. Its population is projected to exceed 11 million by 2020, one of the highest ratios of capital city to national population anywhere in the world.

The massive influx of migrants from the countryside into the main cities places enormous pressures on services, even in a country as theoretically wealthy as Saudi Arabia. Like every developing country of the world, it is poverty that is sucking the poor and dispossessed into the metropolitan centers and spawning in the process brawling, brutish slums on their outskirts. Unlike many other developing countries, however, in Saudi Arabia the migrants into the cities are not only made up of residents of the country itself, but a diversity of immigrants as well, not all legal and hailing from a vast array of countries. In a sense, then, Saudi Arabia's labor market is the first truly global one.

Saudi Arabia is sure to become increasingly restive in the face of all these rapid social transformations, which pose a potentially much more serious risk to the survival of the Al-Saud in the long term than does Islamic militancy, which has the potential to shock but not necessarily destabilize in the near future. At the same time, it would be naive not to see the two issues as intertwined, with a particular irony in the context of the Saudi state: Islamic militarism feeds off desperation and poverty and plays on the same ground as the Wahhabi–Al-Saud alliance by promoting what each claims to be the core values of Islam in its purest form.

The social transformations alone potentially are earthshaking, destabilizing the foundations on which the Al-Saud regime is based. The results of the population boom, urbanization, and unemployment represent a breakdown in traditional forms of social control and constraint. Family, especially paternal, authority is undermined, as is traditional alliance to tribes. Cut adrift, younger Saudis can become unmoored, and opportunities for mischief often are more tempting than those for hard work—especially when the latter is not always rewarded by a system less motivated by merit than personal connections, and when in any case work of any kind is increasingly hard to come by. While official unemployment statistics are not available, the number of jobless Saudis alone is estimated to be as high as 35 percent of the population.

Terrorism is only the most high-profile manifestation of the extraordinary wave of crime insecurity. In 1999, Islamic courts dealt with 616 murder cases, the largest number taking place in Mecca, Islam's holiest city. "People here are totally confused. They don't understand how crime can keep rising in this Muslim society," an editorial in *Okaz* stated, complementing a three-page special on crime. A series of crimes in the space of a few weeks in Jeddah in early 2002 collectively did away forever with the label "crime-free kingdom." Until then, the Al-Saud had justifiably promoted this message as one of the positive aspects of the society its strict Wahhabi religious doctrine had helped to create. Among the crimes during those extraordinary two weeks: Shortly after Friday prayers, an Indian grocery shop assistant was shot in the hand and leg by three Saudi youths robbing his store. Two Saudis nearly killed a British woman when they mugged her in broad daylight in a busy residential area. A local bank was robbed by two machine-gun-wielding men, who overpowered the security guard. In a nearby street, when a policeman tried to arrest a group of Saudi teenagers for joyriding, he came under a hail of rocks thrown by the youths and ended up having to shoot one of them in order to get away.

The last crime should have been particularly troubling for the regime, given the clear disrespect and disregard for official authority it involved. Then again, a bank being robbed by machine-gun-wielding men should also have been of concern, given the possibility that such monies gained may have been used to finance anti-regime terrorism.

What is the Al-Saud regime doing about this challenge? Saudi Arabia still applies a strict form of Shariah law, which includes public beheading for murder, drug trafficking, apostasy, rape, and adultery—and thieves sometimes having their hands amputated (although not nearly as often as anti-Saudi commentary in the Western press claims, and only in extremely limited circumstances). In 2003, more than 50 people were beheaded in public. However, there is an increasing recognition that the death penalty is not working as a deterrent, and a wider debate about the social causes of crime is at last underway in the Saudi media.

One thing is for sure: The days when ordinary people could leave their home unlocked, even when they went on holiday, are gone forever. A Saudi friend in his twenties, after parking his car outside his home in a plush Riyadh suburb late one evening, suddenly fretted that he may have lost his house keys. Such a reaction would be normal in the West. But it was surprising to hear a Saudi talk about how thieves had taken to clearing out apartments in his neighborhood after brazenly parking a van in the street outside, and how he was certain his apartment would be the next target if his keys had fallen from his pocket somewhere in the street. "When my father lived in old Riyadh, Saudis would have gone out of their way to get them back to the owner," he said sadly.

He had every right to be concerned, to judge from the stories about crime that by then had become the subject of daily conversation. Police had only a few weeks earlier arrested a Saudi who had burgled at least 25 houses in a robbing spree in the capital. Students at King Saud University in the capital complained that they were unable to leave their cars in the parking lot, for fear of finding them stripped of valuables after classes had finished. Riyadh police say that in the three years to 2003 they recorded more than 13,000 serious robberies.

Reporting on violent and other crimes, and linking them to poverty and other kinds of social deprivation, was traditionally taboo in Saudi Arabia, while only the punishments themselves were reported—resulting in a paradoxical situation in which the latter implied the former. Everything was perfect, the Al-Saud maintained, apart from these unfortunate (and harshly punished) transgressors. Editors in chief were accused of treachery—of giving ammunition to hostile outsiders eager to undermine "the home of Islam," as the 1930s geopolitical construct of Saudi Arabia is ridiculously referred to—for publishing stories that exposed the darker side of life inside the kingdom.

When I arrived in the middle of 2001, all the journalists I encountered were cautious about printing anything that "reflected badly on the kingdom," and to be fair, to all appearances Saudi Arabia still was relatively crime free. But by the time I left, two and a half years later, most of the local dailies had crime pages.

A highly publicized visit by Crown Prince Abdullah to a slum in a Riyadh suburb in November 2002, broadcast live on Saudi TV, helped put the spotlight squarely on social deprivation, and a personal determination at least on his part to do something about it. A photograph of Abdullah in an old man's filthy home, listening to him rant as he pointed a finger directly at the prince's face, was splashed across all of the dailies the following day. It was widely seen as ushering in a new era and was accompanied by an official announcement of a multimillion-dollar campaign to eradicate poverty.

The scene of an impoverished old man wagging his finger at the prince also spoke of disrespect for authority in a way that perhaps came across more clearly than desired, while doubly reenforcing a sense in the kingdom that Abdullah was nevertheless a man who would listen and even be spoken harshly to by his subjects. All well and good. But while the intent of the prince's visit was to show the attentiveness and benevolence of the leadership, not to mention its openness to dialogue and differing views, it also reinforced the paternalism endemic to Saudi society that is one of the major barriers to economic activity and growth, which are both prerequisites to reducing poverty.

A slum to the south of Jeddah, Kerantina, takes its name from the English world "quarantine," because historically it was the holding area for pilgrims who had overstayed their visas and were awaiting deportation back to their home countries. These days, its winding streets are home to thousands of residents of all nationalities, the majority of whom, however, are Saudis. Prostitution, drug abuse, and alcohol smuggling are rife there, and the area becomes a police no-go area after dark.

When I visited the area, I was at first inundated with offers of everything—from drugs to women to the services of an African who specialized in witchcraft. Although I was accompanied by a Somali and a Saudi, it slowly became obvious that I was not buying, and eventually I was threatened and practically hounded back into my car by three huge Nigerians. In the hour and a half I spent there, it confirmed its reputation as the place where everything officially forbidden in the kingdom—drugs, alcohol, and sex—is available, for the right price.

Only in Kerantina can one find banned substances being sold in the middle of the street in the middle of the day—and without fear in a country where the extremes of such behavior literally can lose you your head in chop-chop square a few miles to the north. The district was teeming with sick people, drug peddlers, addicts, and overstayers. AIDS, which is not widespread in Saudi Arabia, is nevertheless an inevitable byproduct of life in the slum, and an official at a local government hospital has said that he receives up to seven new AIDS cases from Kerantina each week.

A melting pot of colors, cultures, and languages, certain African traditions are also practiced in Kerantina, and the writ of the African tribal leader apparently rules. His orders, according to local Saudi journalists who have spent long periods undercover in the slum, are always obeyed, and he solves all the local problems. A number of residents told the Saudi journalists that the tribal chief was a drug dealer, while others described him as a nice man who goes to the mosque every day. Perhaps he was both. Women meanwhile do all the buying and selling, spreading their wares along every street.

The slum in a southern district of Riyadh where an Irish cameraman was killed and a British BBC reporter was critically wounded in June 2004 by Islamic terrorists is also just a short drive from the bright neon lights, towering skyscrapers, gated royal palaces, and walled residential compounds of one of the world's wealthiest cities. But, as the impoverished epicenter of the kingdom's new Islamic insurgency, it is far from Riyadh's veneer of twenty-first-century modernity.

Nowhere else, apart from in Kerantina, is the shocking division between the haves and the have nots, the super rich and the new underclass, more apparent in Saudi Arabia than in the Al-Suwaidi district, which has a reputation for being a bastion of strict Wahhabism even among the other residents of the kingdom. The slum attracts a steady stream of villagers from the surrounding countryside in search of a better life in the city. The young men of the slum's families hardly need incitement to contrast their own lives with the opulence and indulgence of the Saudi princes and "infidel" Westerners just a few miles away.

Like the residents of Kerantina, the more than half-a-million people already crammed into the district live in a massive entanglement of narrow lanes, pot-holed roads, and open sewers, and suffer frequent power and water outages. Since they are the people most attracted by Al-Qaeda's call to rid the kingdom of corruption and decadence, the slum has predictably become fertile breeding ground for Islamic extremism. It is also a perfect environment for guerilla warfare. Freelance cameraman Simon Cumbers and BBC security correspondent Frank Gardner were easy targets, as the assailants were able to slip away undetected into the maze of back alleys within seconds of carrying out their attack.

Standing in these slums, it becomes apparent just how unsuitable the majlises given by the Al-Saud are when it comes to dealing with fundamental problems such as extreme poverty and massive unemployment among an underclass that is increasingly hostile to the very existence of their Saudi rulers.

Although the rougher parts of Al-Suwaidi, like the other slums on the edge of all of the kingdom's new urban centers, effectively becomes a police no-go area after dark, in the space of eight months it was the scene of at least two armed clashes between the Saudi security forces and suspected militants. When he was shot, Gardner was on his way with his cameraman to film the family home of Ibrahim Al-Rayyes, a terror suspect killed in a shootout with security forces in the slum the previous December. Al-Rayyes was on a list issued by authorities in December 2003 of the 26 most wanted militants, whose photos and names were splashed across the front pages of Saudi newspapers. An estimated 14 of the 26 other listed suspects either originally come from, or had recently moved to, Al-Suwaidi. More than half of them had graduated from the hard-line Imam Mohamed Bin Saud University, blamed for indoctrinating hatred of the West in the minds of its students— as, not coincidentally, did a number of the September 11 hijackers.

In the past, the Wahhabi religious establishment looked the other way as long as the youngsters carried out their jihad abroad—in Chechnya and Afghanistan, for instance. But now they are turning their attention to the home front. The combination of hard-line Islamic dogma, hatred of the West, poverty, and a perceived corrupt pro-Western ruling elite has created a monster in the very heart of the Al-Saud's third empire.

A surgeon and emergency room doctor at the King Fahd General Hospital in Jeddah, where the Indian grocery store assistant shot in the hand and leg was treated, told Saudi journalist Essam Al-Ghalib, who covered the story for *Arab News,* that he used to see one or two shooting incidents each month, most of them accidents, but now he sees the victims of up to seven stabbings and shootings a week. Doctors at Jeddah's King Abdul

Aziz Hospital similarly said they are treating a neverending stream of domestic and child abuse cases. One, according to Al-Ghalib, claimed that
wives with cigarette burns, broken bones, and cuts are being seen more
and more often. Ironically, husbands are the ones who come in with the
most serious injuries, a direct result, according to the doctor, of revenge
attacks by the families of the wives.

The Saudi authorities not only acknowledge that these problems exist,
but are even trying to reinvent their policing tactics to deal with them. The
kingdom has held conferences and published studies on child abuse, a previously taboo subject, and has opened a number of drug rehabilitation centers in its three major cities. Drug busts are now so common that they are
no longer guaranteed to make the front page. There is even an anti-drug
campaign running on national TV. Security forces announced in 2002 the
arrest of Saudi Arabia's biggest drug smuggling gang, along with the confis-
cation of 2,480 pounds of hashish and an unspecified number of firearms.
The number of people convicted for drug possession rose from 4,279 in
1986 to 17,199 in 2001, according to the latest published statistics, which
probably only reveal the tip of the iceberg.

In many other reported cases, mainly concerning Jeddah and Riyadh, a
number of drug-filled prayer beads and prayer rugs, and even opium stuffed
between the pages of the Qu'ran were seized by local customs officials from
"fake pilgrims." All this confirms a surge in demand for drugs and alcohol
in the local market, which has long been penetrated by international traf-
fickers. Many young Saudis relax with a joint after work, and students I
taught would casually say that if I wanted drugs they knew where to get
them. Society weddings see the segregated male and female guests sometimes swaying to the music in ecstasy-induced bliss. My Yemeni doorman,
apparently unconcerned about legal consequences, always spoke through a
mouthful of qat, a mild narcotic plant most Yemenis are addicted to.

The police, of course, have more pressing things to worry about than
plant-eating Yemenis. At least three districts of the capital city—Batha,
Olaya, and Badia—are today safe havens for alcohol and drug smugglers, as
is Kerantina in Jeddah; the main city on the Iraqi border in the al-Jouf region,
Arar; and Jizan near the Saudi-Yemeni border in the south. Such is the extent
of the problem that Saudi authorities were able to frame six Britons—released
in October 2002 after a royal clemency—for a series of bombings by saying
they were part of a feud over illicit alcohol trading. The men had been "convicted" after one Briton was killed in November 2000, and several other
Western expatriate workers were injured when their cars blew up. In 2002, a

Briton and a German were killed in what were said to be related bombings three months apart in Riyadh. Several more incidents followed. In 2003, a British man came under fire as he drove in Riyadh, and an Australian man was fired at while jogging in the southern garrison town of Khamis Mushayt. Not even the authorities tried to blame these last incidents on alcohol.

In fact, it is inconceivable that all these incidents—or for that matter, in many expatriates' eyes, any of them—could have been related to alcohol smuggling. But by pinning the blame in this way the Al-Saud was able to achieve two goals: reinforce the stereotype of the Westerner corrupting the local society with his decadent ways, and put off admitting to what later became the undeniable fact that these and other Westerners were being targeted by Al-Qaeda.

Heroin, hashish, and speed are the most commonly used drugs in Saudi Arabia, according to Maj. Gen. Sultan Al-Harithi, director general of the country's antinarcotics department. He has said that in the kingdom drugs are considered "a phenomenon, not a menace," perhaps an indication of nothing more than that there are limits to how much officials are willing to address the problem publicly. There are nevertheless officers responsible for curing and rehabilitating the addicts, and there are three specialist hospitals in Riyadh, Jeddah, and Dammam to treat addicts and reintegrate them back into mainstream society. They will never be questioned or punished, according to Al-Harithi, since they are the victims of a "malady."

In 2002, the general director of Saudi prisons, Lieutenant General Ali Hussein Al-Harithi, announced measures aimed at reducing the number of non-drug-related offenders serving sentences in overcrowded jails. Penalties, he told reporters, would be eased for petty crimes, and social work and fines would eventually replace jail terms. However, despite these public pronouncements, human rights organizations accuse Saudi Arabia of continuing to engage in arbitrary arrests, the torture of detainees, and the barring of prisoner access to family members or lawyers.

More than a year after Ali Al-Harithi made his remarks, there was still such massive prison overcrowding that more than 200 inmates and staff were killed or injured when a Riyadh jail caught fire. An investigation by the Qatar-based Al-Jazeera news organization quoted several sources who said it "threw light" on prison life in the Al-Hair prison and the conditions that might have led to the tragedy. The father of one dead inmate and a Saudi academic living in the kingdom talked about the "shocking conditions" inside the ill-fated prison. Risking persecution and incarceration by the Saudi authorities, both decided to speak out in the hope of improving conditions for surviving prisoners. In what was indeed a rare public criticism of the government by a national inside Saudi Arabia, the academic, Dr. Said Al-Zuair, told Al-Jazeera that ordinary Saudis have no confidence in the Interior Ministry. "We just don't trust it," he said in the week after the fire, adding that many of the prisoners that died were from "the poor and oppressed."

Al-Zuair criticized the injustice of imprisoning many without trial, legal representation, or indeed any semblance of justice. "Some inmates do not see the light of day or relatives for months at a time," he said.

As the kingdom gets ready to join the World Trade Organization, few Saudis—princes or commoners—seem to have grasped the extent to which entry is likely dramatically to increase poverty and unemployment, and thus undermine still further the traditional system of welfare and patronage—the bedrock of the Saudi state since its foundation.

Naively championed by Saudi reformers as a means of imposing, from outside, a series of binding agreements on the Al-Saud regime—affecting especially the legal system and business transparency—the WTO and IMF regulations will result in dramatic cuts in subsidies to key economic sectors, which will be privatized, and the phasing out of work contracts that guarantee civil servants especially a lifelong job with few demands. Increased internal competition, along with the opening up of vital sectors to international markets, will by default necessitate a more streamlined and efficient performance from workers and employees alike, and a dramatic reduction in the reliance on cheap foreign labor.

The IMF reported in 2002 the following recommendation regarding the management of Saudi Arabia's economy: cuts in government spending, the introduction of income tax for both expatriates and nationals, and the establishment of a timetable for privatizations. Each of these proposed changes comes with massive potential for instability. When the IMF encourages hard-pressed governments to cut back spending and downsize government departments, it usually means in practical terms a rise in unemployment and a cut in wages.

Cuts in government spending risk putting the brakes on an already-sluggish economy that relies on the state—not the private sector—for much of its momentum. Badly needed infrastructure projects might be delayed, and reductions in subsidies or the generous cradle-to-grave welfare system that Saudis have come to expect as their right would be inevitable—all of which will likewise inevitably lead to even higher levels of crime.

The United States has pushed through negotiations with Saudi Arabia, which has been quick to step up its efforts—at least officially—to create the trade guidelines and economic legislation required to join the WTO. More recently, though, the kingdom itself has made a series of unilateral moves to bring the economy into closer alignment with WTO standards, including on the crucial issue of insurance reform. (For decades the Al-Saud had told ordinary Saudis that insurance was religiously forbidden, because everything is willed by Allah.)

The feeling among proglobalization figures seems to be that Saudi membership would be a watershed event, a historically unprecedented move to diversify economies in the Middle East. But the rules of economic globalization—including free trade, deregulation, privatization, and structural adjustment—have, as many an antiglobalization campaigner would be just as quick to point out, destroyed the livelihoods of millions of people in the Third World, often leaving them homeless, landless, and hungry, while removing their access to even the most basic public services such as health and medical care, education, sanitation, fresh water, public transport, job training, and the like—all of which the Al-Saud had traditionally taken upon itself to provide for free as a way of buying the loyalty of its subjects.

Together, then, WTO- and IMF-imposed reforms would, if implemented as quickly and ruthlessly as their more erstwhile proponents would prefer, spell the end to the cradle-to-grave Saudi welfare state, the demise of which would be the biggest recruitment aid Al-Qaeda could pray for.

Chapter Eight

THE SEGREGATION OF THE SEXES

Shopping malls are a familiar destination the world over. While their primary function may be consumption—the purchase of various commodities, whether or not needed—they are also meeting points, not least for youths who have too much time on their hands and too little stimulation. At the mall, these youths are both away from their parents and yet in a relatively controlled environment.

The glass and marble shopping malls of Jeddah—which resemble any you would happen upon in any major American city, selling pretty much the same range of branded clothes and electrical items—are no different. They have long served as a meeting place for Saudi boys and girls, who slip each other bits of paper with their names and mobile-phone numbers scribbled on them. They do this surreptitiously, however: Nowhere else—not in the schools, not in clubs or the like—are they able to meet.

There is a fission of risk and rebellion, natural enough for youth exploring boundaries and new relationships, but here burdened with greater risk, not so much from parental disapproval, though in a conservative society that can be tough enough, as from the morality police who are arguably more feared than the parents: The morality police, should the sensibilities of its members be offended, can drag any young man or woman off to the local police station for questioning. Nevertheless, after chatting by phone, some of these male and female teenagers do meet up again in the family sections of the city malls' many Western-style restaurants, where mingling of the sexes is sometimes tolerated.

This, of course, is where differences begin between malls in the United States and those in Saudi Arabia. For all the apparent similarities between the social interaction at the mall, what sets Saudi Arabia apart is the efforts to keep the sexes segregated. There are, given the customs, understandable reasons for doing so. Honor is of crucial importance, and nowhere is protecting honor more important than in maintaining the purity of females, who are—to the Saudi male mentality—always temptresses, whether or not they seek to be, and vulnerable to the uncontrollable passions of males. It says something about attitudes toward both sexes that there is so little confidence in either's ability to negotiate what other societies consider normal, namely social interaction and friendships between members of opposite sexes. But given the implications of honor impugned or invaded, including "honor killings" or murders of women and girls whose actions, or asserted actions, offend family honor, and revenge attacks against either the male "responsible" or his family, segregation may in the end be if not necessarily for the best in Saudi Arabia then at least the most practical option.

Which is not to say that the effects are what the authorities might expect.

With desires dammed in one direction, they not surprisingly flow in another. Since Saudi Arabia's public sphere is overwhelmingly male—and in the Wahhabi heartland exclusively so—the holding of hands and even exchange of light kisses among men is considered normal, and carries no obvious homosexual connotations. But it is obvious, at the same time, that this is a world that prisoners or sailors in the West would easily recognize, as they, too, live in environments where enforced segregation from women forces men to turn to one another for comfort and sexual gratification.

So malls in Jeddah, as well as in Riyadh and Dammam, have predictably become the preferred haunts of another group: males seeking sex with other males. Unlike the boys and girls seeking to mix, they do not have to hide their intentions. Indeed, they stroll certain of the malls and supermarkets openly making passes at each other. They are dressed in variations on Western fashion that would, in America, be considered outrageously queer, but in Saudi Arabia raise eyebrows only among those who insist on "Islamic"— that is, Bedouin—dress at all times. These young men openly cruise, often exchanging comments in loud voices with their friends when a desirable object comes into view.

Even the dress codes of the boys has been altered as a response. In one mall, a Saudi I was with pointed out that all boys past puberty in Western clothes were wearing an untucked t-shirt or shirt that was long enough to completely cover their rears. When asked why, he replied: "They know what the older boys want from an early age, and if they show their ass it's a kind of advert." An openly "gay"—which is to say passive—boy, he went on, is treated by his peers with extreme lust and utter contempt by turns, indicating presumably nothing more than that schizophrenia is as evident when it comes to this subject as it is when it comes to every other one in Saudi Arabia. Ultimately, though, they inevitably try to bed him, the Saudi claimed. Doing so, being the "active" partner, is not seen as being homosexual. Rather, it is a confirmation of being a man, being superior and dominating other men. Power, that is, inheres in the act.

How much truth is there to such claims?

Ultimately, since there are no opinion polls or cultural surveys in Saudi Arabia, there is no way of knowing. But what is for sure is that gay and lesbian discos, gay-friendly coffee shops, and even gay-oriented Internet chat rooms are flourishing in the three big Saudi cities. In the chat rooms, gay and lesbian Saudis discuss the best places to meet people for one-night stands.

Traditionally, self-identified gays and lesbians openly declaring their sexual preferences would have lived in mortal fear in Saudi Arabia, and they are still viewed with absolute contempt by the vast majority of Saudi men. Homosexuality has long been illegal in the kingdom, and, in theory, the official punishment for sodomy is death. But the young population of the cities is mushrooming, and now includes many young Saudis who returned after September 11 from a lifetime abroad. These "returnees" combine the traditional Saudi tolerance (turning a blind eye to sex between males that, as in prisons, is not viewed as homosexual inherently but instead circumstantial and transient) with a more subversive attitude that homosexuality is part of an identity and, as such, has political components. As a result, a small, confused "gay community" is establishing a space for itself.

The number of gay-themed Saudi websites especially has exploded in recent years. Some of these sites are blocked by those responsible for censoring the Internet, but software to avoid the blocks is easily purchased in local markets. Most sites exist for one reason only: to facilitate meet-ups. Even gay pornography is freely available to anyone who has a satellite dish in their bedroom, which is to say all middle-class Saudi boys. An illegal card on the black market costs only about $2, and gives unrestricted access to XXL—a hardcore sex channel that features a gay sex night once a week. It also beams in a channel called Gay TV. The cards, which are openly sold by Sudanese expatriates in the lanes behind the main supermarkets, often do not expire for a year or two, meaning that Saudi Arabia almost certainly offers the cheapest access to hardcore pornography anywhere in the world.

That fact gives some credence to the arguments of Islamic hard-liners, who complain that satellite dishes are responsible for a lowering of moral and cultural standards, and for the eradication of Islamic culture by the un-controlled import of "Western" licentiousness.

The Jeddah gay community frequents malls, supermarkets, restaurants, and a disco catering to gay men, the existence of which is an open secret. One Jeddah restaurant features young Filipinos plastered in makeup and ob-viously taking hormones, possibly in preparation for a sex-change operation. The young Saudis who eat there do so to try to pick up the waiters, not be-cause the food is especially good. At the disco, north of Jeddah, gay men gather each week to drink beer, itself an act in contravention of Islam, to dance together to Western music, and to introduce their partners to friends. Many of the disco-goers are young returnees from the United States, but there are also older Saudi businessmen who have lived in the kingdom for years, and Saudi princes.

One evening, the disco even featured two Saudi drag queens, who made a dramatic entrance onto the floor. The question everyone wanted answered was how they had managed to get there while in disguise: On the one hand, women are not allowed to drive, while on the other these two "women" could surely not have hailed a taxi on the street.

Without an official complaint from the government or from Saudi citi-zens, the religious police will not raid the disco. At first glance, this seems (to say the least) a somewhat strange and paradoxical situation, since the very same religious police go ballistic even at the hint of a boy looking at a girl who is not his direct relative. But here again the only explanation is in-deed that there exists a fundamental paradox, in the sense that everyone in Saudi Arabia (including the religious police) seems to be in agreement that boys going with boys is an inevitable consequence of keeping girls pure until they are married, and in that sense a worthwhile trade-off—however much the gay behavior may itself, when it actually becomes an issue, con-travene Islamic laws. The trick seems to be not to mention the subject, not to acknowledge its existence, and therefore not deal with it as an aspect of reality.

Such a state of denial leaves a great deal of space for personal freedoms, even in public. In a crowded local fast-food restaurant in Jeddah, three mid-dle-aged Saudis called over a group of feminine Filipino men who were about to leave. They said something flirtatious, and exchanged phone numbers. When I asked the (straight) Saudi I was sitting with what the religious police would have to say if they witnessed such antics, he was outraged— not at what we had seen, but that I should even raise the subject as an issue. "They are men talking to other men," he declared. "And so it is not anybody else's business."

This, it needs to be pointed out, was a stunning statement. A similar statement about men talking to women would, of course, be impossible. And given the close watch the religious police keep on social mores, the open display of desire by Saudi men for one another could readily be cause for a crackdown should the authorities so decide.

"I don't feel oppressed at all," one self-identified gay man, a 23-year-old returnee from the United States, nonetheless told me at a meeting in a coffee shop with a group of gay Saudi friends, all dressed in Western clothes and speaking fluent English. "We have more freedom here than straight couples. After all, they can't kiss in public like we can, or stroll down the street holding one another's hand."

He was right: It is the kind of behavior that raises no eyebrows in the kingdom, which generally hates homosexuality, but only when it is defined and made an issue of. Otherwise, everyone is content to exist in a state of denial, just as they can state that prostitution is nonexistent as they visit prostitutes and just as they state that Islam treats all Muslims as equals as they casually exploit foreign Muslims because they happen to be from South Asia.

Some gay returnees arrive with dreams of establishing a Western-style "gay rights" movement. One gay Saudi went so far as to call, privately, for gay Saudis' right to marry one another, and even faxed off a letter to Amnesty International in protest at his young Filipino lover being arrested.

Such demands, while understandable on the personal level, are doubly absurd in Saudi Arabia on the practical one. First, no one has any rights in Saudi Arabia: it is not a democratic country founded on any notion of the freedom of the individual; instead, it is a second-rate totalitarian regime incorporating some primitive feudal traditions. Heterosexual males enjoy no greater "rights" than women and gays. That is to say, the differences in freedom flow not from government-issued rights, but from more-or-less established privileges.

Demands for gay liberation are also nonsensical in a second, and more immediately practical, respect: in many ways Saudi Arabia is a social environment that is very accommodating to homosexuality, as long as homosexuals keep things relatively private and leave all the gay rights rhetoric back in the closet—as many of the returnees realize after a few months in the kingdom. For, away from the self-consciously "gay" subculture, homosexuality is almost as ubiquitous in Saudi Arabia as the wearing of long white robes.

One Friday night traffic came to a standstill at a main junction in Jeddah when drivers queued and jostled to snatch a look at a particularly beautiful young Filipino, who was strutting his stuff on the sidewalk in tight jeans and a cut-off t-shirt. They honked their horns. They screamed at him through the window to get in. They showed no shame whatsoever. The drivers stopping for a closer look were not obviously "gay." Indeed, far from it. Many wore the traditional *thobe,* sported a beard, and drove what were clearly their family vehicles—large SUVs, sometimes with blacked-out passenger windows to shield their women from prying eyes.

Most male Western expatriates between the ages of 20 and 50 have experienced being propositioned by respectable-looking Saudi men in such cars, at any time of the day or night, quite openly and usually very, very persistently. One anecdote has it that Westerners who go jogging find that cars often slow down on the road beside them, as a young Saudi man dangles a bunch of bananas out of the window in a crudely symbolic display of his intentions.

Problems arise when homosexuality does become an issue, after being brought out of the closet. Then gays become perfect victims for a classic witch hunt, as became apparent in May 2001 in Cairo when several hundred police descended on a floating discotheque on the Nile, the Queen Boat, which was allegedly holding an informal gay night. The police selectively arrested Egyptians, leaving undisturbed several male foreign tourists who were enjoying the dance.

The 52 detained men (35 arrested on the boat and 17 from other areas of Cairo) were subjected to torture, and some were badly beaten. Even the youngest, only 15 and who was not at the disco when he was arrested, told a journalist he had been beaten with a "falaka"—a thick stick—across the legs and feet. This instrument of torture frequently leaves its victims unable to walk for days.

Within a week, several Egyptian national newspapers had published a list of all those arrested, together with their photographs and places of employment. The press also accused them of practicing devil worship, being funded by foreigners, having links with Israel, and taking part in sex parties. These accusations, which somehow seemed to be related to one another, were leveled even before the trial had begun. The trial itself was sheer pandemonium, as families and relatives were denied entrance to the court and the morale of the prisoners slumped as they discovered they were to be tried before a State Security Court (originally set up to deal with cases of terrorism and espionage) with no right of appeal.

Egypt was in the middle of an economic recession at the time, and it was widely believed that the local dictator Hosni Mubarak was using the gay trials to divert public opinion. It is only a matter of time, perhaps, before those gay-defined Saudi youngsters find themselves in the same boat (as it were) as their fellow travelers across the Red Sea.

In a nonpolitical context, when the law mobilizes in Saudi Arabia, as it does infrequently (and, it seems, reluctantly), it does so only when the behavior has become so obvious that it is impossible for the religious police to continue turning a blind eye.

Late in 2003, Saudi authorities raided a house in the city of Medina and arrested dozens of what may have been "gay men." Apparently, the men had gathered to witness the wedding of a Saudi man and his Sudanese partner. But there again, conflicting reports muddied the waters. For a start, it would be normal practice for a man to stand in for the woman at the actual wedding ceremony, which like everything else is segregated. Subsequent reports also said that several men had "married" one another at the event. This suggested that something very visible was taking place on a large scale, and that it was the blatancy of the conduct—rather than the conduct itself—that had drawn the ire of the authorities.

The Saudi treatment of gay men received international attention when an Interior Ministry statement apparently reported in January 2002 that three men in the southern city of Abha had been "beheaded for homosexuality." The report provoked widespread condemnation from gay and human-rights groups in the West—and a swift clarification from an official at the Saudi embassy in Washington. Tariq Allegany, an embassy spokesman, said the three were in fact beheaded for raping boys. He said: "I would guess there's sodomy going on daily in Saudi Arabia, but we don't have executions for it all the time." Apparently, just every once in a while—and strictly when it is not consensual and therefore is prosecuted as rape.

Such nonchalance, coming from an official spokesman, was extraordinary. He was obviously addressing an American audience in English with comments that would never be reported back in Saudi Arabia itself in Arabic, a classic Saudi trait of saying one thing for the outside world and quite another—or nothing at all—about the same subject at home. However, a Riyadh-based Western diplomat who knew of the details of the case at the time confirmed that Allegany was right: the men were indeed beheaded for "rape."

In any case, when the Interior Ministry reported in August 2004 that three more men in Asir had been beheaded for the same crime, the statement that time round was clear to emphasize that the victim was a young boy—and that the crime for which the three were beheaded was specifically "rape." The punishment for rape—of a boy or a man or a woman—is indeed public execution by the sword, so in that sense there was nothing odd (by Saudi standards) about either of the group beheadings, although the fact that six men have been beheaded in Asir in the space of two years for raping young boys is a subject that might interest social anthropologists.

Some gay foreigners were deported in the 1990s, but no one in Saudi Arabia has ever been prosecuted for "being a homosexual." The concept just does not exist. However, periodically gay Westerners in the kingdom have been fired from Saudi companies where they were working. One long-term Western expatriate told me employers have told friends of his, "You have 24 hours to leave the kingdom, or we'll inform the authorities of your behavior."

But the authorities for the time being mostly look the other way. Riyadh even seems to have informed some of its officials to show tolerance when they comment on homosexuality.

Ibrahim bin Abdullah bin Ghaith, head of the religious police, acknowledged in 2002, in unusually tempered (but wholly negative) language, that there are gay Saudis. What is more, the kingdom's Internet Services Unit, which is responsible for blocking sites deemed "un-Islamic" or politically sensitive, unblocked access to one website's homepage for gay Saudi surfers after being bombarded with critical e-mails from the United States. Saudi Arabia seemed concerned about the bad publicity blocking the site would bring, according to A. S. Getenio, the manager of GayMiddleEast.com, a website devoted to homosexual issues in the Arab world.

At the same time, though, it is unwise to attribute too much design to anything the Saudi government does at any one time. What initially looks like a trend one day may seem like a fluke the next, depending on who makes what decision in the Byzantine command structures and warring internal factions of the regime. In the end, it could just be that the apparently liberal attitude of the head of the religious police might have been nothing more than his personal reluctance to discuss the issue with journalists.

Perhaps the most useful parallel for the kingdom's official treatment of the phenomenon is nineteenth-century England, prior to the trial of Oscar Wilde in 1895. There, too, a large number of men, many of them married, habitually engaged in sex with other men. Male brothels were widespread. More importantly, there existed, nurtured by the all-male boarding schools and universities, a pervasively homoerotic climate. Except in a small number of high-profile cases, the authorities turned a blind eye, partly because many members of the establishment had come up through the same schools and universities as those who engaged in gay practices. Many, indeed, continued to do the same when in positions of authority.

So long as such behavior was not spoken of publicly, or was spoken of only in coded language comprehensible to the initiated among a scholarly-literary elite, it did not subvert existing norms, and so was not perceived as a threat. At least in Saudi Arabia, no such coded language or gestures are needed, and there is no scholarly-literary elite. Again as in nineteenth-century England, the only real crime when it comes to this issue—as with many others—is getting caught.

In Saudi Arabia today, then, it is understood that same-sex relationships need not mean a loss of masculinity for those engaging in it. Similarly, in nineteenth-century England, great emphasis was placed on the manliness of such pursuits. Taking their cue from the Greek emphasis on athleticism, proponents of the cult of the young man would tend to argue that an all-male world made if anything more of a man out of a young man than the promiscuous mingling with women, which many of them felt had a polluting, emasculating influence. It was a man who spent too much time with women, rather than a young man who spent all his time around boys or men, who was suspect.

Wahhabism, too, sees women as in themselves seductive and essentially corrupt, so that the enforced segregation of the sexes is not merely a means of vouchsafing the purity of women but also a way of protecting men from emasculation. This may be one reason that present-day Saudi fathers, like their historical counterparts in the British ruling class, are happy to let their sons experience the same homoerotic education they themselves underwent in their time. While certainly not actively encouraging homosexual relations, they are clearly prepared to close their eyes to their existence and willing to perpetuate a system that makes them well-nigh inevitable.

It is practically impossible for a man to know what goes on between women in Saudi Arabia. Total segregation, as well as a welter of social taboos, mean that no man can see first-hand what happens between women behind closed doors. Nor can he ask the important questions which, even if he could, nobody would tell him the answers to. But there is plenty of anecdotal evidence that what is sauce for the goose is sauce for the gander, meaning that Saudi women and girls too, by being kept away from men, may turn to one another for sexual relationships, especially in their youth.

Carmen bin Laden, the sister-in-law of Osama bin Laden, recently published a book, *Inside the Kingdom,* which is a look at the life of the idle Saudi rich. In it, she tells stories of lesbian affairs among the kingdom's wealthy women—fueled, in her interpretation, by the enforced idleness that their exclusion from the public sphere brings with it. The Hijazi anthropologist Mai Yamani meanwhile has shown that all-female discos catering to rich Saudi women are often covers for lesbian get-togethers.

In 2002, two female reporters for the downmarket newspaper *Okaz*— the nearest the kingdom has to a yellow press—broke the taboo at home by writing a full-page report about lesbians in the kingdom. The article began with the "brave confessions of Laila," a woman in her thirties who recalled how, when she was 14 years old, she became deeply attracted to an aunt who was only a few months older than her. "I used to create any kind of excuse so I could get to my grandmother's house to meet my aunt," Laila was quoted as saying. "We would play bride and groom in the afternoon. It became a kind of addiction."

The Saudi gutter press affects a deeply conservative disapproval of anything that departs from strict "Islamic" norm, and under cover of such disapproval it is at liberty to report, at length and often fancifully, on what is usually translated as "deviance." The tension between prurience and condemnation, however, at times makes it less than clear whether the intent of such stories is to titillate or censure. To be on the safe side, this particular feature explained homosexual and lesbian behavior as addiction or mental illness, frequently with the help of a quote from one of the kingdom's surfeit of underemployed religious scholars.

The paper also justified the article with a reference to a Riyadh judge, one Ibrahim Al-Khudairi, who had called for a discussion of "female perversion." The paper reinforced the idea with a cartoon illustrating the article. An unveiled woman, blonde and bold, was shown in the foreground, while an image of the same women was seen in the background fully covered by a veil and in tears. The devil hovered between them, suggesting that to choose lesbianism was to descend into evil, pure and simple.

The authors first interviewed a gaggle of "sociologists and both male and female teachers" as this was, they said, "the best way of dealing with the matter."

One of them, a teacher identified only as Hanan, told the writers lesbian sex was "a very serious matter" in Saudi colleges. "One day a student came to me saying that she had seen two students in a shameful situation. I went out with her to see for myself," the indomitable Hanan told the paper, "and it was true." And she was in for another shock. "I was taken aback to hear one of the two girls tell me in a very impolite way: 'Just leave us alone to do what we're doing.'"

Manifa, another teacher, had observed "peculiar patterns of behavior" in the school toilets during breaks, and when she investigated found that four girls were up to some kind of sexual activity (the report was vague), and called them in for a meeting.

But, instead of mending their ways, she said, the girls simply moved to another school, presumably in order to carry on their affairs.

The report culminated with the story of L.S.N., described by *Okaz* as "the strangest case" because she identified herself as "a lesbian" and said she would never give up "the addiction."

"It started with a kind of love and mutual admiration between me and another girl in the first and second years of high school," she said. "It developed into a special relationship which continues to this day. Although she has now graduated from university, we still visit one another. In fact, we can't live without each other."

Sociologists interviewed by the paper said the best way to tackle the issue was through frank sex education in schools—aware, perhaps, that the kingdom's current policy of sweeping the matter under the carpet is doing nothing more than helping to keep it alive. All of them, without exception, spoke about lesbianism in entirely negative terms. It was said by a variety of experts to have both social and genetic causes.

Only Judge Al-Khudairi had a Wahhabi explanation: "Women are a seduction in themselves, and therefore also a temptation to their own sex."

Attitudes such as Al-Khudairi's are unfortunately all too common in Saudi Arabia, where women are hidden, constrained, and repressed. With men unable to control their urges while being uncertain and insecure, nothing is more threatening to the established order than a confident and successful woman.

Take, for example, Rania Al-Baz. In 2001, she created a stir by being the first female announcer on Saudi television, a pioneer in a country where zealots continue to believe that no circumstances justify a woman showing her face in public. Any woman who does show her face, in newspapers or elsewhere, is identified on Islamic websites as a prostitute and an infidel by self-appointed Islamic scholars, many barely out of their teens. Women are required to wear the abeyya—a neck-to-ankle black robe—and cover their hair with a black scarf. But many cover every inch of their bodies, even the face. In restaurants, banks, and other public places, women must enter and exit through special doors.

In contrast, Al-Baz's publicity photos from the time show a pretty woman with a slightly pinched mouth in a bright orange headscarf and matching makeup, the colors alone a provocation to hard-liners. It was not, however, her television appearances that put Al-Baz on the front pages in April 2004. And the photograph of her this time was not pretty. It had a washed-out, coarse quality that suggested it had been taken with a mobile phone—it was attributed to "hospital staff"—and showed the bruised, swollen, broken, and bleeding face of the unconscious announcer.

Her husband, the accompanying story said, had beaten her to within an inch of her life, and then dumped her at the gates of a private hospital in Jeddah before speeding off into the night. Al-Baz survived, but with 13 fractures to her face and a steel pin inserted in her nose to replace the ruined cartilage and allow her to breathe.

What had she done to provoke him?

The story, as Al-Baz told it, was that her husband, identified as a singer whose career was on the skids, had become incensed "when she answered the phone" and told her that this time she had gone too far. With the maid and their young son looking on helplessly, she had pleaded with her husband not to hit her, but he quickly pinned her to the floor anyway and started beating her. Later, she said, he stopped just long enough for her to say the *shahada*—the Muslim declaration of faith—and make her peace with God, "because," he said, "you are going to die."

He proceeded to slam her face repeatedly into the marble floor, until he thought she was dead. He then wrapped her in a blanket and bundled her insensible body into the trunk of his car, apparently to bury her along a quiet stretch of the beach.

Al-Baz says she woke up in the car and started moaning, and when her husband heard her he became frightened. Luckily for Al-Baz, he was driving along Tahlia Street, a main commercial center in Jeddah, at the time, and Bugshan private hospital was nearby. Hospital staff said the husband dragged her body to the main entrance and then ran away, saying she was an accident victim and he was going to "get others" before disappearing.

The husband, Muhammad Al-Fallatta, had beaten her before. By all accounts indeed he was a classic wife beater, having become increasingly frustrated when his career as a singer petered out just as Al-Baz's as a TV presenter was taking off. For nearly killing his wife, Al-Fallatta was sentenced to six months in prison and 300 lashes, but the wife forgave him when he had served three months, which meant under Islamic law that she had effectively opened the door to his cell, and he was let go.

The story dramatically blew the lid on the abuse of women, the public discussion of which had thus far been among Saudi Arabia's many social taboos. Such cases had been treated as "domestic cases," and rarely reported in the media. If they were, it was usually in the form of ill-documented, anecdotal stories quoting only the head of some police station saying the perpetrator—husband or father—was "mentally disturbed," the catch-all explanation for crime until recently in a "perfect Islamic society" where only insanity could officially account for any transgression.

But here was Al-Baz, a prominent Saudi woman, giving interviews from her hospital bed, allowing pictures to be taken that put the veracity of her account beyond doubt. In the outcry that followed, a significant number of Saudis, in the text messages and on the websites that constitute public debate, pointed out that Al-Fallatta was not a true Saudi—the surname suggests North African ancestry. No true—that is to say tribal—Saudi, the implication was, could do such a thing, and if the crime could please therefore conveniently be blamed on foreigners, we could all go back to "normal." But it did not work. The floodgates were open, and commentator after commentator in the newspapers pointed out that Al-Baz's case was not even the tip of the iceberg.

Jowhara Al-Anqari, a prominent member of the kingdom's newly formed National Human Rights Commission—a fig leaf most of whose directors happen to belong to the Saudi religious and political establishment—visited Al-Baz in the hospital, and the wife of Mecca governor Prince Abdul Majeed vowed to shoulder the entire cost of Al-Baz's treatment until she recovered.

Al-Baz continued to give plenty of fodder to all sides of the debate. Some were disappointed that she was not being tougher on her husband, others said she must have provoked Al-Fallatta and was now sorry. Her lawyer, perhaps sensibly, had wanted her to keep silent altogether until the case was decided. "She knew the story was going public, and she did not do that for publicity, she did it to help other women—because no man has the right to beat a woman," a male sympathizer declared.

While the debate was ongoing, France was busy expelling an Imam who had told a French magazine that Islam gave men precisely that right, especially if the woman had been unfaithful, though he did add they should not be beaten in the face. Many in the kingdom, alas, thought likewise. It is, incidentally, perhaps testimony to the unique confusion in the Saudi leadership that the religious police excised an article about the case by Saudi journalist Essam Al-Ghalib in *People* magazine before it hit the stands in the kingdom, despite the fact that it contained nothing that the same journalist had not written in the Saudi media itself.

That women should remain dependent on men, whether for the former's protection or the latter's power and pride, is evident in the Saudi refusal to allow women to drive. When in 1990 a group of women famously went for a drive, Prince Naif placated enraged clerics by saying the women had committed a "stupid act," rather like a teacher making peace by saying that an offending child had been stupid rather than wicked.

Oddly, when it comes to the issue of women's rights it is impossible not to give Naif some more credit. In 2001, he used his clout with the conservatives to push through separate picture identity cards for women. Previously, women were named, but not pictured, in their husbands' or fathers' ID, which deepened their dependence on them even in some situations where the presence of a legal guardian was not strictly required, simply because they had no independent means of identifying themselves—they had, in a word, no separate identity. The picture ID in principle changed all that, allowing women, for instance, to make purchases and appear in court on their own cognizance.

However, many reactionary judges refused to accept the cards, insisting that women appear fully veiled—and silent—before them in the presence of two witnesses to their identity. When this was brought to Naif's attention, he simply reminded people that the IDs were a legal form of identification and the law of the land required everyone to accept them. He may have been motivated by pragmatism rather than a desire to make the lives of women easier, but, even so, he had done more to improve the position of women than any number of reform-minded idealists. In fact, the biggest hurdle to their widespread acceptance turned out to be women themselves, who largely balked against getting the ID cards because the photographs on them would show their faces unveiled.

The immediate reason why the IDs could no longer be delayed was the massive fraud the old system gave rise to. Women were habitually cheated out of their inheritance. Nothing was easier than taking any veiled figure into a courthouse in the presence of two interested parties testifying she was so-and-so and was giving them power of attorney. The judiciary, while not actually colluding in this, certainly seemed not to go out of their way to prevent it. A Saudi lawyer speaks of one inheritance case involving some $120 million in which male claimants are alleged to have run off with their female relation's share with the help of impostors, false documents, and no photographs. Now, at least in theory, that would no longer be so easy, and as the more reactionary judges die out and acceptance of the new ID grows, there will be at least some safeguard and a measure of independence for women who own property. To qualify for an ID, a woman must be at least 22 and have the written consent of her guardian, as well as a letter from her employer if she is working. If she is not working, there is little perceived need for an ID.

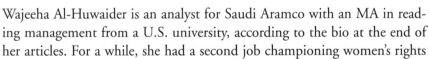

Wajeeha Al-Huwaider is an analyst for Saudi Aramco with an MA in reading management from a U.S. university, according to the bio at the end of her articles. For a while, she had a second job championing women's rights in her column in *Al-Watan* (in Arabic) and *Arab News* (in English), in her peculiar excitable style, until Crown Prince Abdullah gagged her with a telephone call to her editors. Instead of going quietly, however, Al-Huwaider went to where all the real debate in the kingdom goes on: the Internet.

On the British Arabic website *Elaf*, which deals with current events, she wrote an article titled "A Call to Arab Women: A Single Life is a Thousand

Times Better than Marriage to a Man in this Miserable East." She was responding to reports that the number of unmarried women who passed 30 years of age at the end of 2002 reached 1.8 million out of the nearly 7 million women in the country. In other words, close to one-third of the women in the kingdom are considered old maids, mostly because of the prohibitive cost for Saudi men, in terms of dowry and wedding expenses, to marry Saudi women.

Good news for the unmarried women, said Al-Huwaider.

"Most Arab men have been emasculated since they were young," she wrote. "They have no power to give, and therefore they are incapable of granting a respectable life to anyone."

From here Al-Huwaider embarked, together with her female readers, on an extraordinary journey around the Arab countries, beginning with Saudi Arabia. According to Al-Huwaider, Saudi men are afflicted by an "impotence complex," spending more on impotence drugs than men anywhere else in the world in a desperate effort to regain their masculinity. These "pathetic" men need to lord it over women in order to feel complete or intact. "They are afflicted by a chronic germ that has determined that guardianship (of a woman) is a sign of masculinity, and that without it their limbs will not be in balance. . . ."

Therefore, Al-Huwaider's advice to women is that "there is nothing that should arouse in you the feeling of shame at being single, or regret about the years of solitude. The land of the Arabs is full of men who are losers, men who are not worthy of you or of your status."

However polemically, Al-Huwaider points to a stereotype that is perhaps not entirely unfounded, of the brittle pride that afflicts many Arab men, forever bristling at some slight, real or imagined. That, of course, is the definition of an inferiority complex. And the inferiority complex of Arab men is being fed daily, not least by pictures showing the sexual abuse of Iraqi prisoners and an endless stream of reports highlighting the impotence of the Palestinians in the face of Israeli oppression—alas, the single galvanizing issue that holds the Arab world together.

In the end Saudi women, Al-Huwaider wrote, have only themselves to blame for their bondage. "Most of the women in the Gulf states are opposed to an improvement in their conditions. The women complain about the fact that society denies them the right to decide, whether it's a decision about whom to marry or agreement to have lifesaving surgery done. They naively believe that society will grant them these rights without a specific demand on their part. Women will continue to be the dead half of society as long as

they run after the newest products of cosmetics companies or the latest fashion in clothing."

Saudi women have in fact made significant advances over the past few
decades, although always within defined limits, and at times seemingly
apologetically. In March 2004, a five-member delegation of Saudi women
scientists visited India to "shatter the myth" surrounding women in Saudi
Arabia. It was headed by Dr. Samheera Al-Abdullah, the dean of the drug
monitoring unit at King Abdul Aziz University in Jeddah. Marking International Woman's Day, they attended a conference titled "Women in Sci-
ence: Is the Glass Ceiling Disappearing?"

The Saudi visitors were said to be bent on challenging the perception
that they are treated as second-class citizens at home. Unfortunately, their
approach was entirely defensive. When she was told of the marital abuse
a large number of Indian women are subject to—from being psychologically tormented to being burnt to death—Dr. Hana Al-Nuaim, the head
of computer sciences at King Abdul Aziz University, complacently sighed:
"Compared to the abuse they face, I think we are living in heaven at
home."

Weeks later, Rania Al-Baz's story broke.

While the Saudis attending the event in India acknowledged that Arab
women have made little progress politically, they were super quick to point
out that the West also has residual difficulties in this area. "Even the United
States has not had a woman president so far," one delegate said.

When confronted with the image of Saudi women as oppressed—as evidenced by the need for a male guardian in all manner of official transactions
and the fact that they are not allowed to drive—the Saudi delegation insisted
things were changing. "Over the past decade, we have become more visible
in various professional fields," said Maha H. Al-Qunaibit, an assistant professor in chemistry from Riyadh.

Delegates denied, too, that this progress was due to international pressure on Saudi society, saying that if Saudi women had not pushed for their
rights, Western pressure would have had no effect. In the climate of intense anti-American sentiment in Saudi Arabia after September 11, it is
certainly true that any association with U.S.-inspired "reform"—whether
it is related to feminism or anything else—is fast becoming a hindrance
rather than a help.

Inevitably, they were confronted with the abeyya question. Al-Qunaibit dodged it, saying "even Saudi men" adhered to a dress code. "The dress-design developed primarily because of the weather conditions, and now it has become a part of our tradition and identity," she said.

The topic of the abeyya will not go away, and even as more and more of the privileged women who find themselves interviewed for the international press say that it is not the issue, there is a real possibility that it is at least a substantial part of it. There is no doubt that the dress code developed as part of Bedouin culture. In the modern cities, women constantly stumble on steps, and the press reports traffic accident after traffic accident caused directly or indirectly by abeyyas, often of women who are run over at night because they are difficult to see in the dark. Perhaps, one commentator suggested, they should wear reflector strips on their robes? It is unclear if he was being sarcastic.

"I don't think the abeyya is an issue in our country," said Samar Fatani, a local radio host. "We really value our Islamic traditions. And Saudi Arabia has a special place in the Muslim world, so I think as Muslims we need to set an example. There is no debate over that issue."

Fatani's comments came only weeks after she had attended the Jeddah Economic Forum in Jeddah in early 2004, where the abeyya unfortunately was one of the most controversial issues, at least in the eyes of the reactionary male participants. A number of women set off a political and social storm when they shed their abeyyas and scarves and wore contemporary clothes. The women, who mingled freely with the men attending the conference, were there with the blessing of the Saudi government, which sponsored the event.

But they spurred an angry edict from the grand mufti condemning the female participants and saying women should adhere to stricter standards of modesty—such intermingling would lead to "catastrophe," he said. This was taken up a while later when one of the Imams of the grand mosque in Mecca, Abdul Rahman Al-Sudeis, singled out women as he recited a catalogue of sins responsible for a drought the kingdom was experiencing. Their sins, he said, included "unveiling, mingling with men, and being indifferent to the hijab."

Al-Sudeis and the grand mufti are pillars of the Wahhabi establishment and were only saying what would be expected of them. Nonetheless, as a result of their outrage, editors in chief of the local newspapers were told by the Ministry of Information to go easy on women's rights for a while. But then Rania Al-Baz's story broke, and women's issues showed themselves to be as uncontrollable as a balloon that, squeezed in one place, will bulge in another.

King Fahd's wife, Princess Al-Jowhara bint Ibrahim Al-Ibrahim, was, also early in 2004, reported to be a "champion" of women's rights. In a festive hall at the royal palace, she hosted a reception to discuss women's needs at King Saud University, the largest and oldest of a mere eight universities in Saudi Arabia. Surrounded by more than 100 lecturers and professors, all of them women, the princess listened as her guests outlined how her grants of $12 million have been spent or allocated at the Riyadh-based university.

"We have our own traditions, but they do not prevent women seeking education," the princess said. "At the start of the reception," journalist Mona Megall wrote in an article on the event, "some of the guests stood up to thank their publicity-shy benefactress for her backing for female education at their university while others lobbied for new projects. Princess Al-Jowhara, the recipient of an honorary doctorate, has frequently urged Saudi women in private gatherings and at graduation ceremonies to take advantage of the higher education programs that were not available in her youth."

There was also an important caveat: the princess "has also called on women to put their education to use, as long as they remained within the bounds of tradition and respected the moral code of Islam."

So far, so good.

But Megall also reported that "the soft-spoken princess" liked to be addressed as "Umm Abdul Aziz." "Umm" means "mother of," while the "Abdul Aziz" in the princess's name is her son Prince Abdul Aziz bin Fahd, once briefly notorious as the richest teenager in the world. Only a few progressive women in the kingdom, mostly the highly educated and privileged, are known by their own name. Elsewhere, it is thought to bring shame on a Saudi man if his wife's or daughter's name is uttered in public, and women are referred to as "Umm"—mother—of their first-born son or, if they are unmarried, they are not referred to at all.

The princess's call for women to put their education to use "as long as they remained within the bounds of tradition and respected the moral code of Islam" is Saudi Arabia's favorite room-emptier. It means effectively that whatever the received wisdom—and that means the wisdom of the Wahhabi establishment—deems "the moral code of Islam" applies, and any further debate is unnecessary. It pays mere lip service to a concept—women's rights, human rights, political participation—while implying that nothing is going to change. Both so-called reformists and conservatives use this godsend of a phrase "within the limits set by Islam" to avoid either sticking their neck out or doing anything to bring about tangible improvements.

The princess concluded by saying that a suitable field for women to find gainful employment in was nursing.

Only a few months later, after the wife abuse debate had made the subject appear in a very different light, this softly spoken champion of women's rights shrilly berated "liberated" women.

"Islam's enemies and the fainthearted women who follow in their footsteps," she said at yet another university function, "do not tire of waging war against our Muslim traditions, trying to incite Muslim women to shed these norms on grounds that they restrict their freedom."

The princess perhaps thought that the debate had gone too far.

On the opposite end of the spectrum, too, some were baffled. One of them was Sheikha Altakhafi, a writer based, like Al-Huwaider, in the Eastern Province. "I am amazed at the sudden gush of liberal sentiment in the media," she wrote in *Arab News* in March 2004. "For centuries women in our society were marginalized and denied the right to represent their case or claim to have one. The principle was that we were the perfect society, period. . . . However, some of the hypocritical Western media have targeted Saudi Arabia, exposing the poor conditions of women in the country, as if it were a sudden discovery and not a natural result of lack of civil liberties. Do we owe this awakening to the terrorist attacks of September 11, the invasions of Afghanistan and Iraq, and most recently the savage bombings of civilians' homes in Riyadh? Unfortunately, the answer to all is yes."

Altakhafi scoffed at women like those who attended the academic delegation to India, "sent abroad in SOS missions to salvage our damaged reputation and polish our tarnished image." She was also scathing about privileged women who try to minimize the severity and deep-rooted nature of discrimination against women by blaming it on the failure of "extremists" to understand "the fundamentals of our great religion and its humane message." These women, Altakhafi concluded, do not "represent women in this country or even echo their slightest concerns. It is unwise to put words in our mouths and defend a way of life that not every woman here chooses. Restrictions rarely apply to women of wealth and status, and good readers of history know that fundamental changes are championed by the less fortunate segments of the society."

That was the last article Sheikha Altakhafi ever published in *Arab News*. She spoke honestly about some ugly truths, and nothing in the Saudi media is such a challenge as plain honesty, especially if it is directed at the upper-class section of Saudi society that dominates the media industry and in this instance included the wife of the editor in chief.

The reality is that, in stark contrast to the rest of the Gulf, Saudi society, even after the turn of the twenty-first century, was if anything moving ever nearer toward total social segregation of the sexes, as evidenced most obviously in the fact that the new skyscraper in Riyadh, the Kingdom Tower, has a women-only floor. And most women seem to prefer it that way. For instance, there was general relief in June 2004 when the Saudi cabinet decided to ban male staff from women's lingerie stores. Some women-only shops with blacked-out windows have existed in the kingdom's malls for a decade, but in many other stores for women it was still customary, until that cabinet decision was taken, to find male sales staff selling women's underclothes. *Al-Watan* reported a 70 percent increase in business at shops where saleswomen assisted women customers.

The only reliable research into women's lives, carried out in a methodical fashion, is from the Dubai-based NFO Middle East and Africa group, which in 2003 revealed that increasing numbers of Saudi women want to work (only 39 percent of all respondents readily agree that "a woman's place is in the home with her family," still a shockingly high figure by Western standards), and the job sectors they want to work in—outside the socially acceptable ones of nursing and teaching—include architecture, law, and private enterprise, which are only slowly opening up to women. The survey, somewhat predictably, found frustration among young women, but more strikingly identified a group of "Saudi feminists" (12 percent of the female population) who articulate in women's lib terms their belief that women should have more independence.

There are also, to return to Altakhafi's point, a thousand reasons why nobody knows what the underprivileged think in Saudi Arabia, or if they even know what to think themselves. It is commonplace, as Altakhafi says, that the elite in a totalitarian regime have little to complain about. Meanwhile, the millions of hostages that make up the bulk of the population to an extent internalize the propaganda they are fed. It is also true that such a system in the long run leads to intellectual bankruptcy among those who have to operate within its limits, and the bulk of Saudi intellectuals, both men and women, are so compromised that what they write and say is no reflection of anything that is being thought in private. At the same time, the spectrum of available opinions is bound to atrophy for want of stimulus when there is no public debate of any sophistication, and as a result some may actually hold the opinions they profess to hold simply because they cannot imagine that alternatives exist.

What is known is that in Saudi Arabia depression is endemic, according to the hospitals, and the victims are all too often women. According to the head of the psychology unit at King Fahd Hospital, depression is the most likely problem to afflict women after years of abuse.

"Often they don't even know that anything is wrong with their lives," she has said. "They think it's normal."

She cited the starkly revealing case of a woman who complained to the hospital not because her husband was beating her, which he had been doing for years, but because on the last occasion he had beaten her with a slipper—a sign, of course, of utter contempt in Arab society. "There is very little the hospital can do," she said. "Mostly we tell them to take up a hobby so they don't think about their situation too much."

Hospitals list a catalog of indicators for spousal abuse, including "large families with multiple wives, little education, straightened economic circumstances, and insufficient familiarity with the true teachings of Islam"— circumstances that describe a majority of Saudi households in the twenty-first century. Mainly, the victims are poor, uneducated women. Literacy among women in the Arab world is 50 percent, and Saudi Arabia did not introduce education for girls, on a voluntary basis, until the 1960s, around the same time it abolished slavery. Both were the work of King Faisal—an elite private women's college in Jeddah that appears to wage a solitary battle against the Saudi curriculum is named after Faisal's wife, Queen Effat—during the brief thaw his reign represented. Now, however, the majority of graduates from the kingdom's universities are women.

More lurid stories about Saudi women find their way into the media. In February 2004, the local papers reported on a middle-aged widow who had been admitted to the hospital in a state of skeletal emaciation and continued to display an abnormal appetite, so that other patients were giving her their dinners after she had finished her own. The woman said she had for years been kept in a locked room by her family, her only human contact her sister, who sometimes did not come to see her for weeks. Her family, she said, had cheated her out of her inheritance, from both her parents and her husband, and were feeding her leftovers and fruit peel, a probable reason for the emaciation. The woman was clearly disturbed and neglected (one report said she "stank"), and the papers made no attempt to verify her story by contacting her family or neighbors. What could be verified, however, was that the hospital removed some gold jewelry which she had somehow managed to insert into her womb, apparently to prevent her family from taking the last of her belongings from her. She had fainted several times in the attempt, she reportedly said.

Such inhumane treatment of relatives is not rare, though mostly the victims appear to be a man's children from an earlier marriage. Divorced women usually have to resign themselves to a solitary, profoundly restricted life dependent on handouts from their own family or some form of alimony from their ex-husbands, who can stop it any time they like. The children stay with the husband. This creates particular problems for some Western women who marry Saudi men, generating "not-without-my-daughter"–style copy for a great many mid-market tabloids in the United States. Frequently not very well educated either, American women whose romance with a Saudi has gone sour throw themselves at the mercy of their embassy, which reluctantly negotiates on their behalf. In the vast majority of cases, they apparently extract some kind of promise of visitation rights, but the children stay with their father—with whom, in the understanding of most Saudi judges, they belong. Abductions by Saudi fathers in such cases, too, are commonplace, with both American women and Saudi fathers feeling that they are merely enforcing their God-given rights.

Some abused Saudi women are lucky to have access to rough justice: they send their brothers around to beat up their husband—though these things, too, can go wrong, and the prisons are full of brothers who got carried away. Women without brothers, or whose fathers have died or do not want them around, often put up with a husband's abuse because they have nowhere to go. It is a familiar story all over the Third World, and for that matter in much of the First. When hospitals see an abused woman in Saudi Arabia, they can make a report to Social Services and the police, who may act on it. But often they do not, or the case stalls as soon as it reaches a judge. Police tend to treat abuse as a "domestic" problem as they did until very recently in the West, and do not like to interfere. When the husband, who is also the woman's legal guardian, comes and signs the woman out, there rarely is anything the hospital can do to stop him. Of course, only the worst cases eventually get to hospital, since others may never be beaten hard enough to require emergency care.

Sometimes the woman's family can help. One husband went to the papers to complain that a hospital had performed an abortion on his wife without his consent. The hospital said it explained to the man that his wife's life was in danger, and still he refused to consent. The hospital then asked the woman's father, who agreed and signed his daughter out once the operation was done, and when the husband returned to the hospital he found his wife gone. The article did not say whether the woman was filing for a divorce, far less if she would get one. But at least she was still alive.

For ordinary Saudi women in predicaments as absurd as these, then, the abeyya probably does come fairly low down on their list of priorities. The essential thing for them is to be able to look after their own affairs without being at the mercy of a male guardian if they even want to leave the house, let alone travel. Those who can afford it, some say, frequently fake illnesses and travel abroad for treatment, for a brief respite from the restrictions at home.

Others are genuinely ill. Obesity is a huge problem in the kingdom, among women in particular, and recent attempts to introduce physical education in girls' schools hit a brick wall in the form of the religious establishment. Many of those unable to afford membership in a gym—a growing number as per capita income continues to shrink—resign themselves to a sedentary lifestyle and heart disease, exacerbated by the fact that eating is often the only pleasure available to them.

In a country without proper civic institutions, hospitals take on a disproportionate role as the only port of call for many of the distressed. Another such pivot of civil activity are the chambers of commerce. Almost insignificant in the West, in Saudi Arabia they are as important as the medieval guilds. And here, too, women are finding support. Again, this is not motivated by any idealism, but the leveling nature of commerce means that these bodies are increasingly gender-blind when it comes to their supreme purpose of helping their members to make money.

They found that the present system is not doing all it can to generate business. Some studies estimate the bank balance of Saudi women at more than $30 billion, which remains idle because of the massive restrictions on which businesses women can legally operate, and how. Women need to be represented by an agent in all their dealings, and opening a business is hampered by endless red tape. On discovering this, the chambers of commerce immediately became committed feminists and began badgering the government to remedy the situation. A number of chambers have now opened women's branches, and the Saudi Arabian General Investment Authority opened a one-stop investment window for women investors to make it easier for women to put their money to work.

The government, too, is beginning to see sense. The guess was that the numbers of Saudi businesswomen would grow by at least 200 percent during the five-year development plan that began in 2001. In June 2004, local media declared that the time when Saudi businesswomen in Riyadh were neglected had disappeared forever, now that more than 3,000 active businesswomen could benefit from the women's branch of the Riyadh Chamber of Commerce, the first of its kind in Saudi Arabia. It was the culmination of 10 years of demands by Saudi women to be recognized as a vital factor in the Saudi economy, after the Saudi government approved a nine-point plan to create more jobs and business opportunities for women in the kingdom.

The same month, Abdul Wahid Al-Humaid, Labor Ministry Under-Secretary for Planning Affairs, emphasized that all areas of work are open for Saudi women. Saudi Arabia lifted a ban that kept women from jobs in most fields by making a landmark decision allowing women to obtain commercial licenses. Previously, women could only open a business in the name of a male relative, and religious and social restrictions excluded them from all but a few professions, such as teaching and nursing. Some 55 percent of university graduates in the kingdom are females, but the overwhelming majority stayed at home because of the ban and a general lack of job opportunities. Only 5.5 percent out of some 4.7 million Saudi women of working age are employed. The cabinet also ordered government ministries and bodies to create jobs for women, and asked the chambers of commerce to form a committee for women to help train and find jobs for them in the private sector. It also decided that land will be allocated for the establishment of industrial projects to employ women.

But, alas, Al-Humaid's encouragement was appended with that classic Saudi room-emptier, "as long as the jobs do not conflict with the Islamic teachings and traditions of the society or lead to the mingling of men with women"—which, better translated into English, means as long as nothing really changes and everything stays the same.

"If the past and present are biased toward men," a Saudi economist has been quoted as saying, "the future will definitely be on the side of women."

That is too optimistic, but it is clear that in Saudi Arabia, as in China and elsewhere, economic liberalization must be relied on to spearhead political liberalization, and will help at least middle-class women achieve a form of independence. Majed Gharoub, a prominent lawyer and attorney, has said Islam granted women the right to own and manage their own business. "As long as women have the ability to run their own businesses, complying with Islamic regulations, I do not see any problem," he said.

There it is again, the caveat.

Women are finding in Islam, too, an ally in their struggle for greater freedom. It is perhaps a measure of the degree to which the Islamists have hijacked public debate in the Arab world that Islam is the only basis for any kind of intellectual (rather than economic) argument for progress available to women now. But if it was Islam that got them into this mess, it will perhaps be Islam that gets them out of it.

There is already a wave of women who have turned their backs on the largely ineffectual liberal arguments and embraced Islam with a vengeance, adopting the methods of their natural opponents, the ultraconservative religious fundamentalists. Those women—a cross section of doctors, businesswomen, professors, artists, housewives, and social workers—want to reach back to the ancient roots of Islamic law, viewing the Prophet's era as the golden age of women's rights. Before Muhammad, women on the Arabian Peninsula were considered chattel, inherited along with land or livestock. Some Saudi historians who are women now believe that the Prophet's own tribe initially opposed elevating their status. His favorite wife, Ayisha, led men in battle.

"It was as if she had absorbed all the principles of Islam that women should not sit back and do nothing if they see something that is unjust," one of those historians, Hatoon Ajwad Al-Fassi, a professor at King Saud University, has said. "At the time of the Prophet, laws were simple, direct, and were more accurate in terms of the spirit of Islam, freeing women from being demeaned."

She argues that the Prophet responded directly to women's grievances with revolutionary changes in property ownership and other laws. After women started to protest that too many Qu'ranic verses focused exclusively on male believers, more verses began to refer to women. The scholars have started to comb through Islamic texts to muster all the religious arguments that support greater rights for women, believing their strongest argument, perhaps, to be that women often petitioned the Prophet directly during his lifetime. They believe their efforts could serve as the basis for new laws, clearly not derived from the West, and, more important, to pare away what has developed as tradition over centuries of desert life.

Traditions, this argument implies, are not sacred. Only the Qu'ran and the Sunna are sacred. Saudis think they have the right to reinterpret them. But they should not be used as a weapon to exclude women from the public arena. That indeed is the crux of the matter: Wahhabism claims that interpretation is not allowable, as only the pure Islam is acceptable. That concessions and compromises with the modern world have been made is obvious. But the dominant interpretation of the Qu'ran and Sunna is intended as a weapon, and interpretation is a form of power—as is denying that interpretation. Whatever the hadiths used, and they clearly differ, it is the power of the men generally—and the clerical elite in particular—that is being both sustained and challenged by the status quo.

Perhaps it is only away from the political battlefield that real change is happening. In Jeddah, the daughters of wealthy businessmen, many of whom have spent at least some time abroad, help their boyfriends with their homework. "My girlfriend did this," one of my students told me proudly, handing in his take-home assignment.

His admission that he had a girlfriend was momentarily shocking; the shock that he admitted relying on her assistance was sustained. That the paper was infinitely better than anything he could have produced himself, on the other hand, was not all that much of a surprise. For the reality is that like many of the oppressed, Saudi women have to try more than twice as hard to be seen as half as good. Women may find that by thus proving themselves indispensable in a rapidly changing social environment, they will get where they want to be much faster than through open struggle.

Chapter Nine

WHO'S CENSORING WHOM?

In October 2002 an unprecedented letter of complaint appeared in *Asharq Al-Awsat*, a leading pan-Arab daily published in London exclusively with Saudi funding, a fact that minimizes the possibility of it ever publishing anything overtly critical of the Al-Saud and the Wahhabi religious establishment. Wrote the kingdom's former intelligence chief, Prince Turki Al-Faisal, then in political limbo but now the Saudi ambassador to London: "I read my article published by your newspaper on September 18, which was translated from an article I wrote in *The Washington Post* . . . and I was appalled by . . . the deletion of some sentences from the original text."

Sentences deleted from the *Washington Post* article included a striking one that celebrated the abolition of the Wahhabi-controlled Presidency for Girls' Education following a Mecca school fire the previous March, in which 15 girls had died after the religious police refused to let male passersby rescue them as they were not direct relatives. *Asharq Al-Awsat*'s deletion of these sentences took on an air of unintended irony, as elsewhere in the article the liberal-minded Turki had tried to emphasize that there was a new freedom in the kingdom's press (information that was included in the *Asharq Al-Awsat* translation).

Saudis well-enough educated to have read the original article in English on the web, and then the censored article in Arabic the following day in *Asharq Al-Awsat*, were outraged. Why, they asked, if Americans are allowed to read what Saudi officials say about our country, are we forbidden from doing so?

The shortest answer to that question is that there has always been a marked difference between what Saudi officials say abroad and what they think suitable for domestic consumption, in the same way that there has been a difference in the hedonistic and wanton way many Saudis behave in the West and the highly reserved way they behave back in Riyadh or Jeddah. In a strange inversion of the saying that dirty laundry should not be hung out in public, or that internal problems should not be discussed in the foreign media, Turki had gone public in the United States rather than Saudi Arabia. That he had claimed in the *Washington Post* that the Saudi press was freer than it had been previously was, of course, the real point of his op-ed. And the real irony was that *Asharq Al-Awsat* helped to undermine that argument in its truncated translation.

Most editors in Saudi Arabia, when pressed to say something—*anything*—on the record about the awful hand they have been dealt by the Al-Saud regime, tend to say that censorship is not only a question of government red lines but also of an unwillingness among editors themselves to take full advantage of the new freedoms they have been given. Such a construction, at first glance, is strange. That the government can set down "red lines," topics such as criticism of the ruling family or religious norms, should at the least be a subject of discomfort. That the government "grants" freedoms, likewise. But an admission that not all these freedoms are taken advantage of—well, that is bizarre. Except when one considers that what the government giveth it can taketh away, and editors, like all Saudi journalists, ultimately work at the whim of the government. So the editors' collective answer about where the blame for censorship and generally shoddy journalism lies is as true as any of the various other answers they might give.

There is, moreover, plenty of evidence to back it up.

Turki's comments left no doubt that it was the newspaper, and not Turki himself or the minions in the Ministry of Information, that had decided to act as censor. The actual censor himself was, according to an insider, a long-standing editor of *Ashraq Al-Awsat*. When I subsequently published a dispatch from Jeddah in *The Independent,* which discussed the widespread support enjoyed by London-based Saudi dissident Saad Al-Faqih among the kingdom's youth, I was told that it was the very same editor—rather than the Saudi Embassy in London, whose job it technically should have been, and where Turki is now based—who took it upon himself to telephone Crown Prince Abdullah's office in Riyadh to complain that I had "overstepped the mark."

Previously unaware of the article, Abdullah's secretary was left with no choice but to request a translation, a process which at the best of times amounts only to a crude summary of the main ideas. The resulting turmoil resulted in me being summoned for a dressing down by the representative of a concerned local official in Jeddah in the middle of the night, and being pressured to sign a letter that stated that I would never publish a similarly critical article again. I was saved from being put on the next flight out, I believe, only because a more logical summary of the article's contents by my own boss at *Arab News* was accepted by the powers that be.

As ever in Saudi Arabia, inside the media world and everywhere outside it, it was connections, and the personal nature of relationships, that led to the degree of influence needed to resolve the situation, rather than any laws or principles that may have existed (and that probably did not).

The *Washington Post* incident has broader implications than might at first seem apparent. An irony not lost on Saudi intellectuals, for instance, is that the average American reader of the quality U.S. press knows more about certain crucial developments in Saudi society then does the average Saudi. Among the issues widely covered in the American press but only sporadically dealt with in the media in Saudi Arabia: the on-going reform debate; historic balancing acts between the West and domestic constituents; the realities of Saudi economic development or the lack thereof; and even self-perceptions among Saudis themselves. While a debate has been raging in recent years in the United States about what is going to happen in the kingdom, the debate in the Saudi media itself has managed for the most part to be only a poor reflection of what is being said overseas. Indeed, Saudi writers often take their cue from articles published in American newspapers, regurgitating the arguments put forward in order to demolish them with immense patriotic and religious passion. It is acceptable for journalists in Saudi Arabia to repeat information revealed in the United States media that is otherwise censored at home, but the rule generally permits this only so long as it has the overriding intention of debunking the main criticisms raised.

The effects, however, have not been entirely what might have been hoped. For such articles have had the unintended effect of, if not developing the criticism exactly, then at least engaging with the arguments about the kingdom put forward by others. That, in turn, fed previously taboo criticism into the local Saudi discourse: a surreptitious way of entering into a controversial debate not uncommon in countries ruled by authoritarian regimes.

The bottom line, then, is that the only freedoms journalists in Saudi Arabia are ever going to be granted by the Al-Saud regime are those their editors fight for on their behalf, and—as many of the editors themselves admit—Saudi journalism needs one thing above all others: bolder editors.

Some, however, are in denial.

"The high rank of the government has started to respond to what the press publishes," the U.S.-educated editor of a main Arabic language daily told me in his Riyadh office. He believed Saudi media, following the September 11 attacks, was at the height of a "Prague Spring," in reference to Czechoslovakia's brief period of liberal reforms crushed by the Soviet army in 1968. "We are proud that many of the issues we have raised have afterward been adopted as government policy," he added, without giving specific examples.

Either he had been deluding himself that evening, or he was exaggerating for my benefit, because the following year he himself was fired.

Having said that, many topics closed for discussion only a few years earlier were indeed suddenly fair game, and the period of openness was taken full advantage of by a small band of columnists writing for the more respectable Arabic-language dailies. The most striking of these topics was Saudi-born Osama bin Laden and his Al-Qaeda network. On strict orders from the Ministry of Information, they were almost completely unmentionable before the September 11 attacks; but afterward news about them screamed from the headlines, in the first clear indication that events were, for the first time in the history of Saudi Arabia, threatening to overtake the Al-Saud. There were subtler calls for greater transparency in government and accountability. Islamic radicalism, and the need to reform an education system that breeds religious intolerance and subservience to authority, was brought out of obscurity. Corruption at home and extravagant spending by some wealthy Saudis abroad were tackled periodically. Mistreatment of the large number of immigrant workers was documented. Youth problems and mass unemployment were discussed daily, and women writers were allowed much greater freedom of expression.

Even the editors' sackings by the government, traditionally not publicly announced, were being covered.

After the *Al-Medina* daily in March 2002 carried an extraordinary full-page poem accusing the kingdom's Islamic judges of corruption, Prince Naif immediately ordered the dismissal of the newspaper's editor, Mohammed Al-Mukhtar Al-Fal. Abdullah Nasser Al-Fawzan, perhaps Saudi Arabia's best known and certainly its most widely read columnist, blasted the self-imposed media black-out of the sacking. "By failing to publish the news of the editor's dismissal," he wrote in *Al-Watan*, "our media has proved that it remains a prisoner of its own weakness."

Idrees Al-Idrees, a gentle man in his sixties who is a veteran journalist and much-respected by his colleagues, could not agree more.

Al-Idrees is a cut above the rest. That is probably one reason why, despite his decades of experience, he had not managed to rise beyond the position of deputy editor at the Riyadh-based *Al-Jazirah* daily.

In an interview in Riyadh in 2002, he told me an anecdote.

Earlier that year, the Arar border crossing between Iraq and Saudi Arabia was set to reopen for trade, he recalled, and he got an independent source to confirm the story. He published it as an exclusive on the paper's front page, in advance of a statement from the official Saudi Press Agency—a government-funded organization responsible for establishing the guidelines for what can and cannot be reported in the local media, and from which editors take their cue when deciding whether to publish discussion on such "sensitive" topics.

"When someone from the Foreign Ministry called me afterward to inquire about our source," Al-Idrees stated, "I told him to mind his own business, and put the phone down on him."

"Is that on the record?" I asked.

"I'm telling you because I want you to print it," he confirmed, revealing that his commitment to getting out the truth, and pushing the traditional boundaries of censorship, had not been undermined by the incident.

I duly quoted him in an article on Saudi journalism for Reuters. Remarkably, he is still in his job, perhaps proving nothing more than his point that there is indeed some freedom to exploit if only editors are not too timid to take advantage of it.

Al-Idrees, moreover, has a track record of speaking his mind.

When he was managing editor of the literary/cultural *Al-Yamama* magazine 15 years earlier, he published a controversial, and still much-talked about, article titled "The Right That Was Given, but Never Taken." It argued that, because editors hold positions of privilege in Saudi Arabia, it inevitably made them a part of the establishment. They were therefore part of the problem rather than the solution when it came to advancing the cause of political liberalization.

Officials tell them to take the opportunity to discuss political and social issues, Al-Idrees still maintains, and the reason they on the whole still do not is that "they have huge salaries, high social status, and people sucking up to them all the time because they have a title. They are cowardly in that, after reaching a high position in life, they fear putting everything in jeopardy by rocking the boat."

Sadly, what Al-Idrees said is spot on.

While everyone knows that the main, overriding problem when it comes to censorship is a regime that fears that a genuinely free press might threaten social stability and its own legitimacy by homing in on the reality behind the facade of its supposedly benevolent rule over a united people, there is indeed an old media culture in Saudi Arabia that is also fundamentally against freedom. Because the editors are appointed by the government, they will always have one eye on what they think the government will like— a vicious, self-defeating circle. It means, in practical terms, that even if an editor kills a newspaper with his incompetence no one can touch him.

Inevitably, the Prague Spring that the sacked editor at the Arabic language daily spoke of, in relation to the Saudi media, was crushed. Readers realized anyway that, whatever scraps they were thrown by editors like Al-Idrees, their local newspapers would never measure up to what they could get from the foreign media. A longstanding joke among the young has it that the sports daily *Arriyadiyah* is the most popular newspaper in Saudi Arabia because it is the only one that prints the truth, and, for the most part, Saudis continue to be force-fed a diet of pro-government propaganda. It lies like a lump of lead in the stomach and results in the vast majority of the locals ignoring the press altogether.

Saudi newspapers therefore continue to experience a distribution crisis, with sales falling to record lows. While some papers regularly sold 120,000 copies in the 1980s, when the country's population was some 10 million, newspaper distribution today almost never exceeds that figure. That is despite the fact that the population has more than doubled. Although ultimately unreliable, as statistics of any kind are inside the kingdom, those available indicate that the Saudi share in the print media is 40 copies for every 1,000 citizens, a very modest figure.

Newspaper sales, of course, are in decline the world over, but one consequence of that in the West has been healthier competition, as different publications try to elevate the standard of their product to win the loyalty of readers. In Saudi Arabia, however, the princes and Saudi businessmen who own the dailies have enough money to continue bankrolling them, even if they do not sell a single copy. Since in Saudi Arabia the newspapers are privately owned, the goal is in theory to make the publications profitable. But for the majority of them, their main overriding purpose as products is not to generate either profits or debate, but rather to put out a carefully selected stream of pro-government nonsense. This serves an obvious purpose if the owner is a prince. If the owner is not, he at least gains access to the powerful by default.

Another explanation for the decline in sales in Saudi Arabia, again as elsewhere in the world, is the new and stiff competition from satellite television and the Internet. However, in Saudi Arabia there are related issues, such as the low standard of professional performance and the widespread corruption in the public and private sector—both phenomena throughout the Arab world. Saudi newspapers, that is to say, would not be in a position to compete with satellite television even if they were granted a level playing field, and the reason is that the latter has a more professional outlook and sophisticated grasp of world events. As the Saudi population becomes more educated and more aware of standards outside the kingdom, they are inevitably growing less willing to put up with the less-than-satisfactory products inside it.

The Saudi Journalists' Association, formed in 2003 among much fanfare as the first independent professional body in the kingdom, quickly appointed to its board—in what nobody but government officials even pretended was a democratic process, and even they had trouble passing it off as such—a gaggle of editors. This organization's emergence was interesting only in that it revealed the creation of an ostensibly autonomous, civil society, which was immediately coopted by the regime. Saudi editors are rarely journalists by training or inclination, and since most have only the worst interests of the profession at heart the association has become, predictably, the last body anyone would expect to look into any matters concerning the media.

It is in the interest of the editors themselves to fiddle with the circulation figures, and not merely from vanity. In a situation that is repeated throughout the Gulf, one daily newspaper in the kingdom sells advertising space on the basis of a circulation figure of 80,000. Its real circulation, though, as its new distribution manager confessed to me after being appointed in 2003 and making it his business to get to the bottom of the matter, is nearer 16,000. Half of those copies are taken by airlines. If returns and other free copies are also discounted, the reality is that only about 6,000 people regularly shell out their 50 cents to read it. There is no shame in such figures per se, although they should give pause to the large American readership who access the Gulf newspapers' websites every day in the deluded belief that what they read, however interesting, somehow represents public opinion in the region. Another reason to give pause on that score, incidentally, is the fact that more than 90 percent of the newspaper sub editors and journalists on every English-language daily in the Gulf are from the Indian subcontinent. At the Jeddah-based *Arab News,* the newspaper I worked for, sub editors were often amused to see columns of Middle East "experts"— Thomas Friedman, Daniel Pipes, and the like—quoting the newspaper's anonymous editorials because they seemingly reflected "a change in the Arab mindset." In fact, they were written by me, a British chap who lives in the south of France, and—when we were not available—by another British chap, who lives in the north of England.

The main reason, though, Gulf editors generally must keep circulation levels and everything else secret is that the companies that publish them expressly link editorial content to advertising revenue. They do so not in the way one would hope, and which is usually the case in the West, which is based on the assumption that a quality newspaper appealing to a large readership will inevitably attract more advertisers. Rather, they reverse the process, demanding of their editors that they do whatever it takes to make advertisers happy. The overall effect of such a policy is, almost needless to say, devastating, both for press freedom and responsible reporting.

As proof, we need look no further than Nabila Mahjoob, a veteran columnist at *Al-Medina* newspaper. She was suspended for over a month toward the end of 2004, and according to a report by her talented fellow Saudi journalist Maha Akheel, the reason was that she had written a column about corruption in one of Saudi Arabia's major financial institutions, in addition to criticizing its general manager. Although she did not name either the institution or the general manager, the manager himself, of course, knew who he was. He immediately contacted the newspaper and threatened to pull the institution's advertising deal if action was not taken against Mahjoob. The editor in chief of *Al-Medina,* the report said, simply panicked; the next day he informed the columnist, through an assistant, that her articles would not be published until further notice.

On any normal day, a third of the local pages of any English-language Gulf daily—from Kuwait to Riyadh to Dubai—are taken up by press releases from one advertiser or another. Out of earshot of their editors, sub editors on one of them floated the idea of going all the way—relaunching their publication as a free newspaper renamed *LG News,* for instance, after the aggressive Korean electronics giant that is considered by insiders to be the worst regional culprit. Another quarter of the space on the local pages is typically taken up by press releases from the various businesses and embassies that pay retainers—in the form of monthly stipends—to the newspapers' Indian and Pakistani reporters, too many of whom are essentially racketeers. They know that, at least this way, they will find a way of getting the stories in on a slow news day, and in the Gulf even when there is a terrorist incident it remains a slow news day.

Many of the Saudis who tried to get jobs as reporters on *Arab News* in Jeddah were post–September 11 returnees educated in the United States, who were as bewildered by life inside the kingdom as any foreigner, if not indeed more so since they were expected to fit in despite having more or less abandoned their traditional lifestyle and values for the hustle and bustle of whatever big American city they had relocated to. They were generally incapable of doing anything but visiting the local chamber of commerce or interviewing the vendors at places where pirated CDs were sold. Once in a blue moon, such articles could turn out to be amusing and informative, since they revealed a side of the local community not often reported on. But the fifth exposé on the subject in a month often proved the final nail in the coffin, and such reporters came and went in quick succession.

Other full-time reporters—with the exceptions of Essam Al-Ghalib, a fine journalist who became the first Saudi to enter war-torn Baghdad and then got a much-deserved break with CNN, and the Dammam bureau chief Saeed Haider, whose powerful exposés on the mistreatment of Third World immigrants went some way to getting *Arab News* its "liberal" reputation—either spoke no Arabic or, if they did, were incapable of writing stories in English. The core of the reporters were Indian expatriates who, during their decades inside the kingdom, had become so entangled in local businesses that they would not have known how to report genuine news if it pointed a gun at them and held them hostage at a residential compound for 24 hours, under threat of beheading if the advertising-related articles in their newspaper were not removed.

And why should they have?

For decades before the press finally opened up, they had been making good money—small fortunes, by Indian standards—by having absolutely nothing to say that could be of the remotest interest to their readers, while any real reporting would only have landed them in serious trouble.

Given such a media climate, the Indian sub editors at *Arab News* did not need to be told what was wanted or not wanted, and expended a great deal of their energy anticipating the editor's every wish—but even to the extent that they often even irritated the charming but embattled editor in chief by never taking the initiative to push the limits of what could be said.

Arab News's main Saudi columnist, Raid Qusti, was meanwhile an example of how the system could, within a short time, make establishment figures out of dissenters. Now a darling of rightwing U.S. newspapers and websites, which fail to understand that his agreement with them that Saudi Arabia is in many ways a basket case in no way indicates that he is in sympathy with any of the neoconservative policies they promote in regard to the Middle East, Raid was once known as a "one-trick pony" (or, as the local version had it, a "one-trick donkey") by his envious and much less talented Saudi colleagues in Jeddah for his insistence on trying "to change the mindset" of young Saudis on the subject of the segregation of the sexes. Week after week, in column after column, he would attack with genuine humor and spunk the way minds in the kingdom are closed to reason and persist in desert customs he thought highly inappropriate and inhibiting for life in the twenty-first century.

These columns were all the more striking because he was only 24 years old when he joined *Arab News,* and came from a poor family in the holy city in Mecca. Raid put in a full day's work, moreover, and juggled that with ferrying his sisters to and from work and school because his family could not afford a driver. He was much loved, and greatly helped, by every Westerner who came into contact with him, all of whom recognized that he was exceptionally gifted, while expressing their astonishment that he had such a solid work ethic. He clearly had the making to become a fine editor in chief at *Arab News* some day.

That potential was no more in evidence than when he was made Riyadh bureau chief of *Arab News,* despite having relatively little journalistic experience. Afterward, his tune began to change. There he was, suddenly attacking non-Saudi Muslims for littering in the Grand Mosque in Mecca, disturbing his devotions with their dirty Third World ways. The Indian sub editors wondered whether he had got religion; but they soon realized it was possible that he had merely had dinner with a prince.

Before he became Riyadh bureau chief, Raid had once complained in his column that, in Riyadh, he was forced to wear a tightly buttoned thobe and immaculately displayed headscarf, rather than the more casual attire he wore at home in Jeddah or Mecca. Now, based in Riyadh, word had it that he had embraced this stricter dress code with a vengeance, wearing the white head cloth usually preferred by middle-aged senior officials and smoking cigarillos while being at all times trailed by a servile Filipino reporter he had been involved in hiring.

In his columns he moved from berating Saudi youth to calling on them to stand "shoulder to shoulder" with their government, and said nothing was more important in these trying times than "national unity." This was from a columnist who, a few months earlier, had launched into a full-scale attack on the kingdom's tribal system as the root cause of all its problems, and who I had made myself censor out of fear for his own freedom and—more importantly—for my own.

He still called for a change in the Saudi mindset, and he was still a huge asset to *Arab News,* but he was now writing from a position within the liberal establishment that makes up the core of Crown Prince Abdullah's supporters, and that made all the difference in the world. Fittingly, in that respect, American journalists have taken to calling Raid "the liberal Saudi columnist" whenever they mention his name, in the same way that Saudi journalists are obliged to write "commander of the National Guard and Deputy Premier" whenever they refer in their own articles to the crown prince himself.

Hassan Tahsin, an Egyptian columnist, was a different kettle of fish altogether, and he proved harder to dislodge than Mount Sinai itself.

Tahsin lives in Cairo, and has long occupied a prime spot on the opinion page of *Arab News* with his column "Plain Speaking." Despite his sub editors' best efforts, that column remains a living testimony to Tahsin's profound ignorance of the world around him—or, rather, to the profound ignorance of the Egyptian journalists whose articles Tahsin apparently relies on for background. He has often combined his distorted world view with terrible, shocking abrasiveness, once going through a phase of attacking what he called "the damned Jew" (in a telephone conversation) so scurrilously that it was finally decided he was likely to be a cause of embarrassment for the newspaper. Instead of the column being spiked, however, it was only kept out of the print edition (which Tahsin never saw) for several weeks while remaining on the website, where of course it did the most damage.

This attempt by the powers that be not to hurt Tahsin's feelings and pride, though "honorable" strictly in the Arab sense of the term, was of course stupid and cripplingly counterproductive in its practical consequences, since a halfway measure is always twice as bad as taking no action at all.

Any attempt to push for the publication of a controversial report at *Arab News* would require the temperament of a terrier, and in such an office climate the Indian sub editors rarely needed to be told to keep their pages as free of potentially offending matter as they could, especially if it was of the kind that directly challenged the status quo rather than helped maintain it by denouncing terrorism.

One Indian editor, for example, spiked a story on the United Nations' Arab Development Report, arguably one of the most important stories for the region in 2003, on the grounds that it was "negative." Among other things, the report highlighted the woeful state of education, infrastructure, and political freedom in the region, including the fact that illiteracy among Arab women stands at 50 percent. Apparently, no instructions were given to suppress the report; the editor simply considered it the safe thing to do. So the story—which formed the basis of much debate throughout the region afterward—initially went unreported in the newspaper.

The Saudi editor in chief himself, possibly responding to complaints from friends or to readers' letters, eventually wrote a column championing the report's findings, but because he was sitting in Jeddah he made not a single mention of the report's central finding: the almost complete lack of press freedom in the media throughout the Arab world.

In effect, then, censorship in Saudi Arabia starts not with the Al-Saud but at the bottom, with the reporters and the columnists and page editors, each of whom anticipate any possible objection from the next level, all the way to the editor in chief second-guessing the Ministry of Information, and the ministry second-guessing the senior princes, who might promote the color white one day and the color black the next. It is a perfect system generated to create an environment in which even the best reporters and editors respond with a high level of paranoia, and rather rationally so, given the lack of clear guidelines (which itself is a highly effective way of creating control through uncertainty). This way, the senior princes can limit themselves to only occasional meetings with editors, during which they berate them for the few genuinely challenging articles that somehow manage to get through. In return for complying with all this, and minimizing the job of the government by making sure nothing truly controversial is published, the obsequious editors in chief are rewarded with massive salaries, frequent appearances in the Western media, and invitations to accompany their beloved crown prince on foreign trips, when they are given to filing three sentences of hail and praise about rulers, which is then combined with wire copy to produce a "dispatch."

Direct orders occasionally come through from the top, by way of a personal telephone call from someone high up in the Ministry of Information, to all of the editors, who find themselves out of a job the following day if they do not comply. On the eve of the first anniversary of the September 11 attacks, for example, editors were told not to print anything that could be interpreted as celebratory. On the day of a historic meeting between the Shiites and Crown Prince Abdullah, it was made clear that nothing about the event could be published, so sensitive was the issue of the rights of the minority Shiites in the aftermath of the war on Iraq. And, when a uniquely wonderful article by the Saudi Press Agency quoted Crown Prince Abdullah as saying George W. Bush goes to bed too early in the evening to see any news, and so should not be condemned too harshly for knowing nothing of Palestinian suffering or anything else that is happening in the world, it was spiked for the domestic media after having proved wonderful fodder for foreign columnists.

If, in the past, Saudis had no choice but to eat whatever they were served, now over 80 percent of the population have satellite TVs in their homes, and over 30 percent of Saudis have online access—numbers that are increasing by the day. While there are several satellite television channels based abroad, like Al-Arabiya, with its spookily rapid access to news of terror attacks, most of them (with the crucial exception of Qatar-based Al-Jazeera) are either owned by members of the Al-Saud or companies close to them, immediately canceling out the possibility of serious, penetrating criticism of Saudi Arabia.

Nonetheless, the emergence of modern technology has proved a decisive factor in the struggle between freedom of expression and censorship, and arguably the newspapers have now lost out altogether to a system of proliferating text messages on cell phones and websites that spread genuine news and wild rumors.

One evening, a call came from Ahmed, a young Saudi friend who would only hint over the tapped phone that he had "exciting news," but said that, if he could come to my home, he would be willing to share it. An hour later, settling down with the remote control for the satellite channels, he fiddled with the controls on the television so that CNN was replaced by Reform TV, a Saudi opposition channel beamed from Europe and run by Saad Al-Faqih—head of the main overseas-based Saudi opposition group, the London-based Movement for Islamic Reform in Arabia, which had started up that month.

"If you want to know what all the young Saudis are talking about, just watch this for an hour," declared Ahmed, a university student. He was experiencing something he understood to be a defining moment in the kingdom's history, in the sense that it was the first time a fierce critic of the Al-Saud had ever appeared on local television screens. He could not take his eyes from the screen, in a way that many in the West who remember watching their first TV program broadcast in color instead of back-and-white will easily be able to empathize with.

A tense, wiry 22-year-old, Ahmed was also wealthy and polite, and preferred speaking English to Arabic. He lived in a huge villa on Jeddah's outskirts near the airport. But he was, in some ways, like a caged animal, brittle with suppressed energy. Before September 11, he could go to the West once in a while to let his hair down. But now he thought—not altogether inaccurately—that much of the world instinctively viewed him and his fellow Saudis as potential terrorists. So his focus was on a life he realized would likely be spent mostly at home, and the idea filled him with horror.

CNN it was not, in terms of professionalism or sleekness; but that did not bother Ahmed. For three hours a day, Al-Faqih appeared live on Reform TV, taking phone calls and responding to faxes and e-mails. His bearded face, a symbol of piety, was guaranteed a wide audience. But no one could have anticipated just how popular he would become. Crowds of youngsters gathered together in the evenings to watch him. Ahmed wailed with delight that night as Al-Faqih called the Al-Saud princes thieves who should be beheaded instead of petty criminals. It was all just too wonderful to be true, he said, and all he could think about when the show was over was what Al-Faqih would dare to say the following evening.

After a decade in exile, in which he used every means of communication available at the time to promote his anti-Al-Saud agenda, Al-Faqih was finally able to talk to Saudis in the privacy of their homes. There he was, settling down to a cup of green tea with us in the heart of Jeddah and calling for an Islamic revolution. Small wonder Al-Faqih appealed so much to a generation reared on the tedious hailing and praising put out by the Iron-Curtain style Saudi TV, which shows Saudi princes meeting endless streams of visitors for hours at a stretch to the accompaniment of classical music.

Al-Faqih's TV show had started as a radio program, itself an offshoot of his website, and when the Al-Saud eventually blocked the satellite frequency it reverted again to a radio broadcast. "This regime survives on secrecy and hypocrisy," Al-Faqih has said. "With the radio we broke the barrier of secrecy and we created a means for people to speak not just to us, but to each other."

The extent of Al-Faqih's newfound influence became apparent in the fall of 2003, when his call for public demonstrations in Saudi Arabia at well-known mosques, listed on his radio station, brought his followers onto the streets throughout the kingdom, leading to hundreds of arrests. A massive and well-organized deployment of security forces kept many protesters away in Jeddah, where I watched as secret police filmed pedestrians near a mosque that was designated as the gathering place, and security officials in plainclothes recorded license plate numbers. In Riyadh, police vehicles blocked access to side streets leading to the designated mosque, and pedestrians were turned away from the immediate vicinity of several of the mosque entrances. Checkpoints were set up on a main road leading to the neighborhood, and the police stopped some cars.

The popularity of Al-Faqih's radio and television program—and of extremist web boards, come to that—is testimony to the hunger for open expression in the kingdom, rather than for any great thirst for a Taliban-style regime. But the slower reforms are implemented, including those allowing for greater freedom of expression, the more quickly the likes of Ahmed are throwing themselves into the arms of the radicals and extremists. Al-Faqih's highlighting of the lack of transparency in the Saudi system, corruption, poverty and a failure to implement Islamic law that allows also for the punishment of royalty all drew a huge response from such people. Desperate for a voice reflecting their concerns, the Saudis are gravitating toward such radicals as Al-Faqih, who basically wants to establish a Taliban-style state while giving people access to modern technology. His use of valid criticisms gains him support and advances his agenda, even though that agenda is inconsistent with liberalization or even the goals of many Saudis who are not liberals. His main selling point is that he, like all Islamic critics of the Al-Saud regime, criticizes the official Wahhabi religious establishment for being sellouts in legitimizing Al-Saud rule through their support.

By using an Internet phone service known as Paltalk, listeners could take part in the program and say what they liked, without risking arrest or harassment. Gradually, genuine callers started to give their full names and mobile phone numbers on air before launching into explicit criticism of the system, as if daring the government to track them down, while it was said that any caller who asked to remain anonymous and spoke in favor of the regime was probably from the secret police.

Reform TV was a huge blow to effective government censorship—until August 2003, that is, when it mysteriously went off the air, a fact Al-Faqih attributed to influence-peddling by the Al-Saud with a number of companies who helped beam it across the globe from "somewhere in Europe."

For a while, articles appeared in the local press damning the channel as "divisive" at a time of crisis, when "real patriots" should be concerned about "upholding the principles of national unity." There was certainly some truth in the accusations, but the articles—because they came from the government-controlled press—merely served to increase Al-Faqih's cult status. Ahmed at the time wanted radical democratic but peaceful change at home, and is the kind of citizen the government must win over as it takes on the Islamic extremists. But he and his friends were lapping up everything Reform TV had to offer, night after night. While it may have been, in the end, just empty gossip, that is all most government-controlled newspapers put out anyway, with their lurid stories of "large numbers" of foreigners being arrested for this or that vice or crime.

As Ahmed and I watched that evening, Reform TV talked about King Fahd's favorite son, Abdul Aziz, once the wealthiest teenager in the world. Al-Faqih said the prince had given a $120,000 tip after eating in a restaurant in Lebanon, and then fled the country after being exposed by Reform TV. An unnamed princess, one caller claimed, had flown to Europe for a $150,000 haircut. That such sums seem ridiculous speaks either to the wantonness of the royal family, if true, or, if false, of the ready willingness of Saudis to believe that their rulers are profligate and corrupt.

As the Al-Saud continues its genuine crackdown on Islamic militants, it has still not realized that Al-Faqih has opened up a reformist front that might ultimately prove more effective than the bullets and bombs of Al-Qaeda-inspired insurgents. Instead, they call him a terrorist who is conspiring to overthrow the royal family and replace it with a strict Islamic government acceptable to Osama bin Laden. In a dossier shared with officials in Washington and London, the Saudis sought to link Al-Faqih to a long list of suspected terrorists and accused him of inciting violence. Then they produced a new smear, contending that Al-Faqih took $1.2 million from an operative of Libyan leader Muammar Qaddafi to help arrange the assassination of Crown Prince Abdullah. Plotting sessions were allegedly arranged by Abdul Rahman Al-Amoudi, an American Muslim leader based in Northern Virginia who ran foul of the U.S. government and is now in jail. During the meetings, according to the Al-Saud, one Colonel Ishmael gave Al-Faqih $1.2 million for Faqih's broadcast activities and personal use.

At the final session in October 2003, they allege, Al-Faqih gave Ishmael the names of four radicals in Saudi Arabia who, he said, would carry out the assassination.

All of this was repeated verbatim in the local media, and is another good example of how the editors of Saudi Arabia's newspapers collude with the government without needing to be given clear instructions to do so.

The day the *New York Times* "broke" the story of the assassination plot, based on revelations from "unnamed officials" in Saudi Arabia and the United States, editors inside the kingdom were given to understand they could summarize it, and if they liked publish it big, once the crown prince's office had made certain cuts to the *New York Times* copy. One excision was the crucial denial of Qaddafi's son, who said Libya wanted regime change in Saudi Arabia, of course, but would not stoop to paying someone to assassinate the crown prince, especially not someone like Al-Amoudi, a shady operator who desperately needed a bargaining chip to get out of jail. Other cuts included the epithet "Saudi Arabia's de-facto ruler" to describe Abdullah, and similar minor details. Otherwise, the story was to go in full.

The more astutely political *Saudi Gazette* and the Arabic newspapers dutifully illustrated it with pictures of Al-Faqih and his alleged co-conspirator, Muhammad Al-Masaari, an even more extreme London-based dissident, who of course were the main reason the government was interested in getting the story out (though Qaddafi, too, has been highly successful in needling the Al-Saud).

Al-Faqih, who was a surgeon in Riyadh more than a decade earlier before he fled Saudi Arabia after being arrested and tortured for calling for reform, denies all the allegations, but increasingly inhabits a twilight world where the line between dissident and terrorist sympathizer—in Saudi Arabia, other despotic countries, and the United States—is increasingly being blurred beyond recognition. Since the September 11 attacks, he has become more influential, but also more of a target. One member of the royal family, he says, hired two local thugs who attempted to kidnap him from his doorstep in 2003.

"I can assure you that the Saudi regime is using every means possible to attack me," he has said. "They are bombarding the British authorities with false stories. And there are elements in the American administration who are conspiring with the Saudis to incriminate me."

All that is likely to be true, and it is these invariably unnamed people who then feed the stories to the American newspapers, which remain almost as willing as any Saudi newspaper to swallow what government flunkeys tell them, all on the condition that they not be identified.

To be sure, the kingdom's press has come a long way from the days when an editor in chief was jailed for a couple of weeks because a page editor let in a syndicated cartoon depicting God. But in the process it has acquired only the bare minimum of a culture of critical expression. That any news at all gets reported, and criticism of the Saudi system published, is almost entirely due to pressure from outside the newspapers, mainly to a rapidly growing society that is bulging out of control of the arthritic government grip and will be heard, no matter what.

If, on some days, the papers are worth reading, it is because of such forces sweeping the newspapers in their wake, not the newspapers leading from the front. Al-Faqih has taken on that motivating role.

Nor are Saudi Arabia's other media thriving. The appalling state of the education system, and in particular its outright hostility to the arts, have meant that all but a tiny fraction of books available in the kingdom are either textbooks for students or deal with Islam—the Saudi state ideology, that is, not the religion. What little Saudi fiction there is, by a handful of authors, is mostly unavailable in this cultural wasteland.

Two recent best-selling novels on Neelwafurat, an online bookstore based in Lebanon, are by Saudi authors. But *Cities of Salt,* by the late Abdul-Rahman Munif and *The Insane Asylum* by Ghazi Al-Gosaibi—the Saudi Minister of Water and Electricity, no less—are not available in Saudi bookstores. These books and other more recent ones by the country's most celebrated novelists, a tiny avant-garde group who often write in realistic detail about life in Saudi Arabia, are banned.

"It's amazing that Saudi Arabia has produced some of the finest writers in the Arab world, given the lack of support they get from their society and the government, and the unhealthy environment they are living in," Youssef Al-Dayni, a Saudi researcher who writes for the local press on literature and religious affairs, has said.

The success of Saudi novelists abroad is casting a fresh spotlight on the tension inside the kingdom between the Islamist state ideology and the principles of free speech. It also illuminates a more familiar divide, the gap between what is officially sanctioned and what is privately watched, read, or talked about behind closed doors. This split is what arguably says most about Saudi Arabia's failure as a cohesive society. It is not that people are in the dark or without opinions; far from it. If you talk to 10 different Saudis on the subject of, say, the education system, you will likely encounter at least three or four significantly different points of view. The problem is that there is no public space where such information and opinions can be shared, and that in any public forum there is an immediate requirement to pretend they do not exist. This reality is so pervasive that, as with everything else, it goes beyond hypocrisy and creates a double-think, verging on the schizophrenic.

Often, by the same token, what is acceptable when it originates outside the country is still taboo when it comes from inside.

Writer Abdo Khal, who has written five novels, has said in interviews with the international media that his books are not sold in Saudi Arabia because they "address the sacrosanct trio of taboos in the Arab world: sex, politics, and religion. But these are the things that make up people's lives."

Essentially, the novels are banned because the Al-Saud have hijacked Islam's most sacred shrines and the royal family's legitimacy rests on their conflation of religious with political credentials. The Al-Saud, that is to say, is held accountable by reactionary factions for upholding strict Islamist values.

But neither the bans nor the criticism are stopping some Saudi novelists.

Khal, an elementary school teacher, publishes overseas like other novelists. According to a report focusing on his and other novelists' plight, he paid a Lebanese publisher $3,000 in 1995 for 1,000 copies of his first novel and brought back a dozen himself to hand out to friends and newspaper critics. According to interviews in which he stated all of these facts with remarkable frankness, he now reportedly has a contract with an Arab publishing company based in Germany. It distributes his books to online bookstores, and physical bookstores in most other Arab countries. Novels by Saudi authors are gaining recognition abroad, and, despite the ban, are often circulated in the kingdom. When some Saudis return from Egypt or Lebanon, they bring in as many books as they can. Others are photocopied and passed around informally.

Mahmoud Trawri, a literary editor at *Al-Watan,* won the 2001 Sharjah Award for Arab Creativity for his first novel, *Maimouna,* a story of several generations of a family of African immigrants to Saudi Arabia, which touches on the racism they encountered and the role of local merchants in the slave trade. The Sharjah award, established in 1998 by the Emirate of Sharjah in the United Arab Emirates to promote literature and the arts in the region, also published 500 copies of the novel. Trawri told reporters he posted several chapters on literary websites and handed copies out to friends, who reviewed it in the local press. While such reviews are rarely of the first or even second order, they do raise a modicum of awareness of what one can do with language other than write poems celebrating members of the royal family or condemning the infidel.

Trawri also provided the Jeddah Literary Society with a copy, which was photocopied, handed out to about 20 members, and discussed in their book club in 2003. But when he received dozens of e-mails and phone calls from people wanting copies of *Maimouna,* he didn't have any left, and was upset at the realization that a writer in Saudi Arabia has to be a writer, publisher, and distributor all in one.

The schizophrenia of Saudi public life is nowhere more apparent than in the tug of war between officials like the reform-minded Prince Turki Al-Faisal, who has urged the media to act as a public watchdog, and those officials who sacked three editors in one year after they printed "unacceptable" material and continue to gag the few controversial columnists that have emerged. As in other aspects of Saudi life, everyone is engaged in a game of shadows, toe-ing imaginary lines. Saudi Arabia's efforts at total control, however, are forever undermined by hopeless incompetence throughout the system and by the whims of the personalities at the top.

The only clear victory for the Saudi press to date came after newspapers launched an unprecedented campaign for accountability after 15 girls died in a school fire in Mecca in March 2002. The religious police prevented male passers-by from rescuing the girls to prevent a mingling of the sexes. "The girls were killed by pure negligence," read the headline in *Okaz.* "Who is to blame?" asked the economic daily *Al-Eqtisadiah.* "There is something seriously wrong and it has to do with those responsible for girls' education," said *Al-Nadwah,* a Mecca-based daily that quoted a survivor as saying that, while the schoolgirls were dying behind locked gates, members of the religious police argued outside with firemen over their respective jurisdiction. Passers-by rushed to the scene with water buckets, but were blocked by the religious police.

One journalist renamed the committee "The Promotion of Death and the Prevention of Life" in his column. Eventually, the head of a religious institution given control of girls' education was forced to resign, the body was abolished, and its responsibilities were handed over to the Ministry of Education. For the first time in the history of Saudi journalism, a newspaper campaign had forced the removal of a senior official. Circulation hit record levels.

Then the Al-Saud told everyone to shut up, with a series of telephone calls from the Ministry of Information.

In Saudi Arabia, as in the United States, the war on terror has provided a convenient smokescreen behind which freedoms can be eroded, much more of a catastrophe for intellectuals in a country, of course, that allowed no freedoms to begin with. The religious police are once again a taboo subject, as are abuses in the kingdom's judicial system. The terror campaign did not bring a clear swing to the liberals, as had initially been predicted, but rather an attempt by the religious establishment to demarcate its own extremism against the extremism of the terrorists—a strategy that once again left the liberals high and dry.

Hardline religious figures feared that pressure was mounting to crowd them out of public life, and a statement issued by prominent clerics claimed that those they considered "extremist writers," meaning unbelievably the liberals themselves, were using terrorist incidents to attack the religious establishment. Sheik Abdul Aziz Al-Asheikh, the grand mufti, publicly rejected calls to dismantle the morality police. The reformers had been silenced, and in true Orwellian style the terms "extremism" and "moderation" were redefined.

In this sense, the Al-Saud has perhaps a unique ability to resist change, to move at once more slowly than expected and then finally to move, if at all, in all (from a logical Western point of view) the wrong directions, in a way that usefully keeps outsiders second-guessing as to what on earth is really going on and results in no real change being introduced at all.

The story of the new sleek and dissenting daily, *Al-Watan,* published by the Al-Faisal branch of the ruling family, and its battle with the religious police and their main supporter Prince Naif, is a perfect illustration of the arc Saudi Arabia's Prague Spring took before the tanks of the war on terror rolled in.

When *Al-Watan* appeared in 2000, it opened up territories previously closed altogether. The newspaper's logo was an arrow piercing a red line, symbolizing a willingness to transgress traditional boundaries. But its soon-unrivalled popularity had as much to do with its editorial professionalism and modern design as its relatively bolder handling of domestic and international issues.

It did not cross the line, for example, by criticizing the Al-Saud directly. But it was always hovering next to it.

Al-Watan also distinguished itself by not being defined by the region it was published in, which happened to be Asir in the southwest. All other newspapers in the kingdom have an almost exclusively regional readership.

Al-Watan's most famous former editor in chief, Jamal Khashoggi, a former colleague of mine at *Arab News,* lasted just a few months in the job.

Religious leaders issued a fatwa calling for a boycott of the daily after he launched a campaign against the religious police and was then fired from his position by Prince Naif. Khashoggi is no ordinary Saudi journalist. He has reported from Sudan, Afghanistan, Algeria, and Kuwait, and covered from the front lines a wide range of conflicts. He is also one of the few, perhaps in fact the only, Saudi editor in chief who has ever made it to the top by working up the ladder and gaining genuine journalistic experience, while never writing a single article of silly hail and praise about the Saudi royal family. He is an intelligent, conscientious journalist who cares deeply about the profession, and deeply about his country. He is also a very pious man, and very pro-American—even to the extent of having thrown his weight behind the U.S.-led war on Iraq. Predictably, he is widely considered by the conspiracy-minded Saudi public to have been bought off by the CIA, and he has no following inside the kingdom.

In the aftermath of the September 11 attacks, when Saudis entered an epoch of introspection, Khashoggi became a strong and outspoken advocate for tolerance and the shunning of extremism. When he landed his new job at *Al-Watan,* he wanted to introduce new ideas to the paper, in particular the positive effects of globalization. But when terrorism hit home in May 2003 and Saudis got a glimpse of its shocking realities, Khashoggi was enraged, and decided to do something about it. And so he launched his campaign against the God squad, alas with about as much subtlety as a bull in a china shop.

An op-ed piece in *Al-Watan* went too far: "The Individual and the Homeland are More Important than Ibn Taymiyya," by Khaled Al-Ghanami, attacked the teachings of the medieval Muslim jurist Ibn Taymiyya (1263–1328), which form some of the primary inspiration for Wahhabi Islam. An attack on him was effectively an attack on the Saudi-Wahhabi alliance. A "tacit understanding" reformers were said to have reached in earlier meetings with Crown Prince Abdullah, not to raise a "loud debate" for fear of an Islamist backlash, was broken.

After Naif sacked him, the Al-Faisals wrapped Khashoggi into a close hug and gave him a job as PR man at large with that other exile, Prince Turki, at the Saudi Embassy in London. Now another example of how "liberals" can be tamed by the Al-Saud, Khashoggi can be heard defending the regime he once set out to criticize, and within days of moving to London he was denying on the BBC that anyone has ever been tortured in Saudi Arabia, or that the Shiites are in fact persecuted. Having said that, he cannot be criticized too much for compromising—at least publicly and in the short term—on some of his principles, if that is indeed what he is doing, in order to save his career. It is easy—far too easy—for those who are not living under a series of death sentences and smears to mock the survival instincts of those who have to worry not only about their own safety but also their families'.

Unfortunately, journalists who did not enjoy the patronage of the liberal Al-Faisals were not so lucky.

In April 2004, the secret police arrested Saudi journalist Faris Hizam Al-Haribi, 27, in his house in Al-Khobar. There was no information on the charges, if any, brought against him. But he remained without access to family or a lawyer. Prior to his arrest, the Ministry of Information had executed an order by Crown Prince Abdullah permanently banning Al-Haribi from working as a journalist in and outside the kingdom. And the ministry ordered all Saudi media inside and outside the country to stop hiring or cooperating with Al-Haribi in any capacity, according to a report by the Saudi Institute.

Since May 2003, he had been a contributing reporter for *Asharq Al-Awsat,* best known for his frequent articles on terrorism and terrorist suspects, many of which apparently did not follow the strict guidelines set by the Saudi Press Agency. He was also working as a producer for a television youth show on Saudi-owned TV MBC based in Dubai. Two years earlier, when he was working with *Al-Watan,* Al-Haribi had spent three weeks in solitary confinement in a Dammam prison, arrested on the charge of stealing official documents after he reported the kingdom was pondering ending its financial support for the Arab League.

Dawood Al-Shirian, a moderate Islamist and the Gulf chief of *Al-Hayat* daily, a London-based publication funded by the Al-Saud, is yet another of the columnists whose writings fell victim to the promotion of "national unity" in the face of terrorism. For years, he was the most consistently credible Saudi journalist around, the only one who had earned an appreciative following both inside and outside the kingdom.

He had been banned many times before, but late in 2003 his column simply stopped altogether. It is only fitting, therefore, that he should be given the last word. This is part of what he told me when I met him in his office in Riyadh earlier that year:

> We don't have much space in which to express our ideas. Be it religion, relations between ethnic groups, women driving cars . . . there are too many subjects where if you write about it you have to go round and round and can't come inside and write about it freely. It's still the case that when a Saudi journalist writes, he fears he might not be able to walk about freely the next day. One person in the Ministry of Information can just pick up the phone and say: Stop your column for three months. He will never give you a reason. I was writing a column in a local newspaper. Sometimes they stopped me for one week or one month because I wrote about mobile phones or the ministry of health. I wasn't talking about politics. I wasn't talking about religion. Just normal things. So I stopped writing. And then I waited for another phone call telling me I can write again. We have a list of things we can't talk about. Not a blacklist. Everything is on the blacklist. What we get is a whitelist. This is just too much. Saudis don't trust their local newspapers about politics. They know we only put one side of the news. Most of the Saudi newspapers only publish positive developments. Anything even a little negative, and they take it out. The government says that it will not give us more freedom because we are still not professional. They say: we'll give you time to be professional, and then we'll give you freedom. But this is wrong. Freedom cultivates professionalism. If you always tell me to do this and to do that, how can I grow up? It's like the chicken and the egg: What comes first, freedom or responsibility?

Chapter Ten

ARE THE SAUDIS SUNK?

There is something both romantic and unsavory about royalty, an odd leftover from bygone days of divine right, deference to authority, and everyone knowing their place. The romanticism, of course, comes from tales of hero kings and queens of days of old. Things were simpler then, and those leaders who apparently single-handedly and bloodily built states and nations, and led armies into battle, can be admired from a distance, their exploits and exploitation safely in the mist of time, when the past was a different country. Their legacies retain some of the glamour—witness the attention that continues to be lavished on the royal family of Britain—and celebrity due to their quaintness, for they reign but do not rule. In an age of complexity, to suggest that one family filled with squabbles and insecurities should govern seems absurd and the opposite of ideal. In the modern age, whatever the drawbacks of democracy, the rough and tumble of the marketplace of ideas, the openness to criticism and debate, and the awareness of people's imperfections offers a flexibility crucial to stability.

Somehow the truth, or at least utility, of this got lost in translation when the message reached the Middle East. The odd continuation of authoritarian regimes, including such "republics" as Egypt and Syria, stands in sharp contrast to the uneasy spread of democracy in other parts of the world. The Arab republics were, of course, twentieth-century constructions, either created by—or in reaction to—Western colonial powers, inventions adapted to the times in which they were created. While they may not seem to be so, given the long history of monarchies in Europe, so too are Arab monarchies a modern creation.

Saudi Arabia is in many ways both the quintessential monarchy and one that is unique. It is unique because, unlike other Arab monarchies imposed from the outside by imperial powers in the early twentieth century (here the Hashemites of Jordan come to mind, and farther back in time the rather short-lived reigns of different branches of the same family in Syria and Iraq), the Saudi monarchy is in the main a classic phenomenon. By that I mean that like the royal families of old, the Al-Saud came to power through violence and conquest, in their case sweeping out of central Arabia to impose their control over disparate and distinctive regions made up of peoples with different cultural and religious values. The founding Al-Saud princes created a classic empire, and they even named it after themselves. But this, too, was done only in the third decade of the twentieth century. Given its global significance, it is sometimes easy to forget just how new a country Saudi Arabia is.

Once one moves beyond the romanticism inherent in the tales of the founders and early leaders of Saudi Arabia, giving them the benefit of the doubt accorded to other state-builders, one may still have a certain respect, even if begrudging, of how the Al-Saud has not only reigned but ruled. The changes the country has undergone in its brief life—still less than a century—cannot be underestimated. The sudden influx of wealth based on the fluke of their country sitting on top of oil has been both balm and curse, the balance always tenuous. A curse because it drew increasing change to a country ruled and administered by a narrow band of men jealous of their place and power. A balm because the wealth allowed them to contract out—outsource—much of the technical and administrative responsibilities inherent in running a complex modern country. A curse because oil made Saudi Arabia of central importance in the global economy. A balm because this centrality meant that deals could be made and protection bought. And the oil wealth also meant that the Al-Saud could provide stunning amounts of wealth to the country's inhabitants, the manna from heaven, proof positive of the legitimacy of their rule—and any challenge to it potentially one that could kill the golden goose. The ruling Al-Saud regime seems to think or believe, like monarchies of old, that the people's loyalty is owed rather than earned. To the extent they understand that loyalty is earned, they seek to buy it.

Interestingly enough, inherent in the belief that loyalty can be bought through money and services is an underlying premise that the Al-Saud's rule is based on some form of social contract, one open to renegotiation and even cancellation. Apparently aware of the need to show attentiveness to the demands of the people, in October 2003 the regime announced plans to hold the first ever kingdom-wide elections, albeit within strict parameters. The elections would be limited to half of the members of the local municipal councils. As that paragon of American politics Tip O'Neill once said, all politics is local, and so ostensibly involvement of the Saudi people in decisions on the local level would be the first stage: crawl before walk, walk before run. Polls were announced as scheduled to take place in November 2004. Then they were pushed back to February 2005, because more time was needed for their preparation and the regime's attention had been diverted by the domestic war on terror. But only those over the age of 21 would be allowed to vote, a directive excluding approximately 60 percent of the population. Women, moreover, would not be enfranchised, reducing still further the number of those Saudis eligible to vote to 20 percent. According to a November 2004 report in *Okaz* newspaper on a poll it conducted, even eligible votes showed little enthusiasm for the electoral process, with only a small minority of the 20 percent saying that they would bother to partake in the elections—or, indeed, had any interest in them. Most cited the councils' lack of real power as the reason for their apathy. Such cynicism should not come as a shock: all the power in all of the kingdom's regions rests in the hands of a single prince-governor, and the half-elected regional municipal councils have no power to check his arbitrary rule. The local councils have little potential to turn into anything more than talking shops, akin to the Shura Council—the "consultative assembly" established in 1993 by royal decree. Its members are exclusively appointed by the king and do not even have the right to examine (let alone debate) the annual budget. In the end, Islamists won in the Riyadh polls.

The ruling Al-Saud regime, by introducing reforms, is playing a dangerous game. Once the genie of democracy is let out, the implications are far from certain and can backfire on those whose wishes are apparently being granted. For by holding up democracy as a value, the Al-Saud is creating a new criteria of judgment and evaluation, one that is open-ended. Today the franchise may be limited to those considered safe, or at least controllable; but such was once the case in the West, where early on only those who owned property could vote but where the franchise gradually became universal (albeit not without great struggle). By accepting in principle that the people should be involved, the Al-Saud is implicitly admitting that they do not have all the answers. By providing the opportunity for debate and for different interests to publicly state their cases, the regime is allowing for contention. It is thus caught on the horns of a dilemma. On the one horn, to allow democracy to flourish is to enable debate, questioning of policies, and the competition of ideologies antithetical to monarchy, whether liberal or fundamentalist. On the other horn, to draw back, after making promises about democracy, by having the form but not the substance, or even by eliminating the form, leads to charges of hypocrisy and of fear of the people's will, with the beneficiaries again being the liberals and the fundamentalists (although for opposite reasons).

As much as the Al-Saud and their well-endowed propaganda machine may seek to convince outsiders of the unity of the people and the regime, and as much as they may believe themselves to be a benevolent, paternal force ruling over an essentially backward, tribal (and thus easily satisfied) people, the reality is different. Empires are inherently fragile, resting on a coherent and unified leadership, the consent or at least obedience of the peoples, and *in extremis* the ruthlessness of the secret police. That empires have a hard time gaining the loyalty of subjects is obvious. One only has to look at the United Kingdom, which has long faced insurgency in Northern Ireland and a long dormant but nonetheless existing regional pride and sense of distinctive identity in Wales and especially Scotland, even though both were conquered centuries ago. But Britain can remain a kingdom united because it is a democracy, where there are rules of the game and a consensus that negotiation is superior to intimidation. Empires not based on such values have a less rosy and more bloody history—the collapse of the Soviet empire being only the latest example. The Communist Party ruled through intimidation and payoffs rather than loyalty, since the people were never enamored of the ideology. Perestroika and glasnost may have been Gorbachev's attempt at reform, but the combination of increased political and economical openness undermined every pillar of the Communist ideology. Once the people grew tired of the bargain, and the party's leadership lost their sense of nerve and conviction, the downward spiral was steep.

Will the same happen to Saudi Arabia? As in the case of Northern Ireland, Scotland, and Wales, the various regions of the Kingdom of Saudi Arabia maintain their own identity. From the cosmopolitan Hijazis in the west to the Shiites in the Eastern Province and the tribes in the southwest, continuing ambivalence toward and resentment of the Al-Saud is tinder. For all the image of a united family, it is clear that the senior members of the Al-

Saud have various opinions concerning relations with the West, especially with the United States, and the extent and pace of reforms, or a Saudi version of perestroika and glasnost. The ruling family is made up of factions, most notably based on maternal descent, and the inherent jealousies threaten to come into the open as the generational transition comes closer in time.

Acutely sensitive to their image, the Al-Saud will go to great lengths to rein in those who are seen as threatening it. In December 2003, Prince Sultan bin Turki, a nephew of King Fahd, told the BBC and Al-Jazeera from his besieged palace in Riyadh that he had been kidnapped in Switzerland by fellow Saudi royals after he set up a group aimed at combating corruption among Saudi princes and high officials. A specially hired Boeing 747 medical evacuation aircraft was allegedly used to smuggle Sultan out of the country, he said, after he had been drugged and gagged. Such measures speak volumes about the fear of exposure, and the deep insecurity any hint of internal division provokes. It may also speak even more loudly of the resistance to reform from within the princely ranks.

One only wonders what the family's leadership thought of the attention received by Prince Turki bin Khalid's purchase of two apartments at the new Time Warner Center in New York City. The apartments must have nice views, being on the sixty-ninth floor. Apparently Turki, a "sports aficionado who works with the Saudi national soccer team," is sensitive to anti-Saudi feelings in America, as one apartment will be used by friends as a *pied-a-terre* and the other will be left empty as he "hopes to use them once American sentiment toward his country becomes more favorable." At a combined $8.1 million, the apartments were not cheap, but the November 21, 2004, *New York Times* noted that while most purchases at the Center are in cash, in this case "the prince got a mortgage." It is tempting to be impressed by his generosity to friends, sensitivity, and ordinariness, and to suspect that having a home in New York to escape to—if necessary—is an indication of his wisdom.

With the coming generational transition in the ruling family sure to generate competition, the strategies that factions will use to gain power will have considerable implications for the stability of the empire. One strategy is already apparent. Reaction in the face of threat to the Al-Saud has historically taken the form of reaffirming and reasserting the adherence of the family to Islam in an attempt, now, to steal the Islamists' thunder. Internally, this means an attempt to buy off the mainstream Wahhabi establishment, with both money and authority. Externally, it means playing up the Islamist threat in an attempt to convince mainstream opinion in the West that there are only two choices when it comes to whom to deal with in Saudi Arabia: the royals or Osama bin Laden. The war on terror and the anti-Saudi campaign in parts of the U.S. media have given the Al-Saud all the ammunition they need to play up (to their own people) that Islam is under attack and (to the West) that, however objectionable the family's nondemocratic rule may be, the alternative would be far worse.

A second strategy is to engage in denial and blame others. The fact that 15 of the 19 hijackers on September 11 had been Saudi nationals was initially repeatedly denied by leading royals, not least by Interior Minister Prince Naif who, one would have thought, would have known better given that his post means he is responsible for all intelligence internally. Once responsibility was crystal clear and such denials became absurd, responsibility in the Saudi domestic media was attributed to a vague "Zionist conspiracy." Even as attacks within Saudi Arabia increased in frequency and devastation, Naif continued to be in denial regarding sleeping terrorist cells inside Saudi Arabia. According to Naif, there simply weren't any, just as there are no Saudi extremists. When this tact became no longer viable, especially after the May 12, 2003, bombings—in which extremists carried out a series of coordinated attacks on Western residential compounds in Riyadh—and the subsequent low-level Islamic insurgency in Saudi Arabia, there have not been enough hours in the day for Naif to express his hatred of home-grown terrorist cells that have clashed with his internal security forces on an almost weekly basis, and appear to have him squarely in their sights.

Consistency has never been a conspicuous attribute in Saudi domestic politics, while blaming others has been. Crown Prince Abdullah has blamed "Zionists" and "followers of Satan" for recent terror attacks, and it is far from clear that he made any distinction between the two. "We can be certain that Zionism is behind everything," he said after the attack in the Red Sea city of Yanbu that killed five Westerners, offering the brief and pathetic qualification that he was at least 95 percent certain. The crown prince's chief ally, Foreign Minister Prince Saud Al-Faisal, has criticized the U.S.-led war on Iraq as a "colonial" adventure aimed only at gaining control of Iraq's natural resources. While that argument could be made quite strongly by anyone else, it is a bit rich coming from any member of the Al-Saud family. During the Iraq war, Saudi Arabia secretly helped the United States by allowing operations from at least three air bases, permitting special forces to stage attacks from Saudi soil, and providing cheap fuel. The American air campaign against Iraq was essentially managed from inside Saudi borders, where military officers operated a command center and launched refueling tankers, F-16 fighter jets, and sophisticated intelligence-gathering flights.

Which is not to say that the war in Iraq does not have the real potential to create a destabilizing blowback for the Al-Saud. More immediately, however, the war in Iraq has brought two real benefits to the regime—one material, the other ideational. The material benefit is the massive windfall from the dramatic increase in the price of oil. By the end of 2004 Saudi Arabia had an estimated budget surplus of somewhere between $37 billion and $60 billion. Out the window went the projected deficit of $8 billion for the kingdom's 2004 budget, a conservative prediction that was based on an oil price of less than half the level it turned out to be. One wonders, given such figures, why Prince Turki needed a mortgage for his New York apartments. The internal implications of this providential bounty have been the enhanced ability of the Al-Saud to rely on its third strategy: to throw money at problems. There have been promises of increased domestic spending on, among other things, massive infrastructure projects. Flush with cash, the Al-Saud regime again seems to be resorting to the tried and true, following the strategy of spending ostentatiously to keep the people happy, or satisfied, or at least not dissatisfied, just as had been the case during the oil boom years of the 1970s.

The regime seeks to be seen as the goose laying the golden egg, but the danger is that it is fools' gold. The massive spending of the 1970s changed the physical character of the country and affected the psychological character as well. What worked back then, when Saudi residents had almost nothing, no longer is likely to work as well now that expectations have been raised as a result of the prior spending, and so many gained little from the earlier boom. The quick fixes in the past did not solve underlying social and economic problems. Indeed, it created many new ones. This time around the Al-Saud seems, once again, content merely to buy time.

The ideational benefit of the U.S.-led war against Iraq has been an increase in antagonism toward the United States among Saudis, with a concomitant devaluation of American credibility in its calls for democracy. Anti-U.S. sentiment inside Saudi Arabia is now at an all-time high, following the outrages at the Abu Ghraib prison in Baghdad and Washington's continued support for Israel's often-brutal suppression of the Palestinians. But this is a double-edged sword. Just as Saudis who went to Afghanistan to fight against the atheistic Soviet Union, with the open encouragement of the regime, eventually returned to the kingdom, so the jihad in Iraq will come to haunt the Al-Saud. Dozens of Saudi jihadis are reported to have been killed in Fallujah, and many Saudi families have visited the Iraqi city to pay their respects to their "martyred" sons. And the tactics employed by the Fallujah insurgents have already turned up in the attacks on Westerners in Saudi Arabia. The two situations are now feeding directly off each other. The worse things get in Iraq, the more support and legitimacy the terrorists in Saudi Arabia are getting. The Saudi terrorists in Iraq will likely provide a huge boost to Al-Qaeda's ranks when they return to the kingdom because of their large numbers and the tactics they have learned. The ideological bonds that tie the insurgents in Iraq and Saudi Arabia have been made explicit. Those who beheaded American Paul Johnson in Riyadh signed their claim of responsibility "the Fallujah Brigade." In the earlier attack in which six Westerners and a Saudi were killed in Yanbu, terrorists dragged the body of one of the victims into a local school playground and forced students to watch it. "Come join your brothers in Fallujah," they shouted, in reference to the city where four American contractors were similarly slain. The Al-Qaeda cell that attacked foreigners in Khobar also dragged the body of a Westerner through the streets. The leader of that group said on an Islamic website afterward that a subsidiary of Halliburton had been singled out for attack because "it has a role in Iraq."

A fourth strategy the regime pursues, perhaps most predictably, is outright repression. Clearly this works in conjunction with the reaffirmation of core values, and the terrorist attacks within the country obviously provide a rationale that might seem reasonable to people both inside and outside the kingdom. For the regular Saudi, like those whose voices inform this book, seeking to get along with his or her life, the disruption and fear created by attacks is far from appreciated. While the radicals' charges of corruption and hypocrisy against the Al-Saud regime resonate, so too does the Al-Saud's appeal of the need for stability and quiet. After all, one of the worst charges in Islam is that of *fitna,* the dissension and the chaos created by rebellion. Nothing specifically Islamic about that, of course, as one can easily see by looking at how the threat of terrorism has provided a rationale (and public acceptance) for the curtailment of civil rights in various Western countries. It should come as no surprise that, in such a climate, calls for reform and democracy in Saudi Arabia fall on fallow ground.

Nevertheless, over time such calls will continue and likely increase. The social changes brought about by the oil wealth of the 1970s are one reason.

Another is the rapid population growth, including the huge cohort of youth used to wealth, seeking opportunities, increasingly educated, and more and more familiar with the West, whether through spending time there or through the media. The limited opening allowed to Saudi media is in part a reflection of the regime's awareness that there are increasing options when it comes to information. The fact that *Okaz* and other newspapers could report dissension over the limited moves toward democracy is evidence that the Al-Saud has not completely closed the door on the chorus of voices calling for real change. As ever, there are crippling limitations on what can be expressed. But there is always greater freedom and opportunity for opposition figures to express their views in the Western press, in which, for instance, Hijazis and exiled opposition figures have dryly and ironically remarked that they appreciate the opportunity to be grateful to the Al-Saud for granting only half of what they enjoyed before their rule was imposed on the area. It was the Al-Saud, after all, who by the 1960s had phased out full municipal elections in the Hijaz and then failed to reintroduce them in that region—and throughout the rest of the kingdom—as had been promised in legislation passed (but afterward completely ignored) in the 1970s.

Discontent is spread through the Internet, chat rooms, phone calls, and countless conversations. Such technologies are, of course, neutral, there being nothing intrinsic about them conducive to democracy. They are, indeed, used equally well by fundamentalists. One of the most important tactics used by supporters of Ayatollah Khomeini before the revolution in Iran was tape recordings of his speeches. Tapes of sermons from various radical Sunni preachers continue to circulate, complemented (if that is the word) by videos of hostage-takings and beheadings. For a population denied power and responsibility, attuned to feelings of humiliation and shame, and frustrated at the inability of their own rulers to effect change and influence events in the region, the strength demonstrated by the insurgents and radicals (combined with their promise of a better future) holds appeal.

The ruling Al-Saud family has long sought to have it both ways: to be a force for controlled modernization while upholding tradition; to be the ally of the West, especially of the United States, while both influencing it and keeping its corrupting influences at bay, and simultaneously backing a Wahhabi establishment it relies on to remain in power but which also ultimately seeks the West's destruction; to provide benefits to the people, paternalistically, while appearing to be just and sage rather than opportunistic and corrupt. One may be a proponent of democracy and nonetheless still be impressed at the delicate balancing act the Al-Saud has performed, as they made themselves seem an indispensable bulwark. The adroitness, if not necessarily the wisdom, of various kings must be admitted.

But, again, there is the blowback. Reliance on the intelligence and adroitness of a ruler is a dangerous game, all the more so when government is highly personalistic. A democracy is based on faith in the people and the rule of law, not individuals. The Soviet Union had an ideological underpinning that, however obnoxious, promised a better day. It also had a party that was regimented and effective, penetrating all sectors of society, providing benefits to those who conformed and costs to those who did not. It, too, had rules understood by all. In a personalistic system there are no rules, only fear—the rulers fear that they can be outbid for support, and the people fear that their benefits can be taken away at a whim.

So the problems facing the Al-Saud regime are numerous and profound. The ideological foundation of the regime, namely strict adherence to Islam, is contested on the right by radicals both within and without. Like any extended family, the ruling Al-Saud have factions competing for power and influence, with allies among the "commoners" internally and externally. Understanding this is crucial to understanding the starts and stops in policies, whether on increasing freedom, relations with the West, or the pricing of oil. The extensive evidence of corruption, whether financial or moral or both, of various princes undermines the image of paternalistic rectitude. In Islam, hypocrisy is among the most damning charges one can bring, a violent character assassination. That some of the worst offenders of righteousness are younger princes does not bode well, as members of the older generation—who remember the period of relative poverty and who sometimes actually worked (rather than simply having things handed to them)—die. At the same time, it is from among the younger princes—princes who learned the art of diplomacy not in tents in the desert but in universities in the West—that the more sophisticated and worldly leadership must emerge, and as quickly as possible. While the Al-Saud are not a political party, as were the Communists, the large number of princes—nearly seven thousand, by some reckonings—are spread throughout the kingdom and some are provincial governors. Ultimately, Saudi Arabia's future is completely dependent on how the royal family decides to face the future, whether it deals with reality head on or continues to bury its head in the oil-rich sand.

As the transition to the new generation begins in the near future, after the death of the ailing King Fahd, it is fully conceivable that different factions will increasingly fight for dominance. It is, of course, possible that through a Darwinian process of competition, or through providence, the leaders of the next generation will be as adroit as some of Saudi Arabia's past leaders, notably King Faisal who famously remarked at the height of the oil boom: "In one generation we went from riding camels to driving Cadillacs. The way we are spending money today, I fear we will soon be riding camels again." One hesitates, however, to bet on any outcome. As competition increases, it is fully possible that the various strategies available to the regime will be tried, and it is quite possible that none will be effective. It is easy enough to observe that a house divided against itself will fall, and perhaps even to hope that the Al-Saud will realize this rather than allow divisions to provide opportunities for others to seize control. For those waiting in the wings who are most disciplined and determined—and desperate to seize the oil wealth and claim all the prestige that comes with the governorship of the two holy shrines—are the followers of Osama bin Laden.

There is another possibility to consider, namely the breaking apart of the Saudi empire. As far-fetched as this may seem, the recent past gives too many examples of a country falling apart when the leadership lost its grip and unity. For the reality is that the fates of such countries as Yugoslavia were not predetermined by essential ethnic hatreds simply waiting to see the light of day. Differences were manipulated and deliberately accentuated by leaders seeking power, creating bases of support, and taking advantage of instability to generate fear. The differences existed, but what they meant changed in changing circumstances. Such differences exist in the empire known as the Kingdom of Saudi Arabia, and they are just as susceptible to exploitation—whether by various princes jockeying for power or by local leaders taking advantage of divisions among the Al-Saud to make a play for power.

Is this alarmist? Perhaps so. Recognizing a possibility is not to advocate it. And while I would like to say that there is something that outsiders can do to decrease the possibility of disaster, I regret that the current path taken by outsiders gives little room for optimism. The American involvement in Iraq is simply providing more ammunition for extremists, both in terms of evidence of the West's perfidy and in terms of opportunities for radicals to gain experience in fighting a guerrilla war. For all of its claims to support democracy, American policy in Iraq seems to run counter to its declarations. That it is the Sunnis, co-religionists of the majority of Saudis, who are bearing the brunt of the fighting and are most likely to lose out in a real democracy in Iraq means that the Bush administration's policies are basically no-win in terms of likely effects in Saudi Arabia.

In my years in Saudi Arabia, perhaps the most important lesson I learned was that the ability of an outsider to influence others is highly limited. I had Saudi friends and colleagues, many of them quite dear to me and, I think, I was dear to them. Some would confide in me, whether because they trusted me or because as an outsider I was less likely to judge, and if I did, my judgment was less important. That, too, was an important lesson, namely that the judgment or opinion of an outsider is far less important than that of someone from the social circle. Precisely because the opinions of outsiders are less important, their ability to bring about changes—in opinions or behaviors of individuals—is far less than the ability of locals to ensure conformity. If I was unwittingly a small part of the struggle for hearts and minds, to borrow that evocative Orwellian term, I can admit that I changed few if any.

In fact, the subtler my approach, the more tangible were the results. One example: My closest Saudi friend, a young man in his late teens, would come to my house once a week or so to watch a Western movie. He was an extremely confused individual, had taught hard-core jihad in his youth at a religious school, but was finally waking up (mainly through his love of English) to the possibility that there could be a life for him that need not involve sacrificing himself for his religion, that could indeed involve him in living among other people. One evening I rented *The Truman Show* from the local video store. In this 1998 movie, Jim Carrey plays an ordinary man, Truman, living an ordinary life, but it's all fake and he serves only the ends of others. Only Truman himself is real. The town that he lives in—including the sea, the sky, the sun, the moon, and even the stars—is just one gigantic TV studio ("the largest manmade structure on the planet, the only structure other that the Great Wall of China visible from outer space") and everyone around him—including his wife, his parents, and even his best friend—are professional actors who play their roles in the most popular, continuously running TV show in the world, "The Truman Show." This wonderful film is, of course, about Truman's realization that he is part of a large plot and his attempts to break free of it—to create his own future, to define his own reality, to reject conformity, and to cease living the life others have chosen for him. My Saudi friend and I watched the film together, and after it finished he said something simple but profoundly significant and deeply touching: "It's all about Wahhabism."

Those in power in the West would be wise, it seems to me, to listen to those who advocate change in the Middle East not by war but by the expenditure of similar amounts of money on language schools, cultural projects, and exchange programs that would give young Arabs access to the best Western culture has to offer. While that may sound naive, there is certainly no reason to believe American or Western politicians, generals, and bankers will succeed on their other course. The bottom line is that if and when there will be positive and welcome change inside Saudi Arabia, it must be internally generated. A moment of self-realization in the mind of a once-radical young Saudi, for instance, after he watches a Western movie. That some of the people I had the good fortune to meet, and whose voices are heard here, are part of that process is surely reason for some kind of hope.

A NOTE ON SOURCES

As this book was written for the general reader, I have avoided giving citations and footnotes in the text.

I would, however, like to acknowledge relying heavily in some parts of Chapter 1, when discussing the history of the Hijaz and the Alireza family in particular, on two excellent books written by specialists on those subjects: *The Merchants: The Big Business Families of Saudi Arabia and the Gulf States* (1984) by Michael Field, and *The Rise and Fall of the Hashemite Kingdom of Arabia* (2001) by Joshua Teitelbaum. Two books by Thierry Mauger—*Arabia: The Painter's Garden* (2002) and *The Flower-Men of Asir* (1996)—were wonderful guides during my trip to Asir.

In chapter 4, some of the details about the Ismaili rebellion were provided by the Saudi Institute, a Washington-based, pro-democracy think tank run by an estimable liberal Saudi exile, Ali Al-Ahmed.

The TV program on "The Jews" discussed in chapter 9 was broadcast after I had left the kingdom, and I therefore have relied on the video clips and translations provided by the Middle East Media Research Institute on its website (www.memri.org).

INDEX